T0064548

BOOKS BY THE SAME AUTHOR

Betrayal: – A Political documentary of our times

The Sands of Time: A book of poetry Vol 1

The Chalice: A book of poetry Vol 2

Nostalgia: A book of poetry Vol 3

Growing Up: a collection of Children's stories and Pet Stories

Conflagration: Documentary of a World in Turmoil

A Book of Plays

Wake Up Dead

Available from author only

From Across the Waters: a Book of Recipes

Study Book Macro Skills –A Teacher's Guide and a Self Help Book for Post-Intermediate ESL learners & VCE students

ANSWER Book 1 R & W

Study Book Macro Skills –A Teacher's Guide and a Self Help Book for Post-Intermediate ESL learners & VCE students with answers Book L&S2

Answer Book L&S

Study Book Micro Skills –A Teacher's Guide and a Self Help Book for Post-Intermediate ESL learners & VCE students

Answer Book Micro Skills

CD format also available for the Study Guides

Web page: https://kovachevich.net

THE
RAPED
EARTH

SOPHIA Z. KOVACHEVICH

BALBOA.PRESS

A DIVISION OF HAY HOUSE

Balboa Press books may be ordered through booksellers or by contacting:

Balboa Press
A Division of Hay House
1663 Liberty Drive
Bloomington, IN 47403
www.balboapress.com.au
AU TFN: 1 800 844 925 (Toll Free inside Australia)
AU Local: 0283 107 086 (+61 2 8310 7086 from outside Australia)

Image Credit: Janice M Davis, Miroslav Jokic, Pixaby and Sophia Z. Kovachevich and free web images

Print information available on the last page.

ISBN: 978-1-5043-2386-4 (sc)
ISBN: 978-1-5043-2387-1 (e)

Balboa Press rev. date: 12/21/2020

NATURE

Aug 16, 2012 8.00 a m
The peace and tranquillity
Of my garden
Reanimates my wracked body
Rejuvenates my soul
Reanimates my brain

The green of the foliage
The varied hues of the blossoms
The beautiful perfume
Of the rose, jasmine and lilac
Intoxicates and brings solace

Nature is, has and will always be
The powerhouse of humanity's health
The generosity of its gifts
Has always been a great boon
To all created beings
Man, bird and beast

Nurture Nature
Glorify Nature
And in that glorification
You glorify the Creator
Sophia Z Kovachevich –*The Chalice* pp229

CONTENTS

FOREWORD

The ancients left us a world inhabited by many beautiful living things – mammals, birds, reptiles, fish, plants and so on. But what did we do with our inheritance - with this gift? We hunted and killed them for our pleasure and indulgence. We squandered our inheritance. Now our world is the poorer for their loss. Now we wish them back. But it's too late for many of those gorgeous creatures.

INTRODUCTION

The earth is not our possession. It is not ours. We do not own it. We are simply the caretakers for this beautiful, variegated earth. We share it with God's other creations. But we reneged in our duty to the earth. We have raped it, abused it and killed many of its creatures mercilessly for pleasure or entertainment or profit. The more we advance technologically, the more we seem to lose our souls, our humanity.

In this book I would like to look at how we came to such a state that even nature has rebelled against our misuse of the earth. Ancient man, it is generally assumed, was not as technologically advanced as we are today. And yet they left behind monuments and other artefacts that awe us even today. They used the earth primarily to help them to survive. They took from it what was necessary. They cared for the other living creatures and had respect for life. But as we advanced, we decided to be the owners of the earth. We began to kill not just for survival (food) but also for pleasure or for profit. Think about the rhinoceros, and elephants and narwhals that are killed mainly for their horns. Or about the sharks whose fins are cut for food and the still alive shark is thrown back into the water to drown. That is cruelty. That is immoral. That is wrong.

It has only been a few generations – since the mid-to-late 1980's – that knowledge of both anthropogenic climate change and the term 'biodiversity' have filtered through to the general public's consciousness. Since then, they have profoundly reshaped both our behaviour and the way in which we see ourselves in relation to our environment. But this is not the whole picture. For some of us there is no change as we continue to abuse the earth and its creatures. But for some it has been a real wake up call. It is now up to those who realise what is at stake to take the message to the whole world and try to redress the wrong as much as possible. It is still not too late!

We live in a biodiverse world. One can only wonder in awe at the diversity in nature and the beauty! Biodiversity is not just how many diverse living organisms are on this planet. Biodiversity is also the diversity in the ecosystems – freshwater ecosystem, terrestrial ecosystem and the ocean ecosystem as well as the genetic diversity.

What are eco systems? They are all the living and non-living things in a specific natural setting – plants, animals, birds, insects, rocks, soil, water and sunlight. All fall under two categories – terrestrial or aquatic. In the terrestrial group are:

Terrestrial ecosystems
- ❖ Forest Ecosystems e.g. tropical forests, rainforests
- ❖ Grassland Ecosystems e.g. prairies, savannas
- ❖ Desert Ecosystems. The common defining feature among desert ecosystems is low precipitation
- ❖ Tundra Ecosystem e.g. a harsh ice-cold environment, low biotic diversity characterises ecosystems in the tundra

In the aquatic group are:
- ❖ Marine ecosystems – have a variety of characteristics
- ❖ Fresh water ecosystems
- ❖ Wetlands – are generally expected to have the highest level of productivity
- ❖ Coral reefs – have the greatest diversity of organisms depending on the type it belongs to (Sandy beach ecosystem; Mangrove Ecosystems;)

- ❖ Salt Marsh ecosystem
- ❖ Estuaries are deepest part that opens into larger bodies of water

So far we have only seen a fraction of what the aquatic world holds but from those that we know we have already killed to extinction a vast number and made a huge number extremely vulnerable or at risk. Had we known or discovered more, more would have been extinct by now.

There are about 8 million animal and plant species on the earth that we know about, but over 2 million of them are endangered. At the present moment the global extinction rate is the highest it has ever been. One reason is our callous disregard for life but another bigger reason is climate change – for which we are responsible to a great extent. It has been estimated that 137 species in the rain forests are driven to extinction every day; and many more are vulnerable; 47% of land-based mammals and 23% of birds are seriously endangered. And the rate is accelerating not diminishing. Most at risk are ecosystems that cannot move – like trees.

In due course of time the ecosystems will look alien to what they now look. This is because:

- ❖ *The average abundance of native species in most major land-based habitats has fallen by at least 20%, mostly since 1900*
- ❖ *More than 40% of amphibian species, almost 33% of reef-forming corals and more than a third of all marine mammals are endangered*
- ❖ *Around 10% of all insect species are threatened*
- ❖ *At least 680 vertebrate species have been driven to extinction since the 16th century*

- ❖ *5% of species are estimated to be at risk of extinction from 2° Celsius warming*
- ❖ *16% of species are at risk of extinction from just over 4° Celsius warming*

If we are not careful and take the present situation seriously and address the issues we will be the greatest of losers if we are alive till then.

Destruction of our biodiversity will be our downfall!!!

PART 1

ANCIENT CIVILISATIONS

We have come a long, long way from the cavemen to today. As we evolved we started living in groups and then in societies and then we established cities and founded civilisations. It has been a long and very interesting journey. And it is only fair to acknowledge what the ancient civilisations bequeathed us.

> ➢ The first known record is of the **Mesopotamian** civilisation. It flourished between 3500BC and 500BC. It was located in the Mesopotamian Delta between the Tigris and Euphrates rivers in modern day Iraq, Syria and Turkey then known as Sumeria, Assyria and Babylonia. There is no record of any other civilisation before this.

The Mesopotamians developed agriculture around 8000 BC and began domesticating animals for food and agriculture. They began writing in cuneiform script. They gave the world the first code of law – Hammurabi's Code of Law. They had one of the finest literature and many of the greatest cultural and literary achievements like the epic of Gilgamesh.

Gilgamesh is an ancient Mesopotamian odyssey recorded in the Akkadian language about Gilgamesh, the king of the Mesopotamian city-state Uruk (Erech). Then there is the Epic of The Flood Tablet, the 11th cuneiform tablet in the series also relating the Gilgamesh epic, from Nineveh, in the 7thcentury BCE. This is in the British Museum, London. It is one of the best and most important pieces of epic poetry from human history, predating even Homer's Iliad by roughly 1,500 years. It also predates the *Lay of the Niebulungs (Nibelungenlied), the Völsung Saga* or even the *Mabinogian* (all these began as oral traditions and was written down much, much later. Gilgamesh was written at its inception.). The Gilgamesh epic tells of the various adventures of that hero-king, including his quest for immortality and an account of a great flood similar in many details to the Old Testament's story of Noah. Besides this epic there were many others among them the heroic deeds of kings like Enmerkar, Lugalbanda and Ashurbanipal. Ashurbanipal (see notes pg. 13) had the tablets of this people collected and catalogued (about 20,720 tablets). They, too, are currently in the British museum.

The Mesopotamians made and used the first chariots and sailboats in the world long before the Norse. The Mesopotamians gave the world the first potter's wheel (around 3500 BC).

This civilisation- the Mesopotamian civilisation - had a lot of very well-known and accomplished rulers. They contributed a lot to the world.

➢ The **Indus Valley** civilisation was from 3300 BC to 1900 BC in the Bronze Age. It was located by the Indus and Ghagger-Hakra river basins covering present day Northeast Afghanistan, Pakistan and northwest India. It was a very extensive area covering 1.25 million km of land. It is also known as the Harappan civilisation and that of

Mohenjo-Daro. It was a sophisticated and technologically advanced civilisation with an urban capital. They were among the first to develop a uniform system of weights and measures and achieved a high level of accuracy in measurement. Artefacts show a high level of proficiency in arts and crafts too. They were also very proficient in urban planning with baked brick houses and a drainage system and water supply. They were also the very first to incorporate urban sanitation. There were clusters of non-residential houses. They also came up with a new technology in handicraft (carnelian ornaments and seal carving) and metallurgy (copper, bronze, lead and tin) and ochre coloured pottery. They also had cemeteries for burying the dead and so avoided contamination. The large cities of Mohenjo-Daro and Harappa were among the five urban centres and were inhabited by between 30,000 and 60,000 people.

➤ The **Egyptian** Civilisation is also called the Nile Valley civilisation. It existed between 3150 BC and 30 BC. It was founded on the banks of the Nile River in present day Egypt.

It was one of the oldest three civilisations and was culturally very rich. It was and is well known for its great culture, its pharaohs, its pyramids and the Sphinx, especially the three enormous ones at Giza. In 3150 the Upper and Lower kingdoms merged together in a political unity.

The history of Egypt can be divided into a number of stable periods with a strong ruler interspersed by weak ones. They were the Old Kingdom of the early Bronze Age, The Middle Kingdom and the New Kingdom.

The Egyptians gave the world majestic architecture and intricate ornaments. The kings had their rules/laws/edicts written in stone tablets in a pictorial script called Hieroglyphics. They made great advances in mathematics, literature, astronomy, engineering, statecraft, medicine, writing on papyrus with pen and ink, in art and science. Their mummification process is one of the wonders of their civilisation. It was so skilfully done that now after thousands of years, even the hair of the mummy is intact, the features are easily recognisable and even the tattoos and scars remain.

They had some great soldier kings. They were the first civilisation to begin worship of one - the sun god Aten who was universal and not just for the Egyptians. However after the death of this king – Akhenaten (Amenhotep IV), they went back to worshipping Amun Ra and the other gods. The Egyptian Priesthood hankered after the old gods and reinstated them once King Akhenaten the Monotheistic pharaoh who wanted all to worship one god – died.

➢ The **Mayan** civilisation existed between 2600 BC and 900 AD in present day Yucatan, Quintana Roo, Campeche, Tabasco and Chiapas in Mexico and south through Guatemala, Belize, El Salvador and Honduras. It was a Mesoamerican civilisation especially noted for their logo syllabic script – the most developed in pre-Columbian America.

They gave us a very complex understanding of astronomy and the calendar as well as mathematics, architecture and astronomy. It was a very prosperous and highly sophisticated empire with a population of 19 million people. By 700 BC they had devised their own system of writing and the solar calendar which was carved in stone.

The ancient Mayans were culturally rich compared to their contemporary civilisations. They, as well as the Aztecs built pyramids, some of which were larger than those of Egypt.

Their civilisation came to a sudden, abrupt end and no one yet knows how or why. Their decedents still live in parts of Central America.

Some of their major accomplishments were in astronomy, agriculture, engineering, communication, building modern cities and having a written language. They worked in gold and copper and had a script which was a form of hieroglyphic writing.

> The **Chinese** Civilisation existed between 1600 BC and 1046 BC. It was located by the Yellow River and the Yangtze Basin. The Yellow river civilisation as it is also called is said to be the beginning of the Chinese civilisation. In 2700 BC the Yellow emperor ruled China and he went on to give birth to many dynasties which went on to rule mainland China. It was a one family rule. They were the Xia, the Shang, the Zhou, the Jin, the Ming and the Han dynasties. It has a very diverse history.

The Chinese Civilisation is also called the **Han** civilisation because this dynasty ruled over China for a very long period of time between the first and last rulers – longer than the other dynasties.

In 2070 BC the Xia dynasty began their rule and was the first to rule over all of China. Under the Zhou dynasty the Mandate of Heaven was introduced to justify their rule. Much of Chinese philosophy, culture and literature developed under this dynasty.

This dynasty was followed by many others until the end of the Qing dynasty. This ended in 1912 AD with the Xinhai Revolution. This occurred during the last Chinese imperial dynasty (the Qing dynasty in 1912 AD). This marked the end of four millennia of rule by the dynasty. It led to the establishment of the Republic of China.

Some of what the Chinese civilisation gave to the world is silk, gunpowder, paper, printing, cannons, alcohol, the compass, fine pottery, agriculture especially millet farming, burial of the dead, specialist craftsmen and administrators. Scholar-officials, proficient in history, calligraphy, literature and philosophy were selected through difficult government tests to carry out administrative jobs.

China has had thousands of years of continuous history and is often regarded as one of the world's oldest civilisations. It is one of the cradles of civilisation.

➤ The ancient **Greek** Civilisation was from 2700BC to 479 BC. It was located in Greece, Sicily, North Africa and as far west as France. It was one of the most influential civilisations. The official rise of the Greek civilisation is from the Cycladic and Minoan civilisations in 2700 BC to 1500 BC but the Franchti Caves show burials from as early as 7250 BC.

The Greek civilisations stretched over a long period of time and so historians have divided it into different periods the most popular being the Archaic, Classical and Hellenistic periods. These periods are responsible for people and concepts that still influence us today. For example they gave us the Olympic Games – a period of time when all the city states ceased warfare and came together to participate and enjoy the games. It also gave us the concept of Democracy and the Senate. Greeks laid the foundation for modern biology, geometry and physics. It gave us the Hippocratic Oath that is still a cornerstone of medicine. It gave us famous people like Euclid, Pythagoras, Archimedes, Socrates, Plato, Sophocles, Homer, Aeschylus, Sappho, and many more. It gave us rulers like Cadmus, Miltiades, Polycrates, Ulysses, Alexander the Great, and many others. Greek inventions, theories, beliefs, the arts of war and peace still influence us today. Greece also gave us many heroes. Greece influenced Romans to a great extent especially in culture and philosophy. It still influences us, today in many ways – democracy, Olympic Games, in the sciences etc. are among some of them.

➢ The **Persian** Civilisation was from 550 BC to 331 BC. It spanned the area from Egypt to the West, Turkey in the North, through Mesopotamia to the Indus valley in the East. It covered all of modern day Iran. This was the most powerful civilisation of its time in the world. The Persians conquered extensive lands even though they ruled for a comparatively short period of time. This civilisation was known for its military strength and wise rulers.

Before 550 BC when Cyrus the Great unified them, they were divided into factions with each ruling their turf. After unifying them, Cyrus conquered Babylon and India. After his death his descendants continued conquering and annexing lands. Under Darius they fought the Spartans. Their power came to an end when Alexander the Great defeated them in 330 BC. Their capital was at Persepolis. Their religion was Zoroastrianism or Mazdayasna which is one of the world's oldest continuously practiced religions. The faith is centered on a dualistic cosmology of good and evil which predicts the ultimate conquest of evil. The religion is based on theological elements of henotheism, monotheism/monism, and polytheism. The spiritual leader Zoroaster (also known as Zarathushtra), exalts an uncreated and benevolent deity of wisdom, Ahura Mazda (Wise Lord), as its supreme being. The main features of Zoroastrianism, such as Messianism, judgment after death, heaven and hell, and Free Will may have influenced other religious and philosophical systems, including Second Temple Judaism, Gnosticism, Greek philosophy, Christianity, Islam, the Bahá'í Faith, and Buddhism.

Their temple is now a world heritage site. The Book of Kings or *Shahnameh* by the great poet and philosopher Ferdowsi is still read today.

> The **Roman Civilisation** lasted between 550BC and 465 AD. It was located by the banks of the river Tiber. In Old Latin, modern day Rome, the capital and largest city was called Romanus or "of Rome". They were the most powerful ancient civilisation of their time. This civilisation encompassed the rules of the Roman Kingdom (753 BC to 27 BC), that of the Roman Republic (509 BC to 27 BC) and that of the Roman Empire (27 BC to 476 AD) when the empire was overrun by the Alemanni (an alliance of Germanic tribes).

The foundation of Rome is the stuff of myth and legend. Traditional stories handed down by the ancient Romans themselves explain the earliest history of their city in terms of legend and myth. The most familiar of these myths, and perhaps the most famous of all Roman myths, is the story of Romulus and Remus, the twins who were suckled by a she-wolf. At the height of its power Rome ruled a huge area comprising all of the Mediterranean and a huge part of Europe including Gaul and Britain.

Early Rome was ruled by kings but only after seven of them had ruled, the people took control and introduced a council called the Senate. They referred to it as the Roman Republic.

Rome had some of the greatest leaders like Julius Caesar, Trajan, Augustus Caesar and antiheroes like Nero and Caligula.

The Roman Empire became so large (through its conquests) that it was impossible to be ruled by one person so it was divided into two parts, one ruled from Rome and the other from Constantinople – the Western and Eastern Roman Empires.

Rome bequeathed to us the designing of arches, the building of cities on grids, the concept and building of aqueducts, sewers, amphitheatres, the great Colosseum, roads and highways, sanitation etc.

It was finally overrun by millions of barbarians from north and East Europe.

The Roman civilisation still influences us today.

➢ The **Aztec Civilisation** was from 1345 AD to 1521 AD. It stretched across the southcentral region of pre-Columbian Mexico. The Aztecs came to power at about the same time as the Incas were emerging as a very powerful force in South America. Around AD 1200's and 1300's there were three powerful rival cities – Tenochtitlan, Texcoco and Tlacopan.

Tenochtitlan was a swampy area but the Aztecs were told that they would found their kingdom when an eagle with a snake in its beak sat on a cactus. This is the place where that incident took place and so the Aztecs founded an empire from there. Around 1325 AD these three cities made an alliance and this alliance then dominated the Mexico Valley. The Aztecs came to power as the Mayans of Central Mexico and Central America collapsed.

Tenochtitlan was the power base and became the centre for their conquest of new areas. However the whole was not ruled by the Aztec emperor directly. Local governments stayed in place but paid tribute to the Aztec emperor and the Triple Alliance. But in the 1500's the Spanish arrived and the heyday of Aztec power was numbered. The Spanish conquistadors under the leadership of the infamous Hernán Cortés made allies of the natives and fought and defeated the Aztecs in 1521 AD. Cortés then claimed Mexico for Spain.

Some of their major accomplishments during their dominance were the establishment of city-states with great pyramid temples, public plazas with huge columns and a complex form of writing. Nahautl was their official language.

> The **Inca Civilisation** covered the time span between 1438 AD and 1532 AD. They were located in Peru but also covered the area of Ecuador and Chile. They were the largest pre-Columbian era empire. They had their

administrative, military and political centre in Cusco in modern-day Peru. These were the ethnic Quechua people also known as Amerindians.

The Incas were a well-stablished and flourishing society. They worshipped the sun god Inti and the king was referred to as *Sapa Inca* or son of the Sun God. The First king, Pachacuti transformed the city from a modest one to the empire's capital with the city laid out in the shape of a puma. He continued and extended ancestor worship. On the emperor's death his son would inherit but conditionally to preserve and maintain ancestor worship and maintain his political power. The Incas were great builders. As skilled stonemasons they used the locally available materials. They cut the rocks using implements made from stone and metal tools constructed out of bronze, copper, pieces of wood and water. They also constructed fortresses and sites like Machu Picchu and the still standing city of Cusco (Quechua) from granite and limestone.

Some of their achievements were the inventions of the flute, drum, and Inca calendar. They were also adept at the making of pottery and clothes. They were way ahead of their time in incorporating imperial policies with ethnic diversity. However they did not use the wheel or have a written alphabet.

Conclusion

All ancient civilisations had a close relationship to the world around them. All of these civilisations respected nature and took care of it. They worshipped different nature deities. This understanding of the natural and spiritual world made it imperative for them to respect all life. Killing for the sake of killing, (whether fauna, flora or marine life or cutting down trees) arbitrarily, was unacceptable. One killed only for food. Or shelter. Or in self-defence. Many of the ancient civilisations like the Egyptians were connected to nature in the physical sense – the lush Nile River lay between two unforgiving and hostile deserts and this was Egypt's life blood. Its annual flooding made the land fertile. They were also connected to the natural world through their religious observances.

Metaphorically, the murals and the tombs of the ancient Egyptians depicted many nature scenes – the sun, the fauna and flora. Their different gods often had animal heads (or the sun, the moon) to emphasise certain virtues.

The Greeks and to a much lesser degree, Romans, too, had great respect for living creatures. In Rome the bull was a spiritual motif and they sacrificed a bull to their gods to honour the gods. But unlike the Greeks, the Roman attitude to many animals was more negative than positive, more callous, as they involved animals in their arena as sport though never the bull which was reserved for sacrifice only. Rome also had the earliest animal enclosure (zoo) for the enjoyment of the Caesars. In a way we can say the seeds of our negative attitude towards the living world began with the Romans. The bear baiting, the dog fights, the rooster fights and all other such reprehensible practices that were very popular around the world and have now been stopped, arose from the Roman arena. Our modern-day zoos are another legacy from the Romans. Of all the ancient civilisations, Rome was the most callous towards the living world.

It is only in our time that we have almost completely lost caring and respect for the flora and fauna. And that is why so many species have become extinct and so many more are endangered. It is also due to our callousness and negligence towards our trees and forests that have led to numerous environmental problems including new diseases and mutated strains of other diseases facing us today.

Unlike today, all these civilisations had a mutually beneficial relationship with the world around them (except for the Romans to a great extent). Those civilisations took from the earth what they needed. They neither over-used nor exploited the earth to the extent we do today. They worked in harmony with the earth. And they were grateful for the earth's bounty. There were wars and conquests but the earth was not abused as it is today. The soil, the seas, the air and the creatures that live on the earth were respected. The rape of the earth was for a far distant time – our time!

Notes

Ashurbanipal the 4th king of the Sargonid Dynasty was the king of the Neo-Assyrian Empire from the death of his father Esarhaddon in 668 BC to his own death in 631 BC. He is remembered as the last great king of Assyria. During his reign the Neo-Assyrian Empire was the largest empire that the world had ever seen and its capital, Nineveh, was probably the largest city on the planet. During his rule, Assyrian splendour was visible in its culture and art as well as its military power. Ashurbanipal created the first known systematically collected and organised library at Nineveh. In more modern times, Nineveh was a tourist hub until the USA bombing of Iraq (1998) and the meaningless destruction of many of these priceless treasures. However, even now the word Nineveh conjures up an ancient, extremely artistically rich, panorama of the ancient Babylonians.

Tragedy of the Native Americans

No one knows for certain when the first Native Americans came to the American continent. However, it is believed it was about 30,000 years ago. It is believed that they came from Eurasia by way of the Beringia land bridge that connects Siberia to present day Alaska during the Ice Age. They then spread southwards throughout the Americas over subsequent generations. Genetic evidence suggests they came in at least three waves to about 10,000 years ago when the land bridge was submerged under the water due to rising sea levels and the ice melt.

American prehistory shows significant European influence on the Americas in the Upper Palaeolithic period. American indigenous cultures developed apace significantly until Christopher Columbus' voyages of 1492 and 1504 and until their conquest.

The conquest of the American Indians beginning from 1492 resulted in a precipitous decline in their population, to a great extent, due to introduced diseases, ethnic cleansing, warfare and most of all, slavery which forced their transfer from their ancestral homeland. They were subjected to warfare, to unfair treaties which the conquerors mostly broke, discriminatory governmental policies and forced assimilation. The native Indians really had no chance with their bows and arrows against the conquerors' guns and far more modern methods of warfare. All this culminated in the trail of tears.

Introduction

The trail of Tears underlines the terrible tragedy of the American Indians – all due to greed and the bitter face of colonisation. On the way to their destination, they were dogged by famine, exposure, starvation and disease. The Old cultures had no weapon to match that of the newer cultures that followed them to conquer and colonise them. And when the old and the new clash, it is generally a forgone conclusion as to who will win. The ancient weapons - the bows and arrows and spears were no match against modern muskets and guns.

In 1830 the then US President Andrew Jackson passed a bill called the Indian Removal Act in 1830 by which Indian tribes including the Creek, Cherokee, Chikasaw, Choctaw, Seminoles, the Southeast Indian tribe, the Eastern Woodlands Indians and other Native American tribes were forced to leave their homes and trek over 5045 miles of trail over land and water through 9 states (Alabama, Arkansas, Illinois, Kentucky, Missouri, North Carolina, Ohio, Oklahoma and Tennessee) to be relocated far from their homes in the South. Their designated territory was west of the Mississippi. This was because gold had been discovered in the Indian Territory and the Indian land was found to be very fertile. Of the 60,000 Indians at least about 15,000 died before reaching their new home – which was actually a reservation that they were being sent to. Many still live in reservations. They are still discriminated against in democratic USA.

The Trail of tears

The Trail of Tears is the Indian Removal Act of 1830 passed by the then President of USA Andrew Jackson. Gold was discovered on Indian Territory and their land was found to be very fertile. Moreover the land was already cleared and ready for planting. So the Native Indians had to be removed. The Trail was a series of forced relocations from their ancestral homes to suit the Euro-Americans' greed.

The British Proclamation of 1763 designated the region between the Appalachian Mountains and Mississippi River as Indian Territory (Georgia). The designated Indian Territory was supposed to be protected area for exclusive Indian use but soon European and American gold diggers and land speculators descended on Georgia. There was not only gold there but very fertile and arable land, excellent for agriculture. The US government ignored all these acts of trespassing on Indian land. In 1829 the Gold Rush in America began. The Euro-Americans demanded access to Indian land and so in 1839 President Andrew Jackson signed the act consigning the Indian to a lot of misery, heartbreak, poverty, disease and death. And most of all, to an enslaved and unfree, miserable future.

Under pressure the Choctaw were the first tribe to give in. They were supposed to be transported to their new territory by the American but the Americans failed to do so. They began their unfortunate journey in 1830. Many Choctaw died on the way of exposure, malnutrition, diseases, and exhaustion. Their removal from their homeland by the Americans was badly planned and seriously understocked. The American who took their land had a very easy time of it as the land was cleared and ready for planting, the soil was rich and arable. And there was gold to boot.

The Chickasaw were more suspicious of American help with transportation and reimbursement of their property. They must have known something about the Choctaw debacle. They sold their properties at a profit and financed their own transportation. They did much better than the Choctaw and other Southeastern tribes, losing less people on their enforced travel.

They began their journey in 1837.

The Creek too, finalised their agreement with the Americans but the Euro-American settlers and speculators moved in too early – before the settlement date. This led to delays, fraudulent land sales and conflicts. So their journey was delayed and they left in 1836. Once again the Federal authorities proved to be corrupt and incompetent. Like the Choctaw, many Creek died on the way of the same preventable causes.

The Cherokee opted for legal measures to resist removal, but failed as the lawsuit was rejected by the American Supreme Court. A few Cherokee leaders wanted to negotiate but the bulk refused. They thought their land rights would be respected. But that was not to be. In 1838 the US military began to forcibly remove the Cherokee from their homes, often at gunpoint. They were kept in extremely bad internment camps before beginning their journey. Many got sick. They were also very poorly equipped for the journey. Those going by river were loaded onto boats passing through Tennessee, Ohio, Mississippi and Arkansas rivers. Eventually they reached their destination – Fort Gibson in an Indian territory designated by the Euro-Americans. Only now were they given much needed food and supplies. About 4,000 of the 15,000 Cherokee that began the journey died enroute. About 1,000 evaded the authorities and founded communities in North Carolina.

A group of Seminole leaders negotiated a removal agreement but this was rejected strongly by the majority. The US insisted that the negotiation should hold. The Seminoles began fierce resistance (1835-1842). Eventually most were captured and removed to the West. Those that evaded the authorities remained in Florida.

The Northeast Indians were more mobile and less united. Separate groups negotiated separate agreements between 1830 and 1840. They ceded their properties but retained the right to hunt, fish and gather wild plants and timber in perpetuity. The Euro-Americans broke those promises too. Groups living in the Lower Midwest surrendered their lands very unwillingly. Some offered armed resistance to the Euro-Americans but were of course defeated. The most well-known of them was Black Hawk who rebelled in 1832. Between a third and a half of the Northeastern Indians were forcibly removed.

The trail of tears was a tragic and devastating blow to the Indians from which they have never recovered.

This is what colonisation does to the natives of a place.

The Native Americans, more than any other peoples had a very special relationship with the living creatures of the earth. The land and its living things permeated every aspect of their lives – from their physical to their spiritual well-being. Most clans and some warriors had their own totems and they highly respected that totem. The totem was the spirit that was the person's special protector, revered by the individuals. The Earth was central to their individual and communal sense of well-being. The earth could not be owned. It was there to supply their needs. In return they cared for the earth and all its creatures. Animals, birds, fish were never killed wantonly. What they killed they did so humanely and for food and clothes. No animals were put in small cages and forced to perform for people's amusement. All that would occur once the Europeans colonies were established. This would happen over successive centuries.

To conclude this part I can only say that the ancient civilisations left us a world inhabited by many beautiful and wondrous creatures - mammals, birds, reptiles, amphibians and fish and many other living things. But what did we do with those gifts?

It was our duty to care for them. Instead we exploited them, hunted them, killed them for our pleasure and entertainment.

Now our world is the poorer for losing those gorgeous creatures. And many of those that are not extinct, they are endangered.

We have failed miserably in our duty. It is time now for us to redress that betrayal by us of our sacrosanct duties – the care of the living earth.

PART II

COLONISATION

One reason for global warming and over exploitation of the earth's resources, in my opinion, is colonisation. Global warming did not take place overnight but over time as we abused the earth appallingly. The colonisers did not care about the colonies or the colonised people. They only cared about raping the wealth of these countries and about profit. So everything was exploited – the land, the forests and the sea. The creatures living on the land, like their human, native counterparts, fared no better as many species began to become extinct and the earth to become more and more polluted.

Colonisation of some peoples by others has been going on from historic times but modern colonisation, that I am concerned with here, began in the 14th century and some form of it still continues to this day.

The main reasons for colonisation were: religious persecution, greed for wealth and power, social unrest, overpopulation and economic problems. The other reason was imperialism and capitalism – to control and exploit the natural resources and the population of the colonised countries. The Age of Exploration and the beginning of expansion and colonisation by European powers was in its heyday. This was led by the Portuguese and then the Spanish followed by the English and the Dutch and the French.

Gilmartin (Gilmartin, Mary, Lecture - *Imperialism*) says that the three waves of colonialism were linked to Capitalism; that the first wave involved the exploring of the world to find revenue and at the same time to perpetuate feudalism. The second wave according to Gilmartin, was all about mercantile capitalism and to bolster the manufacturing industry of Europe. The third (and in her opinion the last) wave of European colonialism was to solidify all capitalistic ventures by the provision of raw material and markets for the finished products.

Waves of Colonization

Introduction

It is <u>presumed</u> that there were three waves of colonisation. I believe there were/are four. The **first wave** was the conquest of the Americas. The **second** was that of Asia. The **thir**d was that of Africa. And the **fourth** is going on now. It is economy based colonisation.

The main European countries to participate in the first wave were the Ottoman Empire, Spain and Portugal. This began the Age of Discoveries as all who could, rushed to explore, discover and conquer new lands and territories. The Ottomans conquered South Eastern Europe and as much of the Middle East as they could and Northern and Eastern Africa between AD 1359 and 1653. Portugal started its colonisation with the conquest of Ceuta, Morocco in 1415 and then, following this, the conquest of some other African islands and territories. While this was going on by the Ottomans, Portugal and Spain went to the Americas basing their claim of the territories on the Treaty of Tordesillas of 1494. According to this treaty, lands outside Europe were to be divided between the Portuguese Empire and the Crown of Castile (Spain). The area Christopher Columbus discovered on his first voyage was along this meridian. He claimed the lands for Castile and claimed Leon for Spain.

The Aztec Empire was destroyed by the arrival of the conquistadores under Hernán Cortés between 1519 and 1521. They brought diseases like smallpox that decimated the Aztecs who had never come across this disease and so had no immunity to it. The invaders' brutality was continued in genocidal policies even in the 19th (Argentina 1829-1852), 20th and 21st centuries against many natives by their colonisers and/or conquerors or where the natives were/are in a minority. For example the Navajos are the third most stricken group by the COVID-19 virus (following New York and New Jersey) today, but the help they get is not from the Federal fund but from other states like New York; the Muslim minority in India have recently had many of their rights stripped away by the Indian Government; and the Rohinga Muslim minority are still being killed off or forced out of their homes and land, in a very brutal and inhumane way under the leadership of the Burmese Nobel <u>Peace</u> Prize winner (1991) Aung San Suu Kyi. All these forced migrations are all for mainly economic but also for political reasons.

The victimisation of the Native Americans is still continuing to this day. David Stannard says: *The destruction of the Indians of the Americas was, far and away, the most massive act of genocide in the history of the world,* with about 100 million American Indians killed in what he terms the *American Holocaust.* Professor Ward Churchill (author and political activist) believes that the Native American was deliberately and systematically exterminated over the course of several centuries, and that the process continues until today as the fate of the Navajos in Arizona and COVID 19 clearly shows. There has been widespread infection and a lot of deaths. They do not have the necessary protection and their living conditions are at best abominable!

The Spanish and Portuguese claim in the Americas piqued the interest of Britain, France and the Netherlands. They went to the Caribbean and North America and staked their claim there. North America also offered a dumping ground of the undesirable elements in Britain. It was a British penal colony much like in Australia. It has been estimated that about 50,000 British convicts were sent to America with the majority landing in the Chesapeake colony of Maryland and Virginia. The Merchant ships that transported them auctioned them off like cattle. Families were separated including children who were sold off separately.

European colonialism was then in full swing.

The Conquest and Colonisation of America

Systematic European colonisation of the Americas began from 1492 when Christopher Columbus under Queen Isabella of Spain's sponsorship sailed west to find a quicker route to the Far East and by chance stumbled onto the soil of America. This was termed the New World. Columbus in his next two voyages also discovered the Bahamas and the Caribbean Islands. He claimed all the land for Spain.

So Spain sent Hernán Cortés to secure the land (America) and bring back gold. The first genocide in history against the king, Moctezuma II and the native Aztecs took place. More than 240,000 Native Indians died. Spain lost between 500 and 1000 men. By mid-16th century the Spanish crown had control of most of West, South and North America, the Caribbean Islands, Santa Cruz and Brazil.

Other Europeans disputed this and so the Treaty of Tordesillas was signed. Portugal, England, France the Netherlands, Sweden, Denmark, Norway and Russia (Alaska) also established their colonies.

There were many other reasons besides the desire for wealth for the establishment of the colonies:

> ➤ *State Sponsorship*
> Spain, Portugal England and France sponsored attempts to colonise different parts of the Americas from 1492 to 1611. Soldiers were offered grants of land if they settled there. Only non-Christian prisoners were allowed to be sold as slaves, and people were needed to work the lands. The native Americans had a bad time of it. Some converted. Natives who became Christians were not allowed to be sold into slavery.

➢ *Search for Wealth*

Seeing the Spanish come back with gold from the Aztec and Inca lands, the colonists also hoped to enrich themselves. Many colonists were sponsored by common stock companies. Many supply missions were sent to the Americas to help the colonists. Later, tobacco became a very important cash crop. There was a dearth of labour and so colonists (and immigrants) sought indentured servants. Their passage to America was paid and they were given food, clothes and quarters for a fixed number of years to work on the properties. In French holdings the economy was focussed on sugar rather than tobacco. In Canada it was fur from the natives (bought very cheaply) to be resold at huge profits. Many of the colonists especially French, became subsistence farmers.

➢ *Religious Reasons*

The first to come were the Roman Catholics from Spain, France and Portugal seeking to make their fortune. They claimed the first lands. Many people emigrated from their home countries due to religious persecution over the years. The 16th century Protestant Reformation broke the unity of Western Christendom and led to the formation of many new Christian sects who were often faced with persecution by the mainstream religious group and by governmental authority. In England the Church of England was established and the Roman Catholics were persecuted (e.g. Henry VIII and Edward VI). The Protestants were also persecuted under Queen Mary (Bloody Mary) Henry the VIII's daughter by Katherine of Spain. Some of the new sects and movements who sought refuge in America were the English Puritans, Anglicans, Dutch Calvinists, English Catholics, French Huguenots, German and Swedish Lutherans, Scottish Presbyterians, Jews, Quakers, Mennonites, Amish, English Quakers,

Baptists, Anabaptists, and Moravians. They, among others, sought to practise their form of worship without persecution, discrimination or interference. So they landed in the Americas. The lure of cheap land, religious freedom, right to improve their lot was impossible to resist. About 20,000 Puritans went to America.

➢ *Forced Immigration and Slavery*
Many local Native Indians were enslaved but a lot died due to diseases, and over-exploitation. The birth rate fell, and that became an issue. So slavers captured slaves from other countries especially from Africa and sold them in Slave markets in America. Slaves were also taken to the Caribbean, Mexico, and Brazil. It has been estimated that about 12 million Africans were traded. A majority of them were taken to sugar plantations and because of better food their life expectancy was longer. They were also encouraged to have a lot of children. Slaves were a valuable commodity on all plantations and the number of slaves a person owned, determined his position in society. They (the slaves) were also sometimes forced to breed.

Man's inhumanity to man
Makes countless thousands mourn
Robert Burns ***Man was made to mourn.***

The number of slaves imported to the 13 first states between 1619 and 1865: *(Miller and Smith, eds. Dictionary of American Slavery* (1988) p 678) was:
- 1619–1700 – 21,000
- 1701–1760 – 189,000
- 1761–1770 – 63,000
- 1771–1790 – 56,000
- 1791–1800 – 79,000

- 1801–1810 – 124,000
- 1810–1865 – 51,000
- **Total – 597,000**

➤ *Disease and Population Loss*

A very large portion of the Native Indians died due to epidemics of the imported diseases to which they had no immunity:

- smallpox (1518, 1521, 1525, 1558, 1589),
- typhus (1546),
- influenza (1558),
- diphtheria (1614) and
- measles (1618)

These diseases killed between 10 million and 100 million of the Native Indians of the Americas. This meant they needed to get slaves from elsewhere to cultivate the fields and keep them rich. It was economically a vital necessity to replenish their work force. The Slavers thrived – capturing or buying slaves from Africa to bring to America (CF. There is a host of books dealing with different aspects of the American conquest and treatment of Native Africans stolen from their homeland and sold as slaves. Listen to *Buffalo Soldier* by Bob Marley or read any of the books on Slavery like *Uncle Tom's Cabin* by Harriet Beecher Stowe or *To Kill a Mocking Bird* by Harper Lee – these give sympathetic insights to the plight of the Blacks of America – the stolen generations. Even now in the 21st century Blacks are sharply discriminated against, killed for the smallest infractions or for no real reason: e.g. the case of George Floyd, Breonna Taylor etc. American jails are filled with Blacks even today. And more blacks get the death penalty than others in the modern American jail).

Imperialism was reborn in the West with the emergence of the modern nation-state and the age of exploration and discovery.

It goes without saying that wherever the European conquerors landed, there was a devastating blow to the indigenous population living there. When Columbus met the Taino Indians on the island of Hispaniola (present-day Dominican Republic), the indigenous population fell from 600,000 to 60,000 in only twenty years. In Mexico, the indigenous population fell from 25 million to one million in just a hundred years.

The conquest of the Americas didn't stop with the Spanish conquest, however. After settling in North America, the Europeans who stayed there eventually broke off from Great Britain (1775-1783) and formed the United States and pushed ever westward following the ideals of "Manifest Destiny." This was the idea that the Settlers in America were born to expand across North America and "to redeem the Old World by high example" (Fredrick Merk – historian). To do so it was imperative to conquer and/or enslave others and take their land and possessions

Professor Ward Churchill of the University of Colorado estimates that the indigenous population of North America fell from 12 million in 1500 A D to 237,000 in 1900 A D. Although the "American Indian Wars" definitely contributed to this significant drop, experts agree that the biggest blow to the population was in the form of economic and social upheaval.

The Age of Imperialism (1870-1914) saw the British colonisation of the Americas. In the 19th century about 50 million people left Western Europe for America. But after the colonisation of the Americas by Britain, the new colonists decided to go it alone free from state control from Britain. The Boston Tea Party of December 16, 1773 set the stage and the war of Independence also called the Revolutionary war and the American Revolution broke out in 1773. Then in 1783 America threw off the yoke of Britain and 13 colonial states joined to form the United States of America under General George Washington. France entered the war on the side of the 13 states and turned a domestic issue into an international one. Other states were incorporated with the 13 first states after the American Civil war of 1861-1865 and in due course it became 50 states under the Stars and Stripes – the American flag.

And American Indians were not the only people they colonised. At the same time and even before, the Europeans had turned their eyes on Asia. There were a few stages here. The first phase was the colonisation in the 16th and 17th centuries of South East Asia by the Dutch, Portuguese, Spanish and French marine spice traders. Each nation sought to gain control of the trade centres, production and markets for finished products. Simultaneously they sought to rape the colonies of the riches and goods that they coveted.

This age was the result of the European nations' desire for expansion of their territorial possessions which in turn meant free raw materials, cheap labour, riches and markets for finished products including the rejected ones from Europe. This was a major result of Industrialisation. The Imperialists believed they had the right – indeed the moral responsibility to colonise and enslave other non- European nations.

There were some other points to this

- Paternalism – the treating of the people of the colonies like children. Basic needs were provided while taking away of their freedom
- Mercantilism – powerful European nations amassed untold wealth from the colonies

- Rape of colonies – colonies were not only raped of their basic rights and natural wealth but also of their heritage treasures and often their very lives
- Assimilation – which forced the colonised nations to adopt the religion, language, way of life etc. of the colonisers whether they wanted to or not.

In the 19th century 50 million people left West European countries for the Americas. The enslavement of the Africans was just a matter of time.

The **second wave** of colonialism began with the annexation of Malacca in 1511 by Portugal and the establishments of its first permanent base there. Then in 1565 Spain conquered The Philippines creating a trade route to Asia via Mexico. They also converted all the natives to Roman Catholicism.

Britain's involvement with and support of the East India Company (1600 AD) in Asia was to counteract the Portuguese influence. France and the Netherlands, not to be outdone, followed suit with their companies and interests.

The Dutch not to be outdone by Britain either, floated the Dutch East India Company in 1603. The Dutch maritime routes were then established. Meantime the British and the Dutch attacked the Portuguese when and where and how they could. It was a free-for-all.

France tried to enter the Indian subcontinent but that led to the Karnatic wars (from 1746 1763) with Britain which France lost.

The French came to Asia later but from 1858 it started colonising. The first was Southern Vietnam followed by the rest of Vietnam, Laos, Cambodia – which together made up French Indochina.

France also colonised the Middle East especially Syria and Lebanon.

Around this time, Britain, not to be outdone by France, colonised vast chunks of the Middle East, India, Hong Kong and many South-Eastern Asian states.

The grab for Asia had begun.

The **third wave** was the Scramble for Africa or as it is also known as the New Imperialism. This new push was regulated by the terms of the Berlin Conference of 1884-1885 (The Congo Conference or Kongokonferenz). It was also called the West Africa Conference. This coincided with Germany's emergence as a major power in Europe and so trade and colonial possessions had to be marked out. This invasion, colonisation, division and exploitation of Africa (1881-1914) left scars behind until today. From a rich continent with immense natural resources it became a poor one after the withdrawal of most of the colonisers. In 1870 where only 10% of Africa was in colonial hands, by 1924 easily 90% of Africa was colonised. The few to still be free were Ethiopia (Abyssinia of ancient name) parts of Somalia (Dervish state) and Liberia.

The European countries with the most colonies in Africa were: Britain, France, Germany, Portugal, Italy, Spain, and Belgium and in South Africa it was the Dutch. Each of these colonial countries had their own reasons for colonising. For example, Germany was empire building and controlled Cameroon, Tanzania, Uganda and Namibia – and of course large chunks of South Africa; while the Portuguese wanted the slave routes, slave trade and slave posts. Britain had many reasons to wish to colonise and spread its influence, get a large share in the slave trade etc. The Berlin Conference awarded large portions of East Africa to Great Britain. By 1894 the list of colonies included Rhodesia, Nyasaland, British

East Africa, Somaliland and the Sudan under British control. The few colonies Britain maintained in West Africa primarily provided support for the British navy. France was not far behind with similar demands. She planned to establish a continuous west-east axis in Africa. Among French possessions was Senegal from where she sent a military expedition to conquer all of Chad and she did.

There were several factors for the colonising of the continent of Africa – social, political, economic and religious, viz.: the desire for natural resources, national pride, the rivalry between European powers for hegemony, and desire for expansion for their version of Christianity. Internal African native politics also played its part in the unfolding of this dangerous game.

The **economic** factor was the acquisition of raw materials and riches, and slave labour. Industrialisation led to severe unemployment, rural displacement, crowded cities, and diseases. The situation led to cheap or unpaid slave labour, markets for badly finished products, human bank (the enslaved populace and the poor) for use as fodder in war.

The **social** factor was just as important – quest for national prestige and to curb social unrest in their own countries due to various factors including economic hardship as a result of industrialisation. Having territories overseas meant this surplus population could be shipped abroad and so avoid unrest at home. So settler communities were set up in Algeria, Tunisia, South Africa, Namibia, Angola, Mozambique, and central African areas like Zimbabwe and Zambia. Eventually the overriding economic and social factors led to the colonization of other parts of Africa.

Religious controversies were in their heyday. Many people wanted to be able to practice their faith without harassment or persecution which was common in England and other European countries at that time. For example 20,000 Puritans migrated to America. Colonies gave them that hope and was the main reason for religious immigration.

For all these factors, it was vital to possess territories. National preeminence was dependent on territorial acquisition.

King Leopold of Belgium began this scramble for Africa with the invasion and conquest of The Congo.

The scramble for Africa became so intense that it was feared it might lead to war among European nations. So Otto Von Bismarck, the Chancellor of Germany convened a meeting – The Berlin Conference from November 1884 to February 1885 to provide guidelines in the inter-nations competition for Africa. Some of the major articles that the subscribers were expected to abide by were:

1. *The Principle of Notification (Notifying) other powers of a territorial annexation*
2. *The Principle of Effective Occupation to validate the annexations*
3. *Freedom of Trade in the Congo Basin*
4. *Freedom of Navigation on the Niger and Congo Rivers*
5. *Freedom of Trade to all nations*
6. *Suppression of the Slave Trade by land and sea*

There was no African input to decide Africa's fate – its conquest, subdivision and colonisation. It was a *fait accompli* from the start. The victim had no say in the matter. The people were enslaved, the wealth of the land forfeited to the conquerors, and the animals were hunted for sport or as trophies. The rape of the land had begun in earnest. Extinction of the fauna and flora was set in motion.

According to Ehiedu E. G. Iweriebor: *The European imperialist push into Africa was motivated by three main factors: economic, political, and social. It developed in the nineteenth century following the collapse of the profitability of the slave trade, its abolition and suppression, as well as the expansion of the European capitalist Industrial Revolution. The imperatives of capitalist industrialization—including the demand for assured sources of raw materials, the search for guaranteed markets and profitable investment outlets—spurred the European scramble and the partition and eventual conquest of Africa. Thus the primary motivation for European intrusion was economic.*

The **fourth wave** I believe is now. "Democratic" Imperialism has been reborn in the West with the emergence of the modern nation-state. It is now the age of exploitation and carnage. It is to this modern type of empire building that I restrict the title "Democratic" imperialism which quite patently, is not democratic at all. Capitalist "democracies" wish to force their way of life, values, norms of social and political behaviour on all who follow a different path. But in actual fact, they mainly target those countries that are rich in oil and natural wealth (Iraq, Libya, Kuwait). And as an added bonus those countries that they feel are "Socialist" (Federal Republic of Yugoslavia) or "Communist" countries. *Democracy is rule of the people, by the people and for the people.* How then is it bringing 'Democracy' by forcing it on others? This is a conundrum that needs to be solved. Look at the number of countries the so-called democracies "liberated" sowing dissension by bombing them and killing off their leaders on one concocted excuse or another. This is certainly a new take on 'democracy.' I believe this is the fourth wave, popular in our times. – control of a foreign, independent state for economic reasons to economically profit the attackers/attacking countries.

Colonisation of Australia and New Zealand

Australia lies in the Southern Hemisphere. This land has been inhabited by the Aborigines who came here from the Polynesian islands between 40,000 and 70,000 years ago. Before the British colonised the land, it had been settled for a long time and the Aboriginal culture developed over 60,000 years making them the custodians of the world's oldest living culture.

The microcontinent Zealandia of which New Zealand is the largest unsubmerged part, most probably separated from Antarctica between 130 and 85 million years ago and then separated from the rest of Australasia about 60 to 85 million years ago. It was populated by the Maoris long before British intrusion.

New Zealand is a beautiful country with lovely places to see and some of the nicest people I have met. They are hospitable and good friends. I have very fond memories of that country. And its people.

Both Australia and New Zealand were part of the continent of Gondwana before its breakup. Now they constitute Oceania and Australasia (with other neighbouring islands). The Maoris of New Zealand came in canoes (waka) from the Polynesian islands in the 1300's in waves. They are among the youngest cultures. There is no record of these two peoples (the Maoris and the Aborigines) meeting anytime before the 17th or 18th century after the European exploration of Australia. As far as Maori language and culture is concerned, the Maori language is common to all of the Maoris and the iwi (People or tribe) is there to represent their culture. The Aborigines of Australia, on the other hand, do not have one common language or tribe but each group has their own iwis and dialects.

Britain was not the first or the only European nation to aim to explore the Pacific Ocean. An estimated 54 European ships from different nations explored the coast of Australia. In the early 17th century, a Spanish explorer almost landed in Australia, but instead landed on the island of Vanuatu.

Prior to British settlement of Australia, more than 500 Indigenous groups inhabited the Australian continent, i.e. approximately 750,000 people in total. Their cultures had developed over 60,000 years, making these people the custodians of the world's most ancient living culture. Each group lived in close relationship with the land and all its creatures. There was respect for the land and all its living creatures. There was no wanton killing or destruction. These people took and used only what they needed. There was also no waste.

In 1770, during his first voyage in the Pacific, Capt. Cook came across Australia and claimed the east coast of Australia under instruction from King George III of England. And so Australia became a part of the Crown as a penal colony. The prisons in Great Britain were overfull and territory was needed to deposit and house the prisoners. Australia was an excellent proposition. There was very little chance of escaping from the island nation. So in 1788 Capt. Arthur Phillip and 1,500 convicts, crew, marines and civilians arrived at Sydney cove. And the colonisation of Australia began.

With New Zealand it was a different story. Time was of the essence as France, too, was eyeing the island nation. New Zealand was never a penal colony. The Pakeha (Settlers) are descendants of the missionaries, whalers and sealers who were the first European settlers in New Zealand. There were about 2000 of them in 1840.

Both countries experienced ongoing internal conflict between the indigenous population and the colonisers but they took different tacks in resolving that. The Aborigines did not use muskets against each other and the colonists but the Maoris did – in the 1807-1839 conflicts. The Aborigines were not given the same rights as the Maoris were. Both had the gold rush on their soil. Both were founded in the same manner but settled somewhat differently. Australia was a penal colony whereas New Zealand was not. Australia was settled by prisoners, soldiers and those who came out with their families. The majority did not come out of their own volition. New Zealand was settled by missionaries, and other settlers who chose to come out here. Both countries are constitutional monarchies with the Queen at their head. Both are commonwealth realms under the Queen but with their own independent heads of state. Both are parliamentary democracies based on the Westminster system. Both are part of the wider Anglosphere. They are both in the Southern hemisphere and both are islands/island continent. They are each other's closest neighbours.

When Captain Cook circumnavigated the 2 major islands of New Zealand, he wrote back that they would be very suitable for colonisation. In 1642 Abel Tasman arrived off the coast of New Zealand and had his first battle with the Maoris. The land was open for the colonists to come and they did. By the 1830's New Zealand became a part of Great Britain. European settlers came in their scores to settle there. The Europeans introduced the musket, new agricultural methods, social structure and also brought new diseases with them. Maori culture and social structure began to disintegrate. The Maoris began to fear their land was threatened. Most were not ready to sell their land. By 1860 though most of the land was still owned by the Maoris, pressure was added with the new influx of settlers. In 1859 a Maori chief without consulting with others sold some land and precipitated war. This ended in 1872 but parts of the country

(King country) remained closed to the settlers. By 1900 New Zealand had become a settler country. The Treaty of Waitangi was signed between the Maoris and the British underpinning the Maori right to their land as well as to British protection and their rights as subjects of the Crown.

But this was not at all the case with the Aborigines. They were killed off either violently or through poison or disease. Their women and girls were raped. Children from these encounters were removed from the family as young as a few months. They too were raped and put to work in service to the colonisers. This was the *stolen generation* that people talk about even today. (See the DVD *The Rabbit-Proof Fence* or read the book *Stolen* by Jane Harrison).

The most immediate consequence of the settlement of Australia was the epidemic of new diseases that they brought with them like measles, smallpox, cholera, influenza and other such epidemics. These spread like wildfire among the local population annihilating and decimating them. The then governor, Arthur Phillip, reported that smallpox had killed half the Indigenous population in Sydney within 14 months of their arrival (Governor Phillip to Lord Sydney, 13th February 1790, Historical Records of New South Wales, I, ii, pg. 308). The indiscriminate sexual abuse of the women led to the introduction of venereal disease in epic proportions.

Colonisation brought with it many ills – some very obvious from the start, others more insidious. In both North America, and Australia the Europeans brought the 3 D'S - dispossession, disease and direct conflict. But it was not so in New Zealand. Though the 3 D's was applied there too, it was to a much lesser degree perhaps because it was settled by missionaries, whalers and others who were not soldiers and convicted felons and who did not take to war and violence at the drop of a hat. In Australia following the advent of Capt. Arthur Phillip in 1788 about 90% of the Indigenous Aboriginal population died within 10 years.

Dispossession: In both Americas and Australia the natives were dispossessed of their land with no rights whatsoever. In the Americas it was first the Spaniards who destroyed the Inca and Aztec civilisations to be followed by the other Europeans. No one knows what happened to the Mayans. The Native Anmericans lost their lands and livelihood to the colonisers, They were moved to reservations. And in Australia Francis Tuckfield, a Wesleyan missionary (1837) had this to say:

"The Government is fast disposing of the land occupied by the natives from time immemorial. In addition to which settlers under the sanction of government may establish themselves in any part of this extensive territory and since the introduction of the numerous flocks and herds a serious loss has been sustained by the natives without an equivalent being rendered. Their territory is not only invaded, but their game is driven back, their marnong and other valuable roots are eaten by the white man's sheep and their deprivation, abuse and miseries are daily increasing."

(**Governor Phillip** to Lord Sydney, 13th February 1790, Historical Records of New South Wales, I, ii, pg. 308)

Disease: For the Indigenous Australians the colonists brought with them epidemics of new diseases like measles, smallpox, cholera, influenza and other such epidemics. These were all new to the Aboriginals, and they had no built-up resistance and so were incredibly vulnerable. Then also the women contracted Venereal diseases due to widespread raping of native women.

And as far as the Native Americans were concerned disease was rampant and ravaged the tribes, like smallpox (1518, 1521, 1525, 1558, 1589), typhus (1546), influenza (1558), diphtheria (1614) and measles (1618) killing between 10 million and 100 million of the Native Indians of the Americas.

Direct Conflict: Both the Aborigines and the Native Indians were killed off with the superior arms and armaments that the invaders brought with them. This is especially true for the Aborigines who had never seen a gun before the coming of the Fleet and British soldiers. In both cases there was a lot of direct conflict. In the long run the outcome was predetermined as of course the natives lost. One major reason for direct conflict was the expansion of British settlements and their encroachment onto Aboriginal lands along with their desire to establish new colonies in the colonised land. The same applied to the Native Indian lands and possessions in America.

The expansion of British settlements, including the establishment of colonies in Van Diemen's Land (Tasmania), Adelaide, Moreton Bay (Brisbane) and Port Phillip (Melbourne), resulted in competition over land and resources, and quickly resulted in violence. Historical records document numerous occasions on which Indigenous people were hunted and brutally murdered.

Massacres of Indigenous people often took the form of mass shootings or driving groups of people off cliffs. There are also numerous accounts of colonists offering Indigenous people food laced with arsenic and other poisons.

In the words of a Britisher who was there and saw it all:

> *"In less than twenty years we have nearly swept them off the face of the earth. We have shot them down like dogs. In the guise of friendship we have issued corrosive sublimate in their damper and consigned whole tribes to the agonies of an excruciating death. We have made them drunkards, and infected them*

with diseases which have rotted the bones of their adults, and made such few children as are born amongst them a sorrow and a torture from the very instant of their birth. We have made them outcasts on their own land, and are rapidly consigning them to entire annihilation." **Edward Wilson, Argus, 17ᵗʰ March 1856**

The Americas, Australia & New Zealand were all colonised but unlike other colonies stayed as part of the British crown (Australia and New Zealand) – language, religion tradition for the most part (America, Australia and New Zealand). British North America became independent after the war of Independence in 1775-1783 but is still mainly an Anglo-Saxon country. Australia and New Zealand are still part of the Commonwealth of Nations – both like North America espouse Anglo-Saxon values, ideals rituals, way of life, customs and traditions etc.

The colonisers raped the lands they colonised without compunction. The colonised lands and its people bled but there was no reprieve until much later – much later they either got back their freedom or became the colonisers chattel – land on which they then became people who were tolerated as second class citizens in their own land having no freedom. They had no say on their fate.

Once all these continents were colonised the fauna and flora were in trouble. Indiscriminate hunting and killing of the fauna and destruction of the flora began. Wood was needed for the houses so deforestation also began. Gold – man's bane - was discovered so, mining too began. The rape of the earth had begun in these colonial countries. It would lead to what we see today.

PART III

THE INDUSTRIAL REVOLUTION

The Industrial Revolution, which took place from the 18th to 19th centuries, was a period during which predominantly agrarian, rural societies in Europe and America became urban, industrialised societies. The transcontinental railroad, the cotton gin, electricity and other inventions permanently changed society. No one is quite sure why urbanisation and industrialisation takes place but it does and did. In the late 18th century Britain went from an agrarian to an industrial society. This had far reaching consequences and set the prototype for other countries to go industrial too. Along with the new technological inventions, mechanisation of labour and the newfound reliance on inanimate sources of energy, the change had profound social implications. There was now a free market in labour as the labourers were no longer tied to the soil. Industrialisation also saw the emergence of a new class – the entrepreneur. Land lay empty and uncultivated while the cities became crowded. There were more workers than jobs and so the workers were exploited.

Some countries like New Zealand and Denmark commercialised and mechanised agriculture. But even so the labourer's lot was hard. There was more opportunity now, but urban-industrial life alienated the worker by making him anonymous. Karl Marx and Emile Durkheim cited this alienation as the high price they paid for freedom of movement. It also had a psychological and social effect. Life was changed completely and drastically. The tasks needed long hours and seemingly meaningless repetition. The fragmentation of family life led to isolation. There was poverty and squalor as the labourers earned a pittance for long hours and lived in crowded, often unsanitary conditions. Disease became rife.

The main feature of this revolution was the use of steam power which, soon, by the 1830's and 1840's spread to the rest of the world from Britain. Manufacturing was overhauled and the revolution saw rapid advances in steel, electric and automobile industries.

As mentioned earlier, Britain was the birth place of the first industrial revolution. Due to its damp climate, there was a long history of producing textiles like wool, linen and cotton. Prior to this revolution, Britain was a true cottage industry where workers worked in small workshops and in their homes. Individual spinners spun, wove and dyed the clothes painstakingly by hand. But now came innovations like the spinning jenny, the power loom, the water frame and so on. Producing cloth required less time and effort. And certainly less manpower!

In manufacturing the mechanisation of production meant that Britain could meet the growing demand for cloth at home and for its many overseas colonies where there were ready-made markets for British products. Britain also adopted the new innovations in its iron industry. This was the smelting of iron ore with coke instead of the traditional charcoal. This is a process by which a new material is made by the heating of coal. This method was cheaper and produced better quality of materials, enabling Britain's iron and steel production to expand to meet the newer demands of the Napoleonic wars (1803-1815) and for the growth of the railroad industry.

Impact of steam power

In the early 1700's Thomas Newcomen designed the prototype of the first modern steam engine, called the *atmospheric steam engine*. This idea was originally applied to power for the machines to pump water out of mine shafts.

Then also in the 1700's The Scottish engineer James Watt added a separate water condenser to Newcomen's model, making it more efficient. He later collaborated with Matthew Boulton to invent the rotary motion steam engine that enabled the spread of steam power to industries like flour, paper, cotton mills, iron works, waterworks, canals and distilleries.

This application allowed miners to go deeper into mines and so extract relatively cheaper energy source. Demand for coal skyrocketed and soon it would be needed not only in factories but also in railroads, steamships etc.

Transportation

Prior to the First Industrial Revolution, Britain's road network was quite primitive. By 1815 there was more than 2,000 miles of canal across Britain.

In the early 1800's Richard Trevithick made a steam-powered locomotive followed by similar locomotives transporting freight and passengers (1830) to and from industrial cities like Liverpool and Manchester. Steam boats were already used widely at this time carrying goods even across the Atlantic.

Communication and Banking

The second half of the first industrial revolution saw key advances in communication methods over long distances. In 1837 British inventors William Cooke and Charles Wheatstone patented the first telegraphy system while at the same time Samuel Morse and others were working on their version in the USA. Cooke and Wheatstone's system was used for railroad signalling as more sophisticated systems were needed.

Banks and financiers became prominent at this time. A stock exchange was established in London in the 1770's. The New York stock market was established in the 1790's.

Adam Smith (1723-1790), the father of modern economics, published his *The Wealth of Nations,* based on free enterprise, private ownership of means of production and less governmental interference.

Working Conditions

The industrial revolution saw a mass movement of people from the villages to the city. Small towns started becoming large cities over a short span of time. This rapid urbanisation brought with it many significant challenges like pollution from being overcrowded, inadequate sanitation, lack of clean drinking water and other problems.

A new class - the middle class came into existence as a man was no longer circumscribed by his birth. His abilities were what mattered.

As industrialisation increased so did a better living standard for the upper and middle class. The poor became poorer. The working class struggled for a living. The mechanisation of labour made work tedious due to its repetition and ensured the anonymity of the labourer. It was also dangerous. Workers were often forced to work long hours for a pittance. Family life became fragmented.

Meanwhile the recent migration of Samuel Slater, (1793) to the USA led to the establishment of the first textile mill there in the USA. The Industrial Revolution had come to the USA. Slater brought with him Arkwright's (inventor of the water frame) idea unlawfully to the States and implemented it there. He came to be known as the "Father of American Industrial Revolution"

America followed its own path forward from there onwards.

Industrial Revolution, Chemicals and World War I

The first industrial revolution changed the world in many ways – an immediate change as well as a gradual evolution to what is now the Fourth Industrial Revolution. It shaped the world, its economy, the beginning of technology, social and political way of thinking and living. In fact it affected all parts of our lives and way of life. Among these was the introduction of modern chemicals.

Toxic chemicals have been around since ages past but the first time it was used on a very large scale was during World War I.

The Industrial Revolutions brought about many changes that made life easier but it also saw the first production of chemicals on an industrial scale – some of which would be used in World War I. Chemical use began with Thomas Henry of Manchester's (1734-1816) production of *Henry's Genuine Magnesia*. This was marketed for its medicinal properties but soon was applied to the pottery industry – another product of the First Industrial Revolution.

Around the same time Henry was also working on mineral water production which was infused with Fixed Air (CO_2) in a pressurised container. Dr. Hagarth of Chester improved on it with the bellows technology. Large scale production of mineral water began.

The idea was then applied to brewing and fermentation. This led to the production of fermentation and brewing processes. Bread and malt liquor were produced, as was *aromatic vinegars* i.e. perfumes made by dissolving camphor, essential oils and acetic acid – again marketed for medicinal purposes – against infections.

It was then applied to the booming textile industry especially in the manufacture of wool, silk, and cotton. At the same time Henry was busy in extending chemical treatment to various products. The French chemist, Claude Louis Berthollet, was also experimenting in developing the fixed agents further to apply to different fabrics.

Henry's sons also worked in the same industry with one son working with sulphuric acid production (vitriol). They laid the foundation for the chemical manufacturing industry of today. Henry and his son extended their research into extraction of metals from ore and the manufacture of glass and porcelain.

Though chemicals have been used as toxic weapons since thousands of years, it was not as toxic as those used in the First World War nor was it used on a large scale. Once the Germans began using it others followed. During WWI (1914-1919) it was used mainly to demoralise, injure and kill the entrenched soldiers indiscriminately. These toxic substances were slow-moving or static and most effective against the hapless soldiers in trenches or on the ground. Some of these chemicals were tear gas which was not as lethal as phosgene, chlorine and mustard gas. The gas did not kill outright but over time. Some estimates put the number of fatalities due to gas in the First Great War at 90, 000 from a total of 1.3 million gas casualties. Gas masks did not really help. This came to be called the Chemist's war due to the extensive use of chemical directly and use as *high explosives.* This was the first time weapons of mass destruction were used.

The use of poison gas in The First Great War was termed a war crime based on the 1899 Hague Declaration Concerning Asphyxiating Gases and the 1907 Hague Convention on Land Warfare as both forbade the use of poison or poisoned weapons in war. The public was revolted by the use of chemical warfare and so there was less use of it in World War II.

The main chemicals used in World War I were: grenades filled with ethyl bromoacetate, bromine, chloroacetate, fragmentation shells filled with chemical irritants and (1915-1919) artillery shells filled with xylyl bromide, chlorine (which caused damage to the eyes, nose, throat and lungs); phosgene and mustard, sulphur mustard (lethal agents also caused burns; internal and external bleeding; sometimes it took a few weeks to die in agony). A nurse nursing soldiers had this to say: *I wish those people who talk about going on with this war whatever it costs could see the soldiers suffering from mustard gas poisoning. Great mustard-coloured blisters, blind eyes, all sticky and stuck together, always fighting for breath, with voices a mere whisper, saying that their throats are closing and they know they will choke."* Another nurse recorded: *They cannot be bandaged or touched. We cover them with a tent of propped-up sheets. Gas burns must be agonizing because usually the other cases do not complain even with the worst wounds but gas cases are invariably beyond endurance and they cannot help crying out.*

> *Gas! Gas! Quick boys! – An ecstasy of fumbling,*
> *Fitting the clumsy helmets just in time:*
> *But someone still was yelling out and stumbling,*
> *And flound'ring like a man in fire or lime*
> *Dim, through the misty panes and thick green light*
> *As under a green sea, I saw him drowning.*
> (Wilfrid Owen - *Dulce et Decorum est Pro Patria mori*)

And this was not only against soldiers but also against civilians. There were between 100,000 and 260,000 civilian casualties of chemical warfare. Tens of thousands of civilians died from scarring of the lung tissues, skin damage, and cerebral damage even years after the conflict ended. Wilfrid Owen who fought in that war and saw first hand how it unfolds, captures it very succinctly in the following lines

If in some smothering dreams you too could pace
Behind the wagon that we flung him in,
And watch the white eyes writhing in his face,
His hanging face, like a devil's sick of sin
If you could hear, at every jolt, the blood
Come gargling from his froth-corrupted lungs
Obscene as cancer, bitter as the cud...
(Wilfrid Owen - *Dulce et Decorum est Pro Patria mori*)

The Second Industrial Revolution

The second Industrial Revolution continued and built on the first one by the end of the 19th century. During this time modern industry began exploiting many natural and synthetic products which were lighter, cheaper and more durable– alloys, metal, plastic, synthetic fabrics as well as new energy sources. Besides these, new machines and tools were invented. The computers were also invented which gave rise to the automatic factory. Segments of factories were almost completely mechanised by the mid-19th century. Automatic operation distinct from the assembly line was perhaps the most significant achievement of the middle of the 20th century. So it was called the technological revolution. It was a time for standardisation and industrialisation. Many events and innovations of the First Industrial Revolution were improved upon like machine tools and improvements in manufacturing methods. The Bessemer Process of steel production was invented. It was a time of standardisation and industrialisation that continued from 1870 to 1914 (beginning of World War I)

Advancements in manufacturing and production technology enabled great strides in technological systems like the telegraph, railroad, water supply system and sewage management. The railroad allowed unprecedented movements of large numbers of people and ideas. Electricity and telephones started being used.

This industrial revolution was especially rapid in Britain, Germany, USA, France, the Low Countries, Italy and Japan. It saw the production and use of interchangeable parts and improved mass production. More and more railroads were constructed; it saw the large scale production of steel and iron, widespread use of machinery in manufacturing, increased use of the railroad and of steam power, use of petroleum and the beginning of electrification. It also saw research in the production of gases.

A lot of these would be used in The First World War – which till then, was to be the war that would beat all wars.

The internal combustion machine and petroleum were used. New material and substances including alloys were discovered or created. Engineering was now science-based.

Ownership of means of production also changed. The restricted ownership of the first Industrial Revolution gave way for a wider ownership where the average person could buy stocks in the means of production.

It was generally regarded as the technological revolution.

Steel: Sir Henry Bessemer invented steel. It was made by removing excessive carbon and other impurities from pig iron by oxidation. This was improved upon by Sidney Gilchrist Thomas. The next improvement was by the Siemens-Martin Process invented by Sir Charles William Siemens who developed the regenerative furnace. With the availability of cheap steel, building of ships, bridges, skyscrapers, railroads went on apace. They used steel also in making steel rods and steel sheets which enabled the building of large high-pressure boilers. It also contributed in the making of car parts – axle, gears, powerful engines and so on. With large amounts of steel it became possible to build much more powerful guns and carriages, tanks, armored fighting vehicles and naval ships which would be used in the Great War. Steel being stronger and more durable also replaced iron in rail and rail transportation.

Electricity: This was first laid out by Michael Faraday who came up with the concept of electromagnetic fields. His invention of the electromagnetic rotary system became the basis for the use of electricity in technology. This led to the invention of the incandescent light bulb. The first large scale distribution centre for home and industrial distribution of light was in London in 1882.

Electrification also led to major developments in manufacturing methods: the assembly line and mass production. It also led to the production of electro-chemicals like aluminium, sodium hydrochloride, magnesium and chlorine.

Machine tools that first began with the first Industrial Revolution were expanded upon and improved on by using metal parts.

The first paper making machine was established. In the petroleum industry, crude oil was refined. Paraffin was also extracted from crude oil. Kerosene oil began to be used instead of whale oil, tallow and vegetable oils which were more expensive.

Chemical: Synthetic dye was discovered. The first modern ship was constructed as disparate technological advances were amalgamated. The first steamship was constructed and floated too.

There were many other discoveries and inventions that would be used later, in World War II as the scientists understood and applied thermodynamics to different spheres of life.

In the socio-economic sphere crop failure no longer meant starvation. Living standards improved vastly for those who could afford it. But machines started displacing men and so there was large scale unemployment. Many businesses failed. But population kept on increasing. Cities were more crowded than ever.

Summary of 1st and 2nd Industrial revolutions

The first industrial revolution, and the second one that followed, had many different characteristics that were important, and in many ways changed the way the world worked.

> ➢ Agrarian societies became urbanised.
> ➢ The industrial revolutions created a great need for factory work under very harsh conditions. This led to the widespread adoption of worker laws and rights.
> ➢ Marxian economics was forged in these circumstances during and shortly after the industrial revolutions, which lead to new political and economic dynamics.
> ➢ Machines replaced the intense physical work that men were originally doing. This lead to a culture of bodybuilding within many different groups. It also led to the adoption of the aesthetics of male physicality in nationalist circles, and another era of glorification of Roman and Greek statues. This is believed to have become part of the Hitler movement later on.
> ➢ Since hard labor was no longer a necessity, some women started to push for a right to be able to work outside the home. The Suffragette movement or the Women's Rights Movement became a major issue in1903 under the leadership of Emmeline Pankhurst in England. Eventually it led to emancipation for women.
> ➢ Countries started to modernize their cultures, and monarchies fell apart or had to adapt. In Germany, this led Wilhelm II to become somewhat of a hedonist, adopting a moderately bohemian lifestyle. The king of England, George V was also a kind of a hedonist, eating large portions of food.
> ➢ The harsh industrial life led to several outdoor cultures, such as the wandervogel culture in Germany, which expressed a desire for adventure, freedom, and

self-responsibility. This later became part of German nationalism, and eventually the groundwork for the Hitlerjugend (World War II).

➤ The French birthrates dropped significantly after the Napoleonic wars. Before this, the French had outnumbered the Germans by a large margin, now the French were almost twice outnumbered by the Germans and their empire. This and the loss of French territory frightened the French into strong nationalism, and a desire to again establish France as an economic powerhouse.

➤ The industrial revolution changed many societies from rural ones to large urban areas and big cities. In these big cities, things were usually a lot more modern, while large parts of rural areas preferred to keep things as they were. This created tensions between people living in urban areas, and people from rural areas. This didn't just stay between rural people and urbanites, a movement called Luddites, a group of early workers, was a criminal organisation that destroyed machinery to protest against the industrial revolution.

➤ The massive migration to urban areas created such a large demand for housing that large areas turned into slums until houses would be built. Flats were filled to the brim with people, and of course disease became endemic.

➤ Rural areas were emptied to such an extent that sometimes 80% to 90% of a population were living in urban areas. Villages were deserted and farmland lay uncultivated.

TIMELINE FOR THE 1ST AND 2ND
Industrial Revolutions

Date	Event
1712	Thomas Newcomen invents the first steam engine. It is rudimentary
1764	James Hargreaves invents the spinning jenny
1769	James Watt improves on the steam engine. It is used to power the first trains, the steamboats and is also used in factories
1794	Eli Whitney patents the cotton gin which makes it much easier to separate the cotton fibre from the seeds. It reduces the time needed for the job. Enables the Southern States of the USA to make more money from cotton
1800	Alessandro Volta developed the first practical method of generating electricity called the voltaic pile
August 1831	Michael Faraday created the first transformer and revolutionised almost every aspect of life of that time in England
1844	Samuel Morse invents the telegraph. Messages can now be sent quickly over the wire. By 1860 telegraph wires stretch from the east to the west coast of the USA
1846	Elias Howe invents the sewing machine. Clothes start being made in bulk in factories
1853	Elisha Otis invents the elevator safety break to stop elevators from falling down if a cable breaks
January 1855	Henry Bessemer invents the process for making steel out of iron. This helps in the building industry. It is faster and cheaper. It also leads to the growth of cities.
1861	Richard Jordan Gatling makes the first machine gun. It will, later, be used in World War I. He also makes the Colt revolver, the screw propeller, the wheat drill, the hemp break machine, a steam plough and a motor driven plough.
January 1860	Louis Pasteur develops vaccines for disease, which prevents diseases and people start living longer.
1865	Joseph Lister comes up with antiseptic surgery used to control sepsis after amputation. He reduced mortality rate in patients.
1866	Alfred Nobel invents dynamite which is a safer way to blast holes for mining, for clearing paths, in building the roads and railroads. Later it will be used in World War I

1867	Lucien B Smith invents the first barbed wire in Kent, Ohio USA
1879	Thomas Edison invents the electric bulb. People can now do a lot of things by night like working at night.
24th November 1873	Joseph Glidden invents and is awarded the patent for the first practical barbed wire in New Hampshire, England. He constructed the barbed wire by using a coffee mill to create the barbs which he then placed along a wire and twisted another wire around them to keep them in place
March 1876	Alexander Graham Bell patents the telephone. Communication is better and faster over the wire.
October 1879	Thomas Alva Edison patents the first light bulb. He also develops the electric power generator, mass communication sound recording, the phonograph, cameras etc.
May 1883	The Brooklyn Bridge the longest suspension bridge in the world at that time, opens in New York
1890	Sir James McKenzie, a Scottish cardiologist used his polygraph which he invents to measure the heart condition of one of his patients.
1901	Wilhelm Conrad Röntgen discovers the x-ray which revolutionizes diagnostic medicine.
December 1903	Orville and Wilbur Wright make the first powered aeroplane and fly it for 12 minutes in North Carolina
October 1908	Henry Ford makes the Model T car. It is cheaper and more accessible to all as it is made on the assembly line.
1914	Garrett A Morgan invents the gas mask as smoke protection which was called the Morgan Safety Hood. Later called the gasmask. It was used as protection from the gas used in World War I.

Sophia Z. Kovachevich

The Third Industrial Revolution

*The Third Industrial Revolution **begins with a dire premise**. The global economy will continue to exist in tatters for decades, extreme political movements will fail to deliver us from the brink, and climate change will further exacerbate our journey to extinction.*
Jun 3 2018 - The Economist

And so it has happened. In every corner of the earth there is turmoil, warfare and natural disasters. Most economies are in dire straits. More powerful countries interfere and create more problems than they solve. Powerful countries sabotage themselves (USA). And adding to the political and economic turmoil, new diseases have taken centre stage. COVID 19 stalks the streets of many nations and attacks without fear or favour where it will. People are sickening and dying in droves. Countries are scrambling to find an antidote. Hope is an expensive commodity until a vaccine is made.

The third industrial revolution saw manufacturing going digital. It was all about computers. From the 1950s onwards, computers and digital systems enabled new ways of processing and sharing information. Transistors, microprocessors, robotics and automation – not to mention the internet and mass communications – that would eventually allow for the ultimate in scale: globalisation.

The Industrial Revolution, powered by oil and other fossil fuels, is spiraling into a dangerous endgame. The price of gas and food is climbing ever more steeply, unemployment remains high, and has increased tenfold since the Pandemic, the housing market has tanked, consumer and government debt is soaring, and the recovery is slowing. Facing the prospect of a second collapse of the global economy, jobs are evaporating, humanity is desperate for a sustainable economic game plan to take us into the future. In his book, Jeremy Rifkin (*The Third Industrial Revolution*) explores how Internet technology and renewable energy are merging to create a powerful "Third Industrial Revolution." He asks us to imagine hundreds of millions of people producing their own green energy in their homes, offices, and factories, (as the solar panels and green energy has already manifested itself) and sharing it with each other in an "energy internet," just like we now create and share information online. Rifkin describes how the five-pillars of the Third Industrial Revolution will create thousands of businesses, millions of jobs, and usher in a fundamental reordering of human relationships, from hierarchical to lateral power, that will impact the way we conduct commerce, govern society, educate our children, and engage in civic life. Rifkin's vision is already gaining ground in the international community. The European Union Parliament has issued a formal declaration calling for its implementation, and other nations in Asia, Africa, and the Americas, are quickly preparing their own initiatives for transitioning into the new economic paradigm. The Third Industrial Revolution is an account of the next great economic era, including a look into the personalities and players — heads of state, global CEOs, social entrepreneurs, and NGOs — who are pioneering its implementation around the world.

The last two chapters of the book discusses what the author calls the Third Industrial Revolution, the changes created by microprocessors, lasers, fibre optics, biogenetics, etc. The author believes this transformation will be even more profound than the First Industrial Revolution which ushered in the machine age at the beginning of the 19th century or even the Second that brought about the age of the automobile, electricity, radio, and large-scale chemical production.

Bestselling author and renowned economist Lester Thurow argues forcefully that globalization is not a done deal and we must seize the moment now if we are to create a new global economy in which all can prosper. In this new book, (*Globalization: The Product of a Knowledge-Based Economy*) Thurow examines the newly–forming global economy, with a special focus on the role of the US and the dangers to the USA's national well–being. But the US under President Trump has abdicated all responsibility and adherence to a global economy. Only time will tell where this goes! Thurow examines such questions as: What's at stake in the global economy? Why is it important that the system be equitable and that other countries prosper along with the USA? What should its goals as a nation long term and short term be? What are the tough choices that need to be made in America's relationship with other countries and world regulatory bodies? What role should America play globally? What are the political, economic, social choices/tradeoffs that will have to be confronted? Thurow contends that the huge and growing US trade deficit poses grave dangers to the value of the dollar and is putting the US economy in jeopardy. As the world economy leaps national boundaries, its hallmark seems to be a rising instability and a growing inequality between the first and third worlds. Financial crises in the third world come ever more frequently and seem to be ever more severe. The first world economies seem to be in ever more frantic boom and bust cycles. Globalization causes riots throughout the world and is one factor in the rise of terrorism against the West. Thurow shows how some nations, including Ireland and China, have embraced the concept of globalization and placed themselves into a position to prosper with growing and productive national economies. He contrasts their positive actions with Japan, whose leaders have allowed the nation to drift into stagnation and have destroyed its prosperity. He argues that this is the time to choose globalization or be left behind, the time to "*build a global economy that eliminates the defects,*" and he provides plenty of ideas for corporations, governments, economists, and citizens to act upon.

The Third Industrial Revolution the global economy shows that it is in crisis. The biosphere's inability to absorb human activity, combined with the exhaustion of natural resources, the endangerment of the fauna and the flora, new diseases and mutations of already existing ones, declining productivity, slow growth, rising unemployment, coupled with racial inequalities should force people to rethink their economic models.

A number of remarkable technologies converged in the third Industrial Revolution– software, robots, new processes like the 3-D printing and a lot of web-based services. For example a product can be designed on a computer and printed on a 3-D printer which can run unattended to print out the required image - in another room or country. The Third Industrial Revolution saw the applications applied to hearing aids – minute contraptions that can barely be detected but which greatly amplifies sound. New technology has allowed doctors to see inside the human body and perform surgery like cutting cysts in the colon, sewing arteries and so on. Bandages are made that have healing properties. This is an example of nanotechnology. Batteries can be made of genetically engineered viruses. We often eat genetically modified food. Most canned food containing oils, starch etc. is genetically modified.

The new materials are lighter. Carbon fibres are replacing steel and aluminum products ranging from things like airplanes to mountain bikes. Additive manufacturing is spearheading this revolution. It is much cheaper than the old hand-made tools and easier to manipulate and use. And it can be mass produced very easily.

Countries now have factories in faraway, low-wage countries to save on wages. Countries import a lot of goods from low-wage countries as they are much cheaper. Cheap labour in third world countries produce the goods of the first world countries. Inequality and exploitation thrive as always.

IPads, IPods are the way to go. One sees children as young as three years of age amusing themselves with such devices. People rarely call on the telephone or send letters or cards. Instead there is Facebook, Twitter etc. Meetings no longer need to be face-to-face. There is Teams (Microsoft), Zoom and other similar programmes for that.

UAV's (Drones) - unmanned aerial vehicles, or drones was first envisaged by Nikola Tesla. Then it was in the realm of fantasy but now it is a common sight.

It was used in World War II by both the Allies and the Axis powers with devastating consequences. After the War it was used by the US military for reconnaissance missions and against the Vietnamese in the Vietnam War. By the 21st century it took on the role of armed drones against enemies controlled from a safe distance via satellite link. This happened in October 2001 when the drone, the Predator was used in a strike in Kandahar, Afghanistan. The age of militarised drones was in full swing. Now in 2020 drones are commonplace with special attack drones for use against countries and their inhabitants without any harm to the attacker.

Now it is often bought even by civilians to fly as a hobby. They are inexpensive. They are used to attack the enemy, to take photo shots, to spy and for numerous other purposes. Its use is only circumscribed by the imagination of the user.

The Fourth Industrial Revolution

The fourth industrial revolution (also called Industry 4.0) is building on the third. It is characterised by a fusion of technologies that has blurred the demarcation lines between the physical, technological, digital and biological spheres.

We are in this technological revolution that has already changed the way we live, think, work and interact with each other. We are cutting ourselves off from others. This transformation of society where each lives in their own bubbles is unlike anything we have experienced before. Everything is available at the click of a button. Many people rarely leave their houses to interact with others. Shopping for goods can be done from home or online. Offices will become more and more uncommon as people distance themselves from each other more and more to live in solitary places. And so it has already begun. Schooling is also now gone virtual. Computers will replace humans and it has already begun (See footnote). With the COVID 19 pandemic more and more people are working and studying from home, using computers. Once the pandemic is over, many will continue to do so. Group meetings are taking place through applications like ZOOM.

This revolution like others before it is disruptive, as is the nature of revolutions. Digital technology has already rocked the world with its new innovations and their applications. Our warehouses have already become futuristic with for example, the forklift doing all the hard work manned by one. Robot nurses are helping out in hospitals. It will only increase. The future will see everything manned by robots. Now one can buy a robot (GPS) and give it long distance commands like which route to take. The robot then follows the instructions. Car doors open automatically by sensory recognition. Robots will soon be used to do all our housework. School curriculum too, will soon be

63

taught by robots. Now we already have distance learning but soon the human input will disappear.

Note:
In 1909 EM Forster wrote a short story The Machine Stops. It encapsulates what is happening today to a great extent. It is a story where machines automatically control all spheres of human life. It is much like what is happening today but goes still further

Another popular appliance is the drones. These drones (UAV - unmanned aerial vehicle) are becoming ever more popular not just with governments but also with individuals. It is not only the military that uses drones, but also the public. Perhaps the ones for public use are not as advanced as the ones the military uses as yet. These UAV can be used to take aerial photographs, deliver parcels and many other things. In the near future, I think a lot of the mundane tasks will no longer be performed by people but will fall on the drones and robots to do.

There are three reasons why today's transformations represent not merely an extension of the Third Industrial Revolution but rather the arrival of a distinct Fourth one in the spheres of speed, scope, and systems impact. *The speed of current breakthroughs has no historical precedent. When compared with previous industrial revolutions, the Fourth is evolving at an exponential rather than a linear pace. Moreover, it is disrupting almost every industry in every country. And the breadth and depth of these changes herald the transformation of entire systems of production, management, and governance.* (Klaus Schwab – Chairman of the World Economic Forum)

In my opinion I believe the strongest one is the fact that billions of people on earth are connected by mobile devices, the web, e-mail, Twitter and so on. Access to knowledge in our times is unlimited and covers diverse subjects. We have made unbelievable advances in AI (Artificial Intelligence). New drugs are constantly being discovered. New software is being used to discover new algorithms on which predictions are based. Digital technology is interacting with biological ones to produce new treatments. Engineers, designers, architects are using computation with additive manufacturing and synthetic biology to produce a symbiosis among microorganisms, in our bodies, what we consume and even the space we inhabit. Digital technology allows you to make doctor's appointments and consultations on line, carry out operation of cysts, tumours within the body as well as the banding in a few short minutes of time. Laser surgery has become a common application. The impossible is now the new possible. Digital technology has totally changed our lives and the way we view things. The Corona virus has speeded up the process of change. Life will never be the same again after this pandemic is contained.

Like the earlier industrial revolutions, this one too has the potential to raise global incomes and improve the quality of life. In fact it is digitalisation that has made that possible, unbelievable breakthroughs in various fields like AI, 3-D printing, Robotics, Medicine, Prosthetic limbs, Internet Of Things, (IoT) autonomous vehicles, quantum computing, biotechnology, energy storage and many other fields. Today we have Artificial Intelligence, self-driven cars, cars that recognise the owners, robots that can work in the house or hospitals or anywhere else you wish to put them to use after being programmed, drones, virtual assistants and so on. The new cars no longer need keys to start. They start at the press of a button. We are moving from strength to strength in this field. Who knows where it will end. Now you can not only predict the sex of a baby but change its genome. Then there are the IVF pregnancies that have changed the lives of infertile couples. And of course there is cryogenics whereby you can be frozen in time to be defrosted and woken up in another time. Digitalisation has

65

been of immense value to students who can now evolve their skills in virtual environments, while simultaneously having access to all relevant materials. Digitalisation has paved the way for complex simulations. At home I see my husband turning an idea into a 3-D house in a very short time. It is fascinating. Products designed and tested on computers cost less and inexpensive prototypes can easily and cheaply be designed. The list is long and exhaustive. The opportunities are endless. It makes the mind boggle.

At the moment, the revolution could go in any direction. It could lead to greater inequality in wealth distribution as machines and robots displace the workers. Or it might end in the opposite direction. I personally think it will be the former. The rich will get richer and the poor will get poorer.

The impact of industrialisation on the environment

Industrial development has affected the environment negatively and severely. The pollution from industries has led to new diseases; manufacturing and transportation has polluted the atmosphere as well as depleting the natural resources at a faster speed than it can be renewed. It is a fact that industrialisation has brought about good things too, like electricity and new inventions and discoveries but on the ecological and environmental front, we have lost more than we have gained. Many species have become extinct, deforestation is taking place at an unprecedented pace, new weapons of war are used that destroy lives and contaminate the soil, water and air. That leads to diseases in humans and animals, and fruits and vegetables are contaminated. We consume those products and further contaminate our bodies. Then every now and again in one country or another there is famine due to extreme weather which is a result of industrialisation as we release many toxic substances into the air. Then there are typhoons, wild storms with cyclonic velocity winds or raging fires that destroy human lives, fauna and flora, property and farmland. Warming seas are causing ice-melts further endangering wild life in those areas and, in the ocean environment, damage to aquatic water environments, ocean currents and thereby further changing the geographical map of the earth.

Our space-crafts fly and contaminate space, planes are a common way of travel, automobiles, buses, heavy vehicles like trucks, factories and industries - all contaminate the environment with their toxic gases. Heavy armoured vehicles destroy the soil by compacting it and polluting it. All these are happening since we became industrialised.

Factory fire Footscray a couple of days later Aug.30, 2019
| Photo by Sophia Z Kovachevich

The soil is mined in war-torn countries. The mined soil cannot support life. Food cannot be grown there. The mines have toxic substances in them that contaminate the soil. Mines kill or maim people. Many of these people then cannot work but need to be supported. Governments are under even more pressure. And industrialised nations are taking war to less developed countries – contaminating, polluting and destroying nations and countries; maiming and killing young and old alike, sick and able-bodied alike and they have no recourse to any appeal to our better nature. Modern warfare is faceless, having no humanity or pity for the beleaguered nations. And non-combatants in those nations suffer the most – even more than before. Racism has once again raised its evil face as minorities are more and more sharply demonised. Leaders are elected who advocate further division, political instability and most of all the rape of nature and man alike. One such entity is President Donald J Trump of the USA.

Our industries produce the latest in technology but these appliances when they are broken or old or useless must be discarded. It goes into the soil and contaminates that with the toxins, metals, plastics, toxic batteries etc.

Global warming and the greenhouse effect are a direct result of industrialisation. And global warming has brought with it a plethora of problems like the ice caps melting as temperatures and sea levels continue to rise. And not just the environment is contaminated there has also been ecological costs. More and more of our forests are lost. Ever more fauna and flora are endangered or becoming extinct. Rockets are going into space and contaminating the air as they travel. The climate around the world has become unstable. Floods, bush fires, forest fires, hurricanes, tsunamis, cyclones, drought have become rampant nowadays. If it is not one thing, then it is another that confronts us.

The air, soil and water are contaminated. This affects human welfare. The ozone layer has got holes in places and that cause skin cancers. Many other kinds of cancers have appeared. Medicine has advanced remarkably but it has also had negative effects. One illness is cured but another, more dangerous one takes its place. Yes, people live much longer but they need more care. In many countries around the world the aged population outstrips the youth. Our aged population needs much more care, so care homes are mushrooming. People are having fewer and fewer children in the more industrialised countries. What will happen when our youth grow old and there are few to support them?

Summing up of the Four Industrial Revolution

All is seared with trade, bleared. Smeared with
Toil;
And wears man's smudge and shares man's smell
The soil;
Is bare now, nor foot can feel, being shod.
God's Grandeur – GM Hopkins

The first three industrial revolutions transformed our societies into modern ones. The fourth has taken us into another dimension.

The first saw the dawning of the age of mechanical production and the urbanisation of society. It saw the invention of the steam engine which was used to power everything from agriculture to textile manufacturing. From a predominantly agrarian society we stepped into an urban one. Steamships and steam trains revolutionised life. Travel became faster and easier. The community centre shifted to the factory. The poor became poorer and there was an over-abundance of workers most of whom were unskilled. They got paid a pittance for long hours and terrible work conditions. Slums grew up in cities. Life became very hard for the poor. But now a new class came into existence - the middle class – the class of skilled workers who were no longer circumscribed by the situation of their birth. And as the cities grew, the industries, and economies grew along with them.

The second industrial revolution saw in the age of science and mass production. Things sped up with the many new inventions – gasoline, engines, airplanes, chemicals and chemical fertilizers, the steel industry, electric bulb and so on. However advancement in science was not limited to the laboratories. Scientific principles powered the factories – the assembly line and mass production. By the early 20th century Henry Ford and his car were well known and affordable. The mass production of the Ford had begun. The ships were made of steel. Different gases (which would later, in 1914, be used in war) were in production. The beginning of the bomb production had come. Science had taken centre stage.

The third industrial revolution was about digitilisation. Digital technology rocked the media and retail industry much as the cotton mills destroyed the hand looms. Factories have already started having less people manning the factories and warehouses. Robots are used instead or stacking of heavy goods is done automatically.

The Third Industrial Revolution beginning in the 1950's also brought semiconductors, mainframe computing, Personal Computers and the internet. The analog TV moved to an internet-connected tablet – or the digital TV. Analog electronic and mechanical devices were supplanted by automate industry. They went digital. Online shopping started becoming the rage.

And this brings us to the Fourth Industrial Revolution which is on today. This has brought about a societal change. From being farm workers, people became urbanised and mechanisation took firm hold. Electricity and mass production changed life forever. Then came the next major transformation change with digital revolution once again altering the way how people lived, worked or communicated. Now we have genetic sequencing and editing, IVF, prosthetics, gene manipulation, robotics, cryogenics and a huge step forward in travel. Going to another planet to inhabit it is not just a dream but a serious possibility. Robots are an in-thing. Our houses have cameras because crime has risen to new heights. Home invasions have become an everyday occurrence.

IVF treatment has made it possible to have children where once such a thing was not even considered. We also have ovarian grafting and freezing the graft for cancer patients that can be reintroduced later thus enabling normal pregnancy. We have come a long, long way. Now you can determine the sex of your unborn baby; you can choose that, colour of eyes etc. You can change your facial features and body shape through surgery.

Prosthetics has made it possible to change your life totally where once you would have had to live a half-life. Prosthetic limbs make it possible for a disabled person to lead a full life.

We have truly come a long way. The impossible has become the possible and acceptable.

We are now planning to go to Mars on a one-way ticket. Of course there are conditions as the final aim is to populate Mars and then contaminate it as we have done on earth. Here we have contaminated the air, the water, the soil - everything. And we are responsible for the rape of the earth, the extinction of many species and the endangerment of many others. Yet we haven't learnt or stopped. After we contaminate Mars then we will repeat the same with our whole galaxy before going on to the next.

We have successfully landed on the moon and even collected soil specimen from the surface of the moon. We have established that there is water on the sunny side of the moon. That means that there is a distinct possibility of life there – according to our knowledge.

But in my opinion one of the most striking and shocking things is cryogenics. We would play god. Many people have been frozen cryogenically. Among them are the following people:

o James Bedford was an US Psychology Professor at the University of California. He was very interested in cryogenics and left $100,000 in his will for further research into cryogenics. He died from a severe form of melanoma in 1967. After death he was placed in a cylinder filled with liquid nitrogen and covered with ice packs. His bodily fluid and blood was drained and replaced with antifreeze.

o Dora Kent (1904-1987) – was an innocent victim of Cryogenics. In 1987 authorities analysed her remains and said it was not a natural death but murder and decided to preserve her cryogenically.

o Dick Clair Jackson, An American TV Personality (actor and producer) died in 1988 due to AIDS. He had no children. He wanted his body to be sent to Alcor, one of the top in-tech companies that get people who wish to be cryogenically frozen.

o Jerry Leaf was a pioneer in Cryogenic Suspension and Alcor's vice president. He asked to be frozen after his death in 1991. He (along with his colleagues) is renowned for creating a bloodstream alternative that could preserve life signs for a few hours after death.

o Fereidoun M Esfandiary (FM- 2030), a Belgian-born Iranian-American, author, teacher philosopher, a futurist consultant, an athlete and a transhumanist writer was cryogenically frozen after his death in 2000 at the age of 70. He published books on various subjects like politics, religion etc. In 1970 he took the name FM – 2030.

o Ted Williams – famous American Baseball Player had some of his body parts cryogenically frozen after he died in 2002. It triggered a massive public outcry.

o John Henry Williams – Ted's son died 2 years after his father of Leukaemia (in 2004). He too was cryogenically frozen.

o   Thomas K Donaldson, a famous US mathematician wanted to be cryogenically frozen when he died. That happened in 2006. He believed that death is just a phase and brain cells can store our memories. No one knows if this is true.

o   Kim Souzzi was an American. She suffered from a rare form of brain cancer. She died in 2013 at the age of 23. She asked for parts of her body and her head to be cryogenically frozen. She spent the last month of her life at a hospital, near the cryogenic centre of her choice in Phoenix, Arizona.

o   Hal Finney was a famous game developer and a tech celebrity. He was one of the creators of the PGP Corporation. He was among the first bitcoin clients. In 2009 he wrote in an article that he was suffering from Amyotrophic Sclerosis and died five years later (2014) at the age of 58. He too was cryogenically frozen.

o   Matheryn Naovaratpong was the youngest person to be cryogenically frozen at the age of only 2 years in January 2015. She was suffering from an unusual type of brain affliction. Her parents who were health care technicians wanted her to have a second chance.

o   JS a 14-year old girl from the UK, passed away from a rare and very aggressive form of cancer and wished to be cryogenically preserved.

In recent years there have been others. And I'm sure there will be more.

This is fascinating and frightening! We would play god!

Medical Advances in the 21st Century

The Fourth Industrial Revolution saw great strides in many aspects of life. Some of those that are most spectacular, in my opinion, have been the following:

❖ **Nano-Bots.** These are miniscule robots that are used to treat diseases and perform operations. They are used quite extensively to treat cancer patients. They are programmed to seek out and destroy cancer cells and deliver treatment to those cells that need the treatment. Nanotechnology is designing and building nanorobots, with devices ranging in size from 0.1–10 micrometres and constructed of nanoscale or molecular components.

❖ **Liquid Biopsy for cancer**: Cancer is one of the most prevalent and from my point of view, frightening of diseases. In the US only, it is estimated that there are about 600,000 cancer–related deaths a year. Biopsy is the process by which fragments of DNA that are shed by tumours into the bloodstream can be used to non-invasively screen the patient for cancer. Liquid biopsy can also measure circulating tumour cells and gauge the patient's chance of survival

❖ **Stem cell therapy** is the use of stem cells to treat or prevent diseases or conditions. Bone marrow transplant is the most widely used stem-cell therapy, but some therapies derived from umbilical cord blood are also in use. Research is underway to develop various sources for stem cells, as well as to apply stem-cell treatments for neurodegenerative diseases and conditions such as diabetes and heart disease.

❖ **Immunotherapy.** Cancer has been treated with chemotherapy and radiation since a long time. The problem with these is they result in nasty side effects like mouth sores, nausea and vomiting, hair loss and some rather malignant side effects. The latest in cancer treatment and control is immunotherapy. Through this method the body's immune response system is unleashed to attack and destroy the cancerous cells.

❖ In 2011, the first immunotherapy drug was approved by the FDA for advanced melanoma. This was used to treat ex-President Carter who had serious advanced melanoma which had spread to his liver and brain. He is now completely cured. Immunotherapy is also used to treat cancers of the lungs, kidney and head.

❖ **Stem Cell Hearts:** Scientists have been working towards stem cell hearts from the patient's own stem cells. Heart transplants are always tricky because one does not know beforehand if the patient's body will accept or reject the heart. With this particular therapy the stem cell is taken from the patient themselves. The doctors then construct a heart from that stem cell to fit perfectly into the patient's body. As far as I know, it has not yet been tried on a person but is well on the way.

❖ **Wearable sensors:** Most people if they need to see a doctor go to the medical centre. But now they are designing wearable sensors by which a doctor can monitor the patient's condition in their own homes, including if they have a fall and need help. So far it has already been developed by a company called Vital Connect. And this Health Patch is compatible with the Bluetooth. It has been cleared by the FDA. Soon everyone can be monitored using this device not just in the States but also in other developed countries.

❖ **Extended Aids Survival Anti-Retroviral Therapy**: Not so long ago Aids and HIV were considered to be death sentences. But now with the anti-retroviral therapy it is a totally different story. The therapy is a combination of medicines that treat the virus at a slow rate. This enables the patient to live longer with the virus under control. Professor Jonathan Sterne of Bristol University with some colleagues found that between 1996 and 1998 there were 16.3 deaths per 100,000. This dropped to 10.0 between 2003 and 2005. The numbers of deaths is much lower now. This shows the huge progress that has been made.

❖ **Smartphone Stethoscope**: is an electronic device that measures and records the heartbeat much more accurately than the manual stethoscope.

❖ **Electronic Blood Pressure machine** measures and records not only the blood pressure but also the pulse. It can store that in its memory for a number of times.

❖ **Robot Nurse Assistants**: Nurses have it rough. Often instead of a kind word for services rendered, they get abused. Such responses could have a negative repercussion on nursing itself. Nursing is a very stressful job. A small mistake could easily have very bad repercussions. The Robot nurse assistant has been created. It is there to help the nurse like transferring the patient from one place to another. This has proven to be a blessing where they are employed. There are less workplace injuries to nurses, patients also have fewer injuries due to improper lifting and there is excellent nurse retention.

Sophia Z. Kovachevich

❖ **Decrease in the prevalence of cigarette Smoking**: This could be because of the anti-smoking patches and because of the aggressive anti-smoking campaign. And in recent years these have been augmented with the E-cigarette and E-liquid Vape.

And finally the impact of industrialisation has permeated into every aspect of our lives and forever changed us and is still changing us. The four spheres that have been in many ways negatively impacted are:

Air pollution as we will see, is the biggest problem and the most difficult to contain. This is caused by smoke emissions generated through the burning of fossil fuels. It is a fact that at least 80 different toxins can be found in industrial pollution ranging from asbestos to lead and chromium. One of the largest and worst industrial polluters is the USA.

Then there is water pollution which is more controllable on island nations rather than continents like Europe and Asia where the same waterways run through many nations. The problem arises when factories are constructed near waterways. Toxins that run into waterways from these factories can come in a variety of forms as solids, liquids or gases. All of these end up contaminating the waterways. Landfills are another source of contamination of local water supplies for example the Nile in Egypt, the Maribyrnong and Yarra in Australia. The Thames in London, on the other hand, is a success story. It was very polluted but now is one of the cleanest waterways.

Another problem is soil contamination from lead and other heavy metals and toxic chemicals. When the soil is contaminated, the food grown in that soil is also contaminated. Landfills are a major soil pollutant.

And finally there is the habitat pollution and habitat destruction. Deforestation destroys forests and the habitats of our fauna and flora. Ecosystems are destroyed to create roads, strip mines and gravel pits. But there are solutions to counteract these. Factories can reduce pollution-causing products and move towards clean energy. Factories can also treat their industrial waste to remove or reduce the toxins in it and dispose of them safely.

We can and should take better care of our beautiful earth!

PART IV

MAN AND HIS ENVIRONMENT

The environment is what is around us - the air the soil the water, the forests everything. There is of a lot of debate on man and his environment. At first the environment dominated and man lived with that but man is very innovative and in due course of time they harnessed nature's power to serve them. Now this is a very complex relationship as all inhere together. The landscape constantly changes due to the movement of the earth, quakes, tectonic plates, floods, ice, course of rivers and so on. Ice covered the northern hemisphere as late as 20,000- years ago, but as it melted it changed the natural scenery.

We who live on this earth change it and are changed by it. We are all interdependent. For example the air we breathe is the product of billions of years of bacteria acting on the atmosphere. But of all the creatures that inhabit the earth, humans have not only changed it but also contaminated it. Early humans lived in the shadow of their environment. His food was what he caught or hunted. Then came the first industrial Revolution and humans started contaminating the environment. We also began serious deforestation of the land. With the fourth industrial revolution of today, humans not only dominate the environment but also abuse it and rape it. Now there are no or very few 'natural' areas left. All are touched by humans – the moors of Yorkshire and Lancashire are changed by sheep grazing and the textile industry. The geography of much of North America is the result of human actions. The evolution of humans was markedly different from other species. Humans have the ability to use tools, think abstractly, envisage ideas and put them into effect. And because of this, humans have a greater responsibility to care for the environment. Humans can understand their surroundings whereas animals react to it. We inhabit a specific niche that has enabled us to develop and change our environment to cater to our needs. That makes us morally responsible to nurture the land and water and air of our earth. We have the foresight and imagination. We have the ability to communicate through language. We have the ability to create tools and harness the environment. Therefore it is our DUTY to protect our environment and not ruin it, rape it, destroy it.

We humans contribute to the extinction of the species in basically two ways – habitat fragmentation and anthropogenic pollution. Everything else falls under these two categories.

Habitat fragmentation: We clear forests to build houses, roads, railway tracks. This leads to the inhabitants of the area – the animals, birds - relocating and finding new food source. They may not find suitable habitat nor be able to raise their young for whatever reason, though often it is predation. This may lead to loss of biodiversity as the species die off and become extinct.

Anthropogenic pollution: Humans pollute and contaminate wherever they go. The burning of fossil fuels pollutes the atmosphere. These energy sources need a very long time to regenerate. We create a huge amount of waste, which we put into our landfills contaminating the area and the air. We use huge amounts of plastics which are extremely difficult to break down. Plastics and garbage in the oceans kill the inhabitants and pollute the waters. Run offs from farms carry sediments with them. The sediments then block out the sun and photosynthesis cannot take place. The fish do not have food and die off. We overhunt and over fish – again contributing to their extinction.

Present Day Environmental problems

Through the various stages of human history there has always been a close relationship between man and the environment. Serious disruption of this bond started from the 18th century with the Industrial Revolution. Man was not in-step with nature. Factories, cars industries, mining started polluting the atmosphere. The poor became poorer, the rich, richer. Extreme wealth was juxtaposed against terrible squalor. The rape of nature began. Whereas the natural environment helped in the development of social structure, now the quality and continuing existence of the natural environment rests with man. Where ever we look, as society is developing apace, the environment is suffering at an even more accelerated pace, with disruption of the earth's natural ecosystem, environmental degradation, pollution, loss of habitat, cutting down of forests – deforestation and forest fires, unprecedented depletion of all natural resources, poisoning of the atmosphere, cancer-causing material in homes and buildings and many other things.

The interaction between environment and society depends mainly on the social and political systems even though the capitalistic and socialistic systems have different perceptions and reactions to the environment.

The continuous increasing rate of exploitation of natural resources, industrialisation, technological growth, unplanned urbanisation and profit oriented capitalism are responsible for the very serious environmental crisis and ecological imbalance that has affected the whole world today. It is truly a sorry state of affairs!

The change in the relationship between man and environment depends upon the change in organisation and the attitude of society. To improve environmental standard and to maintain ecological balance, the followings are some of the issues confronting us today which we must address:

o **Population explosion:**
This puts tremendous pressure on the natural resources and the environment. The fact is population growth leads to poverty which directly or indirectly affects the standard of living.

o **Quality of water**
Our waters are polluted due to human activity - pollution - as a result of the release of harmful substances like chemicals and micro-organisms into the waters. It is imperative to restore the quality of water bodies for their optimum use

o **Sustained increased agricultural growth:**
Without damaging the environment we should increase the agricultural growth for the ever-increasing population. The over cultivation of the soil, results in nutrient deficiency, lack of organic matter, soil salinity and damage to the physical structure of the soil. Rotational farming is a good possibility towards keeping the soil healthy

o **Soil erosion**
Prevent soil erosion by restoring land or soil resources which relate to strategies for the management of land, water and forest.

o **Restoration of forest resources:**
The forest resources are being depleted at an alarming rate in order to meet the ever-growing need for timber and farmland. Vast forest areas have been converted

into barren, waste lands. We need to restore our forest resources through social forestry and afforestation

o   **Control pollution:**
Overexploitation of natural resources, intervention of bio-geochemical cycles and trace element cycles, extraneous release of matter and energy and other such issues cause serious environmental damage. We should find an alternative path to control the pollution that we cause, in order to reduce it

In addition, continuous emission of green-house gas, hazardous chemicals of industry and agriculture, nuclear arsenals; radioactive wastes and biotechnological misuse lead to possible global catastrophe. Therefore prevention of pollution is of prime importance today.

It is clear that human fate is bound to the fate of our environment and our earth. It is now time to try and reverse the process of destruction of all the earth's resources.

Following are some measures to redress this issue of environmental rape:

(a)   Population control.
(b)   Optimum use of natural resources. No waste.
(c)   Conservation and protection of biodiversity.
(d)   Creation of public awareness about the benefits of preserving the environment.
(e)   Top priority for environmental protection. EPA in all countries should put environmental protection before selfish desires and interests.
(f)   Development of ecofriendly technological processes.

(g) Promotion of sustainable agriculture which will not harm the environment.

(h) Use of bio-fertilisers or ecofriendly fertilisers.

(i) Minimum use of pesticides and insecticides and/or use of some form of natural insecticides/pesticides.

(j) Development of waste land by adopting afforestation programmes.

(k) Development of suitable biotechnology to clean up hazardous wastes in the environment.

(l) Having suitable technique to treat pollutants before their discharge into the environment.

(m) Use of solar power, wind turbines to minimise pollution.

(n) Turning wasteland into wetland.

A Brief introduction to endangered & extinct fauna

Animals extinct in the 20th century due to human activity – habitat loss, overhunting for sport or profit - to sell the horns, shells etc., introduction of other species not endemic to the land, shrinking habitat and diseases are some of the reasons for their extinction and endangerment.

As time has gone by our disregard for the earth and its creatures has impacted severely. Many animals have become extinct and many more are endangered, some critically. Man is a part of nature, the apex of growth and development so what we do and how we do it impacts sharply on all. In older societies man hunted for food. It is true that spears and stakes and bows and arrows made it more difficult to kill the animal. For early man hunting was a group endeavour. They shared their kill among the hunters or the village. Early man hunted for food - the meat or flesh as food; the skin for clothes the teeth horns etc. for ornaments or trade. They hunted for survival. Nothing was wasted. There was a balance. But in our time we are disconnected from the world around us. We buy our food, clothes, ornaments from supermarkets and shops. We do not see the sacrilege of hunting for pleasure or profit, killing for the sake of killing animals, birds and sea creatures.

In our modern society money equals to food, drinks, survival. We are often unaware that our survival depends on the world around us. We are depleting the earth and taking away from our descendants. Our abuse and misuse of our world has already impacted on us. Fires, floods, earthquakes, hurricanes have become a regular occurrence. And not only that, we also kill our own kind with shootings every day in some place or the other. We should abide by the law of giving, only taking what is necessary and giving the rest to the general needs of society, by our own freedom of choice. If we do not do that we shall see worse times to come. We have over-hunted, over-fished and cut down too much of our forests. We have also overhunted our birds and now many are extinct. As a consequence of our selfishness many animals and fish have also become extinct and many more are endangered. When there is a shark attack at sea, we go in and kill a shark. It may not be the shark that attacked. It is rather silly because the animal did not attack us in our habitat but in its own. We entered its terrain. It may have seen us as a danger. We should be more carefulof where we go and when we go into the water. We attack and kill animals like tigers, lions which come into our sphere because we think they are a danger to us. So perhaps the same applies to other living creatures. As a consequence of this pointless killing, some species of sharks have become extinct, some more are endangered. Ever since the Europeans started colonising, the fauna and flora became endangered. In the 16th century 30% of birds, plants, insects, molluscs and fish either became extinct or critically endangered in various European colonies. That was when colonisation began in earnest and on a major scale.

In the Caribbean with the arrival of humans, different types of arboreal dwellers and ground sloths and other animals disappeared. The same was repeated in the Pacific Islands. In Hawaii 2,000 bird species disappeared within a short time after colonisation.

In Madagascar nearly all of its endemic megafauna are extinct today. The largest megafauna went extinct due to overhunting, losing of habitat due to an ever expanding human population and hunting for sport e.g. the giant lemur (150 kg) disappeared, 8 types of elephant birds, the giant flightless ratites and 17 other species of lemurs all became extinct. Many were simply butchered, their carcasses left to rot. Most of these megafauna that disappeared were around 150 kg. What a meaningless waste!

Smaller fauna also disappeared, all over 10kg due to hunting, habitat loss and aridification. All of this could have been avoided but we were careless and callous and did not take care of our inheritance.

In the USA 40% of its bird species have disappeared. Some were the **Ivory-bill woodpecker**. It became extinct in the 1940's but was seen (it was assumed) only once again on February 11, 2004. It was a huge bird. It was seen in the Cache River National Wildlife Refuge of Arkansas. It is feared it became extinct due to loss of habitat when the southern old-growth forests were cut down. Another species of birds that died out is the **Bachman's warbler**. These nested in the underbrush of forested swamps by Louisiana up to Kentucky and Maryland and into the Carolinas and Georgia. They used to migrate to Cuba in winter. They were listed as endangered in 1967 but have never been seen since the 1960's in North America.

Still another extinct species is the once abundant **Carolina parakeet**. They nested in large colonies in cypress swamps in the South Atlantic and the Gulf. They migrated up the Mississippi and Missouri Rivers to the Platte and to Ohio, Indiana, Illinois, Iowa, Wisconsin and Nebraska and in the east to Pennsylvania. They were hunted for their beautiful feathers and slaughtered as pests. The last flock was seen in Florida in 1920. They are now extinct.

In New Zealand the Polynesian settlers killed all of the mega fauna birds within a couple of hundred years. Among them were the **moa and ratites**. They also introduced the Polynesian rat that preyed on the smaller species and spread diseases. Europeans came into contact with them in the 18th century and colonised New Zealand in the 19th century. On their ships they brought ship rats, possums, cats, and mustelids that decimated the birds. Most of the native birds were flightless, so easy prey.

The **Kakapo bird** which is the largest parrot only lives in managed breeding programmes. There are none to be found in the wild. The **Kiwi bird** New Zealand's iconic bird is also endangered. As late as November 2020 an eagle was caught in an unstrung loosely hanging clothes line and was totally entangled. If not for the humanity of the men who found him he would have been dead. This kind of action gives us hope that there is still a possibility we can live in harmony with nature.

The **Bald Eagle** is usually quite sensitive to human activity while nesting, and is found most commonly in areas with minimal human disturbance. **Bald eagles** were officially declared an **endangered** species in 1967 in all areas of the United States south of the 40th parallel, under a law that preceded the **Endangered** Species Act of 1973. In more recent times namely under Donald J Trump's presidency the protection of endangered species bill was ended in 2017. According to the (US) National Marine Fisheries Service the cost of the protection measures for endangered sea creatures caught in nets *outweighed the benefits*. So they scrapped that too!! Included in the list of endangered creatures are the **olive-Ridley sea turtles, Leatherback turtles**, and **green sea turtle; Fin, Humpback** and **Sperm whales, short-fin pilot whales** – which are already seriously endangered, (there are only 411 whales left); and common **bottlenose dolphins**, (some species of dolphins have only a few hundred left alive).

In North America there was a sharp decline of the **Passenger Pigeon** in the 1800's due to over hunting. The last passenger Pigeon was shot in 1901. Of the hundreds of millions of passenger pigeon birds, not one is left today.

The Tennessee River has one of the most aquatically biodiverse river systems in North America. Many of its inhabitants are now endangered.

The ecosystems encountered by the first Americans had not been exposed to human interaction, and so may have been far less resilient to human-made changes than the ecosystems encountered by industrial era humans. Therefore, the actions of the Clovis people, despite seeming insignificant by today's standards, could indeed have had a profound effect on the ecosystems and wild life of the Americas which was entirely unused to human influence. Clovis people are also known as Paleo-Indians, and are generally regarded as the first human inhabitants of the New World, and believed to be the ancestors of the indigenous cultures of North and South America.

With the arrival of humans many flora and fauna became extinct. There was habitat destruction on a large scale including the cutting down of forests to clear land for dwellings and timber to make dwellings and for planting crops. The ocean was also impacted with overfishing and contamination. Original local eco systems were displaced due to land clearance and introduced species. Those that were replaced were with non-native species.

Other causes are deforestation, hunting animals for food but also for sport and for profit, pollution, introduction of non-native species and transmission of infectious diseases spread through crops and livestock. Many scholars believe that more land and water species have disappeared during capitalism than at any other time. They put the number at 83% mega wild mammals and 80% marine mammals, 50% plants and 15% fish have disappeared. Currently it appears that 60% of the biomass is made up of livestock, 36% of humans and 4% wild mammals, 70% poultry, and 30% wild fowl.

Megafauna were once found on every continent including Madagascar but now can only be seen in Africa in the wild. However their numbers are a serious cause for concern. It is a question of time before they too become extinct.

The loss of species is a result of human action, directly by killing them or indirectly through habitat loss, pollution, introduction of other animals, industrialisation - release of huge amounts of greenhouse gases like Methane (CH_4) and Carbon dioxide (CO_2). This has resulted in depleted large vertebrates from ecological communities and empty forests.

Following is a brief worldwide toll of the situation now concerning the fauna and flora.

Some extinct species are the following:

Extinct Reptiles

Name/species	location	comment
Jamaican Giant Waspcelestius occiduus (amnguid lizard)	Caribbean (Jamaica, Cuba, Puerto Rico, Costa Rico)	Last seen in 1840's. They were night hunters; shy, mysterious creatures
Cape Verde Giant Skink (Chioninia cocteri)	Cape Verde Islands	Type of lizard. Extinct since early 20th Century due to inability to adapt to resident humans. Killed for its oil. Extinct also because of aridification of its natural habitat
Kawekaweau (Delcourt's giant gecko)	native to New Zealand	Extinct in 1873 when a Maori chief killed the last one. Largest ever gecko over 2 feet long
Rodrigues Giant Tortoises 2 types– Cylindraspis peltastes & Cylansraspis vosmaeri	350 miles off Mauritius in the Indian Ocean	Extinct 19th century – hunted to extinction by man for amusement at its social behaviour
Horned turtle (Meiolania)	Australia, New Caledonia & Vanuatu	Bones discovered in Vanuatu. Hunted to extinction by the local Aborigines

Name/species	location	comment
Giant monitor lizard (Ankylosaurus Meiolania)	Australia	An apex predator 25 ft. long 2 tons, fed on the megafauna e.g. giant short-faced kangaroo. Extinct due to climate change & loss of food source
Wonambi (Wonambi naracoorthsis & Wonambi barriei)	Australia	Over 100 lbs, 18 foot long could kill a giant wombat – a prehistoric snake. Disappeared when the Aborigines came to Australia
Quinkana (long legged, very sharp-toothed crocodile)	Australia	Fed on the megafauna. Extinct due to being hunted as food by the Aborigines & loss of usual prey
Big-Eared Hopping Mouse	Australia	European settlers cleared their habitat for agriculture & they were mercilessly preyed upon by the settlers' dogs and cats
Bulldog Rat	Christmas Island (External Australian territory)	Weighed about a pound when wet. Succumbed to diseases brought by the Black Rat on European ships
Dark Flying Fox	Reunion & Mauritius Islands Brazil	A fruiting bat crowding in caves. Eaten by the Islanders & settlers on the Islands. Hunted for their meat, fat & the young by the natives during summer. In autumn & winter hunted by Europeans with guns.
Indefatigable Galapagos Mouse (Nesoryzomys indeffesus)	Galapagos archipelago	Killed by human settlers, loss of habitat, lethal introduced diseases (from the hitch-hiking Black rats)
Giant Vampire Bat (Desmodus draculae)	South America & Brazil	Slightly larger than the common bat; was a blood sucker preyed on mega fauna. Extinct probably due to climate change

Sophia Z. Kovachevich

Name/species	location	comment
Lesser Stick Nest Rat	Australia	Built large nests with twigs. Hunted as food by humans for its tasty meat. Last sighted in 1970. IUCN hopes some still live in interior Australia
Puerto Rican Hutia	Puerto Rico& Cuba	Believed to have been eaten By Columbus for its tasty meat when he landed in the West Indies; hunted by the indigenous people for years; Extinct due to diseases brought by Black Rats
Name/species	**location**	**comments**
Sardinian Pika Corsican Pika	Sardinia Corsica	They were larger than rabbits. Had succulent meat & hunted by indigenous Nuragici (Sardinian) people. Extinct in the 19th Century.
Vespucci's Rodent	Islands of Fernando de Noronha off the coast of Brazil	Named after Amerigo Vespucci; extinct in the late 19th century due to pests brought by Europeans – rats, cats & mice.
White-Footed Rabbit Rat	Australia	Quite large, the size of a kitten. Made its nest of leaves in tree hollows. Became extinct in the mid-19th century due to loss of habitat and the invasive Black rats and cats

Animals extinct by the 20ᵗʰ century

70% of megafauna of 362 species are endangered. They may never recover

o **Mountain gorillas** - 880 left alive. 60% of the present population of present primate population face extinction (60% of 880 gorillas)

o **Bramble Cay Melomys** became extinct in June 2016 due to climate change more than anything else

o **The Florida panther** is ecologically extinct because the numbers are too low to have any impact on the ecosystem

o **The West African Black rhinoceros** was found in many countries. They were killed for their horn which was to be used for supposedly medicinal purposes. They were also killed for sport and many died due to loss of habitat. Agriculturists viewed them as pests and also hunted them. Poachers descended on West Africa to hunt them also. The last one died in Cameroon in 2006 and the black rhino was declared officially extinct in 2011

o **The Spanish Ibex** (Iberian wild goat – Capra pyrenaica) There were 4 sub-species of it. Only two species survive One species disappeared at the beginning of the 20ᵗʰ century there were only 100 ibex in Spain. By the end of 1980 there were only 14 ibex left. The last one died on January 6ᵀʰ 2000 when it was hit by a falling tree. It was only 13 years old The Portuguese subspecies became extinct in 1892

o **The Portuguese** subspecies became extinct in 1892

o **The Iberian Goat** is a subspecies of the Spanish Ibex. From 50,000 by the early 1900 there were only 100 left. Of these, two species can still be found on the Iberian Peninsula, but the remaining two species are now extinct

o **The Pyrenean Ibex.** Scientists tried to bring it back into existence by cloning but failed. Its population declined due to a slow but continuous persecution and it disappeared from the French Pyrenees in the mid-19th century.

o **Bubal Hartebeest:** this animal once roamed freely throughout North Africa and the Middle East. But when the Europeans came, they hunted the hartebeest for sport and for its flesh. Some were captured and sent to the London zoo. The last one – a female died in 1923 in a French zoo

o **The Eastern Elk** (*Cervus canadensis canadensis*) was one of the largest cervids of North America. The bulls were up to half a ton. The last one was shot in 1880. It is survived by its subspecies including the **Roosevelt Elk, the Manitoban elk** and the **Rocky Mountain Elk**

o **The Irish Elk** *(Megaloceros giganteus).* There were nine species of elk of which this was the largest weighing as much as three quarters of a ton. It went extinct about 7,700 years ago in Siberia. It was probably hunted by the European settlers for its meat and fur. It roamed across Eurasia during the Pleistocene period

o **The Auroch** *(Bos primigenius)* is the ancestor of the modern cow but was then a game animal. The bull weighed about one ton. It defended its territory but was hunted savagely. It managed to survive into the 17th century when the last female auroch died in 1627 in a Polish forest

o **Passenger Pigeon** native to North America has been extinct since the 20th century. When North America was colonised, it led to mass deforestation resulting in habitat loss. By the 19th century pigeon meat was commercialised. The last pigeon died in captivity in 1914

o **The Tasmanian Tiger** (*Thylacine*) was a large carnivore native to Australia, Tasmania and New Guinea. It was hunted to extinction. Besides that there was loss of habitat due to human encroachment, introduction of dogs into its habitat and disease. Most died between 1910 and

1920. The last Tasmanian tiger died in the Hobart Zoo in Tasmania in 1936

- **The Syrian Elephant** (*Elephas maximus asurus*) was an offshoot of the Asian elephant. It was highly prized for its ivory and also in warfare. It flourished in the Middle East for almost three million years and then disappeared around 100 BC. At About the same time the **North African Elephant** *(Loxodonta)* also became extinct. Ivory trade was then at its peak in both areas.
- **The Cyprus Dwarf Hippopotamus** *(Hippopotamus minor)* weighed only a few hundred pounds. It was hunted by the early settlers to extinction for its meat
- The same thing happened to the **Dwarf elephant** in the Mediterranean islands
- **Jamaican Giant Waspcelestius occiduus (amnguid lizard)** was found in the Caribbean Islands. (Jamaica, Cuba, Puerto Rico, Costa Rico). It was last seen in the 1840's. They were night hunters; and shy mysterious creatures
- **Cape Verde Giant Skink (Chioninia cocteri)** was found in the Cape Verde Islands. It was a type of lizard. Extinct since early 20th Century due to its inability to adapt to resident humans. Killed for its oil. Extinct also because of aridification of its natural habitat
- **Vespucci's Rodents** were inhabitants of the Islands of Fernando de Noronha off the coast of Brazil. They were named after Amerigo Vespucci; they became extinct in the late 19th century due to pests brought by Europeans – rats, cats & mice.
- **Indefatigable Galapagos Mouse (Nesoryzomys indeffesus)** was found in the Galapagos archipelago. It was killed by human settlers, loss of habitat, and lethal introduced diseases (from the hitch-hiking Black rats)
- **Giant Vampire Bat** (Desmodus draculae) was found in South America & Brazil. Slightly larger than the common

bat; it was a blood sucker that preyed on mega fauna. Extinct probably due to climate change

o **The Sardinian Pika and the Corsican Pika** were found respectively in Sardinia and Corsica. They were larger than rabbits. Had succulent meat and were hunted by the indigenous Nuragici (Sardinian) people. They became extinct in the 19th century

o **The Puerto Rican Hutia** was found in Puerto Rico, & Cuba. Believed to have been eaten By Columbus for its tasty meat when he landed in the West Indies; it was hunted by the indigenous people for years; it became extinct due to diseases brought by Black Rats

o **Dark Flying Fox** was found in Reunion & Mauritius Islands Brazil. A fruit eating bat crowding in caves. It was eaten by the Islanders & settlers on the Islands. Hunted for their meat, fat & the young during summer by the natives. In autumn and winter hunted by Europeans with guns

o **The Stag Moose** *(Cervalces scotti)* was hunted to extinction 10,000 years ago. It lost its natural habitat to humans. This Stag along with the **Irish Elk** were two of the dozen megafauna that became extinct soon after the last ice age. Its bones were first discovered in 1805 by William Clark

o **The Great Auk** was a large flightless bird found in the North Atlantic and as far south as Northern Spain. The last colony of auks lived on Eldey Islands. They were all killed by 1835. The last auk was killed in St Kilda, Scotland in 1844 because they thought it was a witch

o Another large flightless extinct bird was the **Dodo.** It inhabited Mauritius. It is believed they became flightless due to the abundance of food (seeds, roots, fallen fruit...) and a lack of predators before the Europeans came. They were hunted to extinction by 1680 by the sailors and their domesticated pets and some invasive species the sailors brought with them

o   Another large flightless bird was the **Moa** bird, native to New Zealand. They were hunted to extinction as food by the Maori people.

o   **The Atlas Bear** *(Ursus arctos crowtheri)* was found in Northern Africa from the 2nd century. It has been deemed a different species by scientists. It was relentlessly hunted by the Romans. It was the only African bear to survive into modern times. It became extinct in the late 19th century in Morocco's Rif Mountain due to hunting by the local tribes

o   **The Quagga** was a subspecies of the Zebra. It was half zebra and half horse. It was hunted to extinction in 1883 for its meat and hide and to clear the land for agriculture

o   **The Blue Buck** *(Hippotragus leucophagus)* was the first African game mammal to become extinct in historical times. It had lost most of its habitat due to climate change. But it was also hunted. The last Blue Buck was shot in 1800

o   **Schomburgk's Deer** *(Rucervus schomburgki)* was a native of Thailand. It was doomed by its habitat. During the monsoon it was forced to shelter on high promontories where it was easy to hunt them. Rice paddies also encroached on its habitat. It was last sighted in 1938

o   **The Japanese Honshu Wolf** lived on the Japanese islands of Shikoku, Honshu and Kyushu. It was a small species of wolf. In 1732 rabies was introduced into the island either through dogs or deliberately. These wolves died or were hunted to extinction by 1905. Also they lost big chunks of their habitat to farming and deforestation

o   **Pere David's deer** extinct in the wild caused directly by humans. They only survive in captive populations now

o   **Hawaiian crow** extinct in the wild caused directly by humans. They only survive in captive populations now

- o **Toolache Wallaby** (Macropus Greyi) was a graceful elegant species of kangaroo inhabiting Australia and New Zealand. They were common until 1910 but by 1923 they were rarely found. The last of these beautiful animals died after 12 years of captivity in 1939 and was declared extinct in 1943. They were wiped out due to habitat loss and being hunted by the introduced foxes
- o **The Caspian Tiger** (Panthera tigris virgata) was found south of the Caspian Sea in Central Asia. It was one of the biggest cats on earth. It was officially declared extinct in 1970. Again it was due to overhunting, habitat loss and loss of their food which was other animals that were also hunted to extinction by humans
- o **Mexican Grizzly Bear** was declared extinct in 1964
- o **Javan Tiger** was a sub species of the tigers that inhabited the island of Java in Indonesia. They were a common sight in the early 19th century but as population increased their habitat was severely reduced and they were ruthlessly hunted down. They were not seen after 1979 and were declared extinct in 1994
- o **Zanzibar Leopard** was declared extinct in 2008
- o The last **Northern White** male rhino died on December 14, 2016
- o The last **Male Black Rhino** died on March 19, 2018 and **the female** in 2020.
- o **The Caribbean Monk Seal** (*Monachus* tropicalis) was found throughout the Caribbean Sea, Gulf of Mexico and West Atlantic Ocean. When Christopher Columbus saw them in 1494 he called them sea wolves. They were overhunted and fell easy prey to humans when they were birthing, feeding the pups or resting. They were also curious, trusting animals. They were declared extinct in 2008
- o **The Atlantic gray** whale is extinct
- o **The Atlantic Sturgeon** (Acipenser Sturio) is extinct

- o **The Ship sturgeon** (acipensernudiventris) is on the way to extinction
- o **The Danube sturgeon** is critically endangered on its way to extinction
- o **The Beluga sturgeon (Huso Huso)** was found in the Caspian and Black Sea basins. It was also found in the Adriatic. Its roe is the black caviar. It has been heavily fished. It is now critically endangered
- o **The Leatherback sea turtle** in Malaysia is extinct
- o **The Pinta Island tortoise** (*Chelonoidis nigra abingdonii*) was a subspecies of the giant tortoise that lived in the Galapagos Islands. In the 19th century they were hunted mercilessly for their meat and their habitat was destroyed. By 1971 only 1 tortoise named Lonesome George remained. He died in 2012 making this species extinct
- o **Baiji or Yangtze River Dolphin** was declared extinct in 2006—one or two might still be alive, but not enough to continue the species
- o **Japanese Sea Lion** was declared extinct in 1974
- o **Steller's Sea Cow** was named after George Wilhelm Steller, a naturalist who saw it in 1741. It inhabited the Near Islands, southwest Alaska, and the Commander Islands in the Bering Sea. It was a huge tame creature. It was hunted to extinction 27 years after the European colonisers discovered its existence

Most of these megafauna became extinct by the 21st century.

Various species likely to become extinct in the near future are among others, the **rhinos, nonhuman primates, pangolins, pandas, giraffes and elephants**. They are all critically endangered.

70% of 362 megafauna is in decline as of 2019. Mammals will need a very long time to recover – if ever.

Most of the megafauna above became extinct in the 20th and/or 21st centuries.

There has also been a sharp decline in **insect and animal pollinators** worldwide beginning at the end of the 20th century. Pollinators are needed for 75% of food crops which are declining in abundance and diversity now.

In a study in 2017 Hans de Kroon of the Radboud University stated that the biomass of insect life in Germany had declined by three quarters in the past 25 years. Dave Goulson of Sussex University suggested that we are making the *planet uninhabitable* and that we are fast approaching an *ecological Armageddon* as without the pollinators things would collapse.

In 2019 we have lost 40% of our insects and a third of the others are endangered. Most of this is due to intensive farming along with the use of pesticides, insecticides and climate change – all a result of industrialisation.

For the first time since the demise of the dinosaurs 65 million years ago, we face a global mass extinction of wildlife. We ignore the decline of other species at our peril – for they are the barometer that reveals our impact on the world that sustains us. Mike Barrett, director of science and policy at WWF's UK branch·

Other causes are deforestation, hunting animals for food but also for sport, pollution, introduction of non-native species and transmission of infectious diseases spread through crops and livestock. Many scholars believe that more land and water species have disappeared during capitalism than at any other time. They put the number at 83% mega wild mammals and 80% marine mammals, 50% plants and 15% fish have disappeared. Currently it appears that 60% of the biomass is made up of livestock, 36% humans, wild mammals 4%, poultry 70% and wild fowl 30%.

Megafauna were once found on every continent including New Zealand and Madagascar but now can only be seen in Africa in the wild.

The loss of species is a result of human action, directly by killing them or indirectly through habitat loss, introduction of other animals, industrialisation - release of huge amounts of greenhouse gases like Methane (CH_4) and Carbon dioxide (CO_2). This has resulted in depleted large vertebrates from ecological communities and empty forests.

Following is a brief worldwide toll of the situation now concerning the fauna and flora.

All these are due to overhunting, illegal trading, retaliatory killing, and loss of habitat.

Endangered species

Most species are now endangered due to habitat loss, overhunting for sport or trophies, disease (to a lesser extent), cruel animal traps and loss of prey.

The **bison** was on the verge of extinction when Ted Turner bought farmland to house them. He now has a few herds of wild bison.

The big cat population has severely declined in the last half century according to IUCN (International Union for Conservation of Nature). Among them are the following animals:

- o Lions from 450,000 to now 25,000
- o Leopards 750,000, now 50,000
- o Cheetahs 45,000 to 12,000
- o Tigers 50,000 to 3,000
- o Panthers only 7,100 in the wild and using only 9% of their original habitat they are crammed into small spaces. Panthers need space. They don't do well in crammed quarters

Other animals are:

- o **Bornean Orangutan** –only found in Borneo. Their numbers have decreased by 60% since 1950. Their birth rate is very poor. It takes 6 to 8 years for them to reproduce. The foremost reason for the decrease in their numbers is habitat loss and illegal hunting of the animal
- o **Ili Pika** – this small animal originates from the Tianshan mountain range in China. It feeds on the grass of the mountain slope. It is on the endangered list because of habitat loss, air pollution and livestock grazing on its patch

o **Pandas** – These are gentle giants indigenous to China. Once they were common but due to habitat loss and loss of the bamboo, their staple and only diet they had become critically endangered. They were also heavily poached for their pelts and skins. The rehabilitation programme in the Sichuan province of Chengdu now boasts 124 births and 83 in captivity. They are now listed as vulnerable. These are highly unusual animals in their coloration and behaviour. They have difficulty in reproducing because they are very choosy about a mate. There are very few in the wild

o **Giant Otter** – these are the rarest otters in the world. Their numbers are severely depleted. Few surviving ones are in South America. They feed on fish. They are at risk due to overhunting for their pelts, habitat loss due to pollution and loss of fish/food

o **Eurasian Otter:** once widely seen in Germany was hunted to extinction during the 19th century. They have been brought back due to conservation efforts but are now facing another challenge in pollution which causes acidification of their habitat and food source. They are found from Nepal to France

o **Amur Leopard** – is the world's most endangered cat. It is currently only found along the Amur River in Russia. It is extinct in China and Korea. Currently there are only 60 animals in the world. This is due to poaching and climate change

o **Black–footed Ferret** – is only found in North America. They are endangered mainly because of the plagues and loss of habitat. There are only 500 surviving ferrets

o **Darwin's Fox** - is named after Charles Darwin who discovered them in 1834. They are threatened by habitat loss, hunting and predators

o **The Gray wolf** once widely seen became extinct in Germany in the 19th century. They were brought back in the 1990's. Now there are about 50 wolves in Germany. They are still at risk from hunting even though they are legally protected

o **Sumatran Rhinoceros** – It is the smallest in the rhino family. They can be found in Malaysia, Indonesia and Burma. They are facing extinction due to poaching

o **White-Rumped Vulture** – They have declined shockingly over the years. 99% of these birds have been wiped out since the 1980's. A lot of them were destroyed after ingesting diclofenac in cow remains

o **The Great White Pelican**: is an elegant bird and a high stamina glider. It lives on the Danube Delta in Rumania and the Ukraine. It is classified as rare. Once in large colonies now there are only 4,100 mating pairs in Europe and under 10,000 the world over.

o **Golden eagle**: - is the emblem of Germany. Once it was widespread there, but they are now a rare sight mainly sighted in the German Alps

o **The European Kingfisher was once widely seen**. Now they are threatened by extinction by locals. They are also threatened by loss of habitat and spawning opportunities

o **The European Pond turtle**: is also critically endangered. It is found in Europe and North Africa. On the Danube there are only a few remaining native populations. They are threatened by human disturbances of their habitat, e.g. draining of the swampland & wetlands, urban sprawl, restructuring of the bodies of water, destruction of their nesting areas and often being run over by vehicles. They are also trapped in weirs and so drown

o **Pangolin** – is a night animal found in parts of Asia and Africa. They are vulnerable due to poachers who are after the meat and the scales of the pangolins

o **Saola** – is a mammal herbivore. It is also called an Asian unicorn. It is one of the world's rarest animals. It ranges in the mountain range between Vietnam and Laos. It is critically endangered. They were discovered in 1992 but only 4 have been seen in the wild since then but there are about a100 in protected areas. They too are threatened by habitat loss, hunting and other human activities

o **Vaquita** – is the world's rarest marine creature and is on the verge of extinction. Since 2014 they have decreased by 40% leaving only 60 vaquitas alive. They have been badly impacted by climate change and loss of habitat

o **The Smokey Madtom** was believed to be extinct but since has been sighted (though very rarely) in North Carolina's Great Smokey Mountains National Park in the 1980's. It can also be seen in Little Tennessee River system along the Tennessee-North Carolina coast. It is a venomous catfish and a native of Little Tennessee Watershed. It grows to about three inches in length. It has spines and can deliver a nasty sting if you accidentally step on it. It is regarded as a federally endangered species

o **Peruvian Black Spider Monkey** – is found north of the Amazon River. Their population decreased by 50% in the past 45 years due mainly to hunting, fragmentation and destruction of their habitat

o **Black footed ferret** – is the only native ferret of North America. Their main food was prairie dogs but they were poisoned and so the ferret population declined leaving only 18 in captivity. The breeding programme was successful and now there are about 300 ferrets

o **Red Wolf** of Southeast Florida is critically endangered. There are only 25-40 left in the wild

o **The Sumatran Orangutan** like the Bornean are both on the endangered list due to loss of habitat, illegal logging and illegal poaching

o **The Mountain gorilla,** an inhabitant of the Uganda-DRC (The Democratic Republic of the Congo) border is also on the endangered list. They face constant threats from human encroachment, getting killed in snares and illegal trade. Some of these are under some control by the armed border guards

o **Malayan Tiger** – is on the critical list. They are primarily found in Malaysia. Road developments are a serious threat to their habitat. Angry villagers often kill the tigers

o **Javan Rhino** – is only found in Java. It is one of the largest land animals of Asia. It is also one of the rarest mammals on the earth. It is critically endangered with poachers killing them for their horn. Each kilo of horn gets the poacher or those that employ them USD 30,000 dollars

o **Hawksbill turtle** is found worldwide. It is also on the critical list due to illegal capture of the turtle, pollution and destruction of nesting areas

o **The Black rhino** – is the largest land mammal. Before the arrival of Europeans to the sub-Saharan region there were lots of them. But in the 19th century when the Europeans arrived, there was rampant poaching for game trophies. About 96% of black rhinos were killed. They were declared extinct in 2011

o **Danube Salmon** is the largest species of salmon. It is native to the Danube which has its origins in the German Black Forest. Once widespread in the Danube, now it is critically endangered. The threats to it are overfishing, dams, and pollution

o **Fire Coral** (*Millepora boschmai*) is an animal with a skeleton. It is related to the jellyfish. It is critically endangered. Seven colonies of fire corals were wiped out by the El Niño of 1998. Of the 14 species world-wide, two species are extinct, two more are endangered. Australia has 6 of the species, the exact status is unknown. The greatest threat is from climate change

o **Sharks** are much maligned and 'functionally extinct' at 20% of reefs caused by destructive, unsustainable fishing. This adds pressure to the already over-burdened reefs and impacts on the reef health. Every year about 100 million sharks are killed by people. Many are critically endangered. Among them the 10 most endangered sharks are:

- **Pondicherry Shark** – not seen since 1979. May already be extinct due to unregulated fishing. Its habitat was in the Indian Ocean from The Gulf of Oman to New Guinea. IUCN places it on the critically endangered list and is trying to find some existing populations, so far, without success
- **Ganges Shark** – a river shark in Indian rivers. It is threatened with habitat destruction, pollution, dams and barrages and overfishing. Fishing for this species is now banned
- **Northern River Shark** inhabits the waters between Australia and New Guinea. ICUN estimates there are only 250 in existence, They are critically threatened by commercial and recreational fishing
- **Natal Shyshark** is a very small species of shark (50cm) found in the coastal waters of South Africa. It is critically endangered due to habitat degradation from the industrial and tourist development programmes
- **Daggernose Shark** is also a small species of shark (1.5m). It inhabits the tropical waters off the coast of Brazil and Trinidad. There has been a 90% decrease in numbers resulting from commercial fishing for its meat and as bycatch
- **Smoothback Angel Shark**: is also critically endangered from overfishing and is almost extinct. It is found in the Mediterranean, Sea, Atlantic Ocean and along Southern Europe and Northwestern Africa. Their numbers are very low.
- **Sawback Angel Shark** inhabits the Mediterranean Sea, along West African and Southwestern European

Atlantic coastlines. It is critically endangered due to overfishing and habitat destruction

- **Sand Tiger Shark (Grey Nurse Shark)** ranges around the sandy coastlines, continental shelves and submerged reefs around the North and South American coast, South Africa, Japan and Australia. They are threatened by overfishing, habitat destruction and pollution. They are extremely vulnerable as they have a very low and slow rate of reproduction
- **Striped Smoothhound Shark** – inhabits the coast of Brazil and Argentina. They are critically endangered because their nursery grounds are popular fishing areas and too many mothers and pups are killed there. No effort has been made to rehabilitate them. The fishery continues in their nursery ground
- **Porbeagle Shark** is vulnerable worldwide but critically endangered in the North Atlantic. It is a mackerel shark and highly valued by sport fishermen and commercial fishermen for its meat. It is near extinction due to overfishing

Currently there are **5000 species** that are listed as critically endangered. Since the Industrial Revolution in the 18th century, human activity has increased tremendously. The insatiable demand for raw materials has put strains on the environment through the destruction of forests as well as pollution of the water bodies along with hunting and poaching. Animals have been on the receiving end of the increased destruction to the point where many are increasingly nearing extinction. It is now time for us to be proper caretakers of our planet and save these species.

I am ashamed of being a human learning what we have done to our earth and its creatures. They have as much right as we do to live on the earth. I no longer eat meat, fish or seafood.

IUCN Red List

Species threatened with extinction according to the Red List:

Amphibians 41%	Mammals 25%	Birds 14%	Sharks & Rays 30%
Reef corals 33%	Some crustaceans 27%	Conifers 34%	

Sophia Z. Kovachevich

Why animals become endangered and extinct

An endangered living organism is one that is dying out and that will probably become extinct or lost forever to us. For example the dinosaurs are extinct today. They disappeared 65 million years ago. Scientists estimate that 90% of animals that had lived on earth are now extinct. It is generally a very slow process but in modern times due to a number of reasons they are becoming extinct faster and faster. The world-wide organisation for determining the status of an animal species is the International Union for the Conservation of Nature (IUCN). This body regularly publishes its Red List of Threatened Species. In Australia, various federal and state environmental protection agencies also publish their own lists. The Australian Department of the Environment Endangered Australian Animals List identifies many Australian native animals that are endangered and threatened with extinction. Species become extinct when circumstances arise that they cannot cope with.

Some are the following reasons:

- **Natural disasters**: Like earthquakes that wiped out the cities of Pompeii and Herculaneum with its inhabitants and animals or typhoons and cyclones or even like in 2019-2020 terrible bushfires in Australia that has wiped out many species and made the Koala of Australia, among others, now an endangered species
- **Asteroid strikes:** These are events beyond our control like the asteroid that struck in the Yucatan peninsula in Mexico and which led to the disappearance of dinosaurs millions of years ago. Most of the mass extinctions such as KT-extinction 65 million years ago in the Cretaceous-Tertiary period or Permian-Triassic extinction that occurred 252 million years ago, long before the dinosaurs

were caused due to such events. They are out of our control

- **Climate change:** These are human induced or natural consequence of change which is always going on due to one reason or another (natural or man-made). For example now, the melting of the polar ice is putting a lot of polar animals at risk. Or even the effect of climate change on our beautiful Great Barrier Reef that is killing off corals and many water species that are dependent on the Reef for their existence. Climate change was also responsible for the destruction of terrestrial organisms. During the end of the last ice-age, most of the megafauna were unable to adapt to the changing warm temperatures. They died due to lack of food and due to over hunting by early humans like the wooly mammoths which was hunted to extinction. Our megafauna is going the same way with the threat of extinction due to global warming

- **Human impacts:** Increase in population, technology, man-made contribution to species endangerment and annihilation is on the increase. Humans have contributed greatly to large-scale habitat destruction of the species by agriculture, mining, urban growth, land clearance, pollution of the world's waterways, depletion of the ozone layer, overfishing and overhunting for recreation and commerce. An example of this would be the extinction of the Tasmanian tiger which was regarded as a pest and so hunted and killed indiscriminately

- **Competition & displacement** of native life by introduced species: without considering the impact that this would have on the native species and on the environment. Some examples are the introduction of the cane toad, feral cats, red fox and rabbit and their effect on the continued existence of many native species.

- **Disease:** Many native species have contracted diseases that have either wiped out or severely affected the native species. For example the Tasmanian Devil Tumour wiped out a large number of Tasmanian devils. The chlamydia epidemics rendered many female koalas infertile and severely affected their population. Epidemics at different times have been the cause of extinction of a large population of humans and animals on earth. E.g. the Black Death wiped out one-third of the European population in the middle ages. The SARS, MERS and Ebola and now the COVID 19 have been responsible for large numbers of deaths. All these pandemics are the result of our misuse of the earth and its resources. All originate from non-humans

- **Invasive Species** like the black rats that was responsible for the extinction of many species
- **Better adapted competition** the better-adapted populations win over the ones that lag behind. For e.g., the pre-historic mammals were better adapted than the dinosaurs. The ones which are well-adapted will and do survive, while the others become extinct
- **Lack of food** as the habitat shrinks, food sources dry up. This is one scenario. Then as the prey dies so does the source of the hunter and they too die out
- **Pollution** The pollution from industries and vehicles has led to a drastic change in the oxygen levels in the atmosphere, soil and water. This has led to the extinction of many of the aquatic and terrestrial species
- **Lack of genetic diversity** When the number of species starts decreasing, the gene pool of that species grows smaller and smaller. Eventually, there is a lack of genetic diversity. For example, due to habitat loss, the African cheetahs have a considerably low genetic diversity. The black rhino has disappeared for the same reason
- **Loss of Habitat** All life flourishes in an environment that is conducive to their needs. When this habitat becomes smaller as humans encroach more and more into their

territory, the habitat shrinks and is less able to support them. They start to die out. This scenario has been repeated time after time and is still going on. For example due to deforestation a lot of bird species are lost to us.

Sophia Z. Kovachevich

Fisheries

For the first time since the demise of the dinosaurs 65 million years ago, we face a global mass extinction of wildlife. We ignore the decline of other species at our peril – for they are the barometer that reveals our impact on the world that sustains us. Mike Barrett, director of science and policy at WWF's UK branch

The ecosystem is made up of an interconnected web of living creatures. To a great extent they are interdependent, including humans. It is the biodiversity among the different species that makes the world what it is and that is vital to our continued existence. When one goes out of kelter, it upsets the balance of the whole. When we lose any one species it impacts on the whole and puts life itself at risk. But human beings, it seems to me, cannot and will not live in amity with other living beings that were here long before humankind. They have to hunt and kill as it takes their fancy not just for existence but also for pleasure - though what pleasure there is in taking a life, any life I really cannot fathom!

However ever since the industrial revolutions and the colonisations of peoples by other races, things have changed radically. Human intervention has upset the balance. The ecosystem has been raped time and time again. Species are killed for profit and pleasure not only for food. There is excessive waste and abuse of other living creatures by man. We have endangered many species. Many others are threatened or have been made extinct. At this rate there is not much hope left for life on earth as we have known it.

According to the International Union for Conservation of Nature (IUCN), there are 1,414 species of fish and sea animals that are endangered. Some may soon become extinct unless we stop overhunting these beautiful and rare sea creatures for no good reason. They do not come on land to hunt us. We go into their domain to kill them. This has got to stop. Following are some of the large fish and sea mammals that are the most endangered.

o **Sturgeons** are of economic importance for their roe (caviar) and their flesh for centuries. Of the six types of sturgeon found in the Danube, 2 are already extinct due to over fishing – the **Atlantic sturgeon** and the **Ship sturgeon.** The other four are critically endangered or dependent on stocking programmes. Sturgeons used to range from the Northern Hemisphere through the Atlantic, Pacific and Mediterranean, Black and Caspian Seas, along the Danube and some lakes. Now they are a rare sight.

o **The Atlantic Halibut** is the largest of the flat fish species. It can live up to 50 years. At the moment it is overfished. The Atlantic Halibut population has decreased alarmingly as a result.

o **Beluga Sturgeon** (Huso Huso) is found in the Caspian Sea and the Black Sea. It is an ancient fish. It can live to more than 100 years but due to habitat loss and overfishing, poaching and gill nets the numbers have decreased alarmingly. It is also heavily fished for the eggs -roe or beluga caviar. It is regarded as an endangered species. It always returns to the same estuary each year.

o **The Danube Sturgeon** is also critically endangered due to being heavily fished

o **The Stellate Sturgeon** (Acipenser Stellatus) is critically endangered and extremely rare

o **The Starlet Sturgeon** (Acipenser ruthenus) is dependent on stocking programmes for survival

o **Hammerhead shark (**Sphyrna mokarran) is found in tropical waters around the world. In Australia it is regarded as an iconic species. They are critically endangered around the world including Australia often due to overfishing They are nearing extinction due to the fin trade and their close-to-shore habits

o **The Ganges Shark** found in the lower reaches of freshwater, inshore and estuarine ecosystems is also critically endangered

o **The Great White** belongs to the vulnerable category. In spite of having the reputation of being man eaters, in fact it is not so. They are overfished and often collide with shipping vessels

o **Dusky shark** is also vulnerable and can easily become endangered. It is bronze or silver grey or bluish grey in colour. It too, is overfished

o **Brown Shark** is also on the vulnerable list

o **The Basking shark** is on the ICUN list of endangered creatures. It is a docile, slow moving shark. It does not have sharp teeth. It has a mottled skin that I think is beautiful. It is severely overfished and is often a target of the fishing industry

o **Beluga whale** - It is also called the White Whale or Sea Canary because of its high-pitched calls. There are about 375 Beluga whales left alive. It was declared critically endangered in 2004. A main reason for the low numbers is the subsistence hunting of these whales in Greenland, Canada and Alaska. Along with that is water pollution, noise pollution (movements of ships) and global warming

o **Acadian Red Fish** is found in the North Atlantic Ocean. It can live up to 50 years. It is a slow growing fish and overfishing has decreased the number alarmingly. This violates the IUCN environmental laws. It is among the top 10 endangered species as of 2015. It is a beautiful fish.

o **The Orange Roughy** has habitats around the world including New Zealand, Australia, Nambia and the northeast Atlantic Coast. It can live up to 149 years. Overfishing has led to a dramatic decrease in the Roughy's breeding. Massive numbers have been wiped out due to overfishing. It is an endangered species.

o **Winter Skate** inhabits the northwest Atlantic Ocean from St Lawrence in Canada to North Carolina in the USA. It is harvested and processed into fish meal and lobster bait as well as for human consumption. Overfishing has led to it being classified as an endangered species.

o **Bocaccio Rockfish** is also one of the topmost endangered species of fish. It is also called the Salmon Grouper, Grouper and Slimy. It, too, is severely endangered due to overfishing.

o **The Danube Salmon:** is one of the largest species of salmon – up to 5 feet. It is one of the most endangered fish in the world.

o **The European pond turtle:** is a timid creature but an excellent swimmer. It prefers to spend the cold months in the muddy waters at the bottom of ponds. In the Danube they are few of them left. It is found in Europe and North Africa but they are threatened by disturbances of their habitat and urban sprawl. They also fall victims to weirs and drown.

o **The European Eel** is found primarily in the North Atlantic Ocean, the Baltic Sea and the Mediterranean Sea. It can live up to 50 years. It is critically endangered since 1970 by about 90% due to over fishing and parasites like the Anguillioch crassus.

o **Goliath Grouper:** there are two types of grouper – the **Atlantic Goliath Grouper** and the **Pacific Goliath Grouper**. All species of this fish are critically endangered. It is also known as the Jewfish. It inhabits the subtropical eastern Pacific – from Baja California to Peru and the Atlantic from North Carolina to Brazil. It is a very large fish and can live up to 40 years. It is endangered specifically due to line hook fishing. And like other endangered fish, it is overfished.

- o **Maltese Ray** (or Skate) is found in the Mediterranean Sea, along the Italian Coast, in Malta and Algeria. Commercial fishing vessels target this fish and so it is also overfished. It is the second most endangered fish in the world.
- o **Blue Fin Tuna** is the most endangered fish in the world since 2015 even though there are many Blue Fin Tuna. This is mostly found in the Atlantic Ocean. It is a very fast fish. Due to extensive and intensive fishing it is becoming rare.
- o **The Tennessee River** has one of the most aquatically biodiverse river systems in North America. It also has the greatest number of imperilled species in the USA. There are **57 species of fish and 47 species of mussels** in this river basin that are at risk. Southeastern USA has 90% of the World's species of mussels and crayfish, 73% of all the aquatic snail species, 50% of all freshwater fish. The Tennessee River system alone has 230 species of fish and 100 species of mussels that are endemic to the river system. Among the fish at risk here is the **Snail Darter**, a small fish native to the area. It was declared an endangered species in 1975 and changed to a critically threatened species in July 1984
- o **The Alabama Cavefish** is endangered
- o **The Spotfin Chub** is also endangered
- o The **Palezone Shiner** is also endangered
- o Many **mussel species** including the Cumberland monkeyface, the Oyster mussel, the Dromedary pearly mussel are all endangered
- o Among the endangered snail species is **Anthony's River snail**,
- o There are 4 flower species that are endangered here namely **Green Pitcher Plant, Harperella, Morefield's Leather Flower** and **Mountain Skullcap**

- o In the Tennessee River basin also endangered are these: the **Red-Cockaded Woodpecker** and the **Gray Indiana Bat**, **The Bald Eagle** and the **Gray Bat**
- o Also endangered is the **Hellbender Salamander** which is a giant salamander native to North America. Besides overfishing these species are also at risk from human encroachment and dams

Other sea animals that are endangered around the world are:

- o **Hawksbill Turtle** that is found in tropical regions especially in coral reefs. The population has declined by 80% in the last century. It is heavily trafficked for its meat and shell. They are killed mercilessly. The beautiful shell of this turtle is sold as tortoiseshell. Its egg is harvested even though that is banned. Another reason for its decline is that the coral reefs are dying and so its food source is getting limited. They are vital to our ecosystem. They are also vital for the coral reefs and seagrass
- o **Vaquita** inhabits shallow, muddy waters off the Baja Peninsula in Mexico. It is a member of the porpoise family. It is the world's smallest critically endangered species only 50 years after its first sighting. This is in a great part due to the use of gill nets and extensive fishing. According to reports there are only about a dozen of this species in the world. That is a sharp decline of 90% since 2011.
- o **The Blue Whale** is the world's largest living mammal. It belongs to the group of Baleen whales. They maintain a healthy marine environment. Excessive fishing and commercial hunting has markedly reduced their numbers and now they are an endangered species. An IUCN report says that there are only between 10,000 and 25,000 of them in the oceans of the world. Hunting Blue whales was banned in 1966. Now only between 3%-11% of the whales are alive

- o **Sei Whale:** Like the Blue Whales, they too are endangered. They were massively hunted in the second half of the 20th century even after hunting Blue whales was banned. Commercial hunting of these unlucky mammals was prohibited in the 1980s. In 2002, Japan resumed hunting under scientific permit in the North Pacific, allowing 100 animals to be caught each year. There are only 20% of these beautiful creatures alive today out of their 1937 population

- o **Kemp's Ridley sea turtle**: is also known as the Atlantic Ridley turtle. It is the rarest and smallest of all turtles. They are critically endangered. They mainly inhabit the Gulf of Mexico and migrate to the Atlantic to lay eggs. All the females travel in a group to the same island each year to lay their eggs. But now due to loss of habitat, marine pollution, entanglement in fishing nets, harvesting of their eggs (forbidden but still happens) and over hunting, they have become seriously endangered. There are now research projects that incubate the eggs in laboratories.

- o **Stellar's Sea Lion**: is the largest of the Otariid family and the fourth largest seal species. It was named for Wilhelm Stellar who first discovered them in 1741. By 1768 they were on the verge of extinction. It lives in the cold coastal waters of the North Pacific. It is also called the Northern Sea Lion. They are at risk of predation by Killer whales, fishing and harvesting of their eggs. Its population has declined by 60% since the 1960's. Between 1977 and 2007 the population decreased by 70%. It was added to the endangered list in 2013. It is now showing some signs of recovery after the initiation of the IUCN protection plan

- o **Hammerhead Sharks**: inhabit the waters around the tropical regions. Its head is shaped like a hammer and that's how it got its name. They are aggressive and feed on small fish, squids, crustaceans and octopuses. There are reports of unprovoked attacks on people. These sharks are victimised for their fins. They are caught, dragged on board the ship or large boat, their fins are cut while they are still alive and then still breathing, they are thrown back into the sea. It is a shockingly inhumane practice. Harvesting of their fins is banned but it still happens in the black market. They are an endangered species

o **Fin Whale**: is also called the rorqual. It is the second largest mammal on our planet after the Blue Whale. Like other whales it is hunted by humans. The global population is less than 100,000. It has a very distinctive ridge behind its dorsal fin. Before whale hunting really took off, they were very difficult to hunt. Between 1975 – 1990 hunting Fin whales was banned. It is endangered due to over hunting and marine pollution

o **Humpback Whale** is also a species of rorqual and is listed as endangered. Before the introduction of the moratorium on whales in 1966, these whales were hunted for their fur, flesh and meat, mercilessly. The population had dropped by 90%. Currently there are about only 2,500 humpback whales in the world

o **Baiji River Dolphin** - This dolphin, native to Yangtze River in China, was declared functionally extinct in 2006 owing to industrialization and heavy fishing, although some reports have suggested that isolated specimens still survive

o **Hector's Dolphin** is found along the New Zealand coast around the South Island. It is the smallest of all the dolphins. A group of dolphins have between 2 and 8 members. Their population has dropped significantly as Trawl fisheries and bottom set nets trap and drown them. One of the 2 sub species of this dolphin, the **Maui Dolphin** is the most endangered. According to a survey conducted by the New Zealand Department of Conservation in

2010-2011, there is an estimated population of 55 of this dolphin species left alive

o **The Sea Otter** was once really abundant living in the North Pacific rim. But the beginning of commercial hunting in the 18th century changed everything for them and the population started declining. By the time they were put on the endangered list in 2011, there were only 2,000 animals left. They did recover but the overall population is still shrinking. There are presumably 90,000 of them in Alaska now. This is because of hunting by humans, killer whale predation, and severe pollution. The Exxon Valdez oil spill alone killed 3,000 sea otters. Then there is the acidification of the oceans and climate change

o **Hawaiian Monk Seal**: is a native of the Hawaiian Islands. Unlike other seals it is earless and prefers warm beaches. This is one of the two remaining monk seals species along with the **Mediterranean Monk Seal**. There is an estimated 1,400 left. They are threatened by commercial hunting for their meat, oil and skin. They are also attacked by predators like the tiger shark. Another threat is from marine debris and getting entangled in fishing nets. Their population has been continuously declining since 1983. In 2011, the number of mature animals was 632 and 577 babies. They are solitary animals and threat to them remains high. Their food source is also lessening. Their pups are often attacked by mature males or fall victim to sharks. **The Caribbean Monk Seal** is now extinct.

o **The Green Sea Turtle**: is one of the largest sea turtles. It is a herbivore. It inhabits tropical and sub-tropical waters. It is named after the green coloured fat under its carapace. Like most turtle species it returns to its birth place to lay its eggs each year. Turtles are a popular food item in some countries and so they and their eggs are hunted. Also a threat to them is the loss of sandy beaches, careless fishing methods and overhunting.

o **The Blackfin Cisco** is closely related to the salmon & trout. Once plentiful in the Great Lakes it is now extinct due to a combination of overfishing, predation by 3 invasive species – the Alewife, the Rainbow Smelt and a genus of Lamprey. It was last sighted in 1969 in Lake Michigan

o **The Blue Walleye** also known as the Blue Pike was overfished in the Great Lakes in the late 19th to the mid-20th century. The invasive Rainbow Smelt also preyed on it. As well as that, the industrial pollution from the surrounding factories was also to blame for its disappearance. It was declared extinct in 1983.

o **The Galapagos Damsel** was found in the Galapagos Islands that was the original foundation place for much of Charles Darwin's evolution theory. This fish is one of the most endangered species in the world. This is not directly attributable to man but rather to the rise in local water temperatures that resulted from the El Niño currents in the early 1980's that drastically reduced the plankton population which is the main food for this fish

o **The Gravenche** is found in Lake Geneva – a location that would be expected to have much more ecological protection but that is not the case here. The protection came too late for this fish. The Gravenche is related to the salmon. It is about a foot long. It was overfished in the late 19th century and virtually disappeared in the 1920's. It was last seen in 1950. Apparently, there are no specimens of this fish available

o **The Harelip Sucker** was an inhabitant of the freshwater streams of Alabama. Very little is known about this fish. It was last seen in the late 19th century. It was caught in 1859 and was described 20 years later when the fish was nearly extinct. It became extinct due to large amounts of silt infused into the once pristine, clear ecosystem of southeastern USA

o **The Lake Titicaca Orestias** disappeared from Lake Titicaca in South America in the mid-20th century. The Titicaca Orestias was also known as the Amanto. It was a small rather unprepossessing fish with a large head and a distinctive underbite. It disappeared due to the introduction of trout into the Lake

o **The Silver Trout** was extremely rare even when it was first discovered. They were native to three small lakes in New Hampshire which were most probably the remnants of a larger population that was dragged northward by the retreating glaciers, thousands of years ago. This fish was doomed when stocking recreational fish began. It was last seen in 1930

o **The Tecopa Pupfish** was an exotic fish. It thrived in conditions that humans would find extremely hostile. It lived and swam in the hot springs of California's Mojave Desert where average temperatures are about 110^0 Fahrenheit. The pup thrived under these conditions but could not survive human encroachment. In the 1950's-1960's a large number of bathhouses were built in the vicinity of the hot springs and the water from the springs were artificially diverted. The last pupfish was caught in 1970. It is now extinct

o **The Thicktail Chub** was an inhabitant of the unappealing marshes, lowland and weed-choked backwaters of California's Central Valley. In the 1900 it was a common sight to see this fish in the Sacramento River and the San Francisco Bay. It was a staple in the Californian diet of California's Native American population. It was doomed due to overfishing and the loss of its habitat. It was last seen in 1950

o **The Yellowfin Cutthroat Trout** was a ten-pound trout with bright yellow fins. It was first seen in the Twin

Lakes of Colorado in the late 19th century. It was a strange looking fish. It became extinct due to the introduction of the Rainbow Trout in the early 20th century. The smaller Greenback Cutthroat trout is a much smaller relative of the Yellowfin

Some endangered animals of the Arctic Tundra

Tundra regions are extremely cold, dry, windy, treeless ecosystems. They are the harshest biomes. One example is Greenland. A lot of flora grows in such places as they have adapted to the cold, harsh conditions. Like other tundra regions there are a lot of glaciers here, rocky, barren outcrops and huge icecaps. They are generally treeless biomes.

Animals that live in Alaska's Arctic Tundra face a whole set of different challenges to those that other animals face in other regions. They have to survive in a sort of frozen desert. There is no escaping into the forests for shelter from the cold, biting winds nor from attack. In winter temperatures are easily -34° F. In summer it is a mild day when the temperature reaches to 54°F. The topsoil does thaw but beneath the permafrost the subsoil always remains frozen. But now there is a major problem. With global warming the climate is changing and the permafrost is thawing. This ecological change is endangering the very survival of some species there. Some are endangered due to other introduced species. All are endangered by human behaviour and interference. The following animals and birds are some species that are threatened, endangered or on the verge of extinction.

Arctic Fox: this fox has a snow white coat in the Arctic winter and a thick brown one in summer for camouflage. Its territory is being invaded and they are also hunted by the larger introduced Red Fox. Sometimes the Red Foxes also burrow into the Arctic fox's den and kill its cubs. In Norway, Sweden and Denmark they are also an endangered species due to overhunting by humans.

Polar Bear: is regarded as the icon of the Arctic. It ranges from Northern Alaska to northern Canada and into Russia. It loves pack ice and will travel long distance to jump from one floe to another. They also use the pack ice to ambush seals, a major food source for them. Breeding polar bears also den and bring up their young on pack ice. In 2008 they were listed as an endangered and threatened species.

The Prairie Pigeon: is also called the Arctic Curlew or the Eskimo Curlew. It has been listed as endangered for a long time. It spends the winter in Argentina and the summer in Alaska. It nests in the tundra. It was sighted in south Texas in 1962. This was verified. It was supposedly last seen in Manitoba, Canada in 1996. This sighting was not verified but is accepted as the last time it was seen. It has not been seen since then.

The Arctic Peregrine Falcon: is one of the success stories of the Arctic Tundra. It was listed as endangered as the population was fast dwindling due to human interference (over hunting) and the use of DDT. The birds ate prey that had digested the pesticide and in consequence their eggs were very fragile and often broke during incubation. When DDT was banned from being used the falcons recovered somewhat. They have been spotted in Kenai Fjords National Parks on Boat tours.

Wood Bison is larger than the North American Bison. Once they roamed freely in Alaska but were endangered due to overhunting. They were only found in the wild in Canada. The only other wild herd was located in the Alaskan Wildlife Conservation Centre. From there in 2015 a herd of 130 bison was reintroduced into the Alaskan wild - their original habitat

Caribou: is an endangered species. Its habitat is under serious threat from forest logging, and increased oil and gas mining. They are also poached by humans

Narwhal: is a seriously endangered whale species of the Arctic. It is hunted for its ivory tusk and for the Vitamin C that is present in their skin and which the Arctic dwellers need. If they are not protected they will become extinct very soon

Musk Ox: is a shaggy haired large oxen that has inhabited the Arctic for thousands of years. Due to overhunting their numbers had gone down to only 500 in the wild. Now they are close to 40,000 due to conservation of their species. This is a success story

Beluga Whale: is critically endangered due to increased extraction of fossil fuels in the Arctic. In 2012 there were only 321 of them documented. They have been reduced by 75% of their population

The Pacific Walrus: like the Polar Bear its survival depends on pack ice. The pups are also brought up on the pack ice. Due to global warming, the ice is thawing and their survival is now at stake unless something is done

Life in the Arctic tundra is different from living in other places.

Some endangered and vulnerable animals of the Antarctic

Endangered and vulnerable Antarctic mammals, birds, fish etc.

Southern Right Whale	Sei Whale	Blue whale
Fin whale	Humpback whale	Magellanic Penguin
Emperor Penguin	King Penguin	Rockhopper Penguin
Macaroni Penguin	Adelie Penguin	Chinstrap penguin
Gentoo Penguin	Amsterdam Albatross	Antipodean Albatross
Tristan Albatross	Southern Royal Albatross	Wandering Albatross
Northern Royal Albatross	Sooty Albatross	Buller's Albatross
Indian Yellow-nosed Albatross	Shy Albatross	Chatham Albatross
Campbell Albatross	Salvin's Albatross	White capped Albatross
White-bellied Storm Petrel	Antarctic Tern	Subantarctic Fur Seal
Imperial Shag	Southern Elephant Seal	Blue Petrel
Northern Giant Petrel	Soft Plumaged Petrel	Kermadic Petrel
Abbott's Booby Petrel	Northern Right Whale	Great white Pelican & others
European Kingfisher	European pond turtle Found also in North Africa	Danube Salmon

Information from: Environment Protection and Biodiversity Conservation Act 1999 (Australia)/

Antarctic Blue Whale was hunted to near extinction in 1970. There were just a few hundred of them left. Now though the population is somewhat better it is still regarded as rare and endangered. It is the largest sea animal. Whales mostly eat krill.

Of the 13 whale species 6 are regarded as endangered (see above) due to whaling as the main reason. But they are also negatively affected by climate change, pollution especially the noise of drilling and the pollution from the oil drilling and the boats. Another important threat to them is bycatch – they get tangled in the nets and lines and drown especially the blue whales. Other threats are habitat loss, climate change and continuation of whaling in spite of them belonging to the protected group. The whales most at risk are the **North Atlantic and North Pacific Right whales.**

Of the 18 **penguin** species, 10 species are considered endangered. Of the other 8 species 2 – **the Emperor Penguin and the Magellanic penguin are near threatened; the Macaroni and Southern Rockhopper** penguins are vulnerable and of least concern at the moment as are the **Adélie, Chinstrap, Gentoo and King penguins**. Penguins face many threats from introduced predators, diseases, natural disasters like volcanic eruptions, pollution and getting tangled in fishing nets and drowning, climate change and severe weather conditions.

Albatross too are critically endangered in the Antarctic from fishing lines and trawling cables. About 100,000 albatross are killed each year. They are now regarded as critically endangered. In general seabirds are amongst the most threatened group of birds in the world today.

According to the EPBC Act (Environment Protection and Biodiversity Conservation Act) all seals and sea lions in Australia are protected under EPBC Act 1999; Section 248. Killing, trading or harming these animals in any way is regarded as an offence that is punishable. Seals are mostly found along the coast, the majority living in the Arctic and Antarctic waters. One species lives in the Mediterranean and is critically endangered. It is believed that less than 600 of them survive. In 1997, two-thirds of Mediterranean seals were wiped out due to a virus.

Snow petrels are also endangered. They nest far inland on rocks surrounded by ice in the Antarctic about 325 km from the sea. They have to travel in order to find food. They are at risk then.

A species of petrels also breed on Macquarie, but they have been adversely affected by the introduction of the black rats, mice, cats and rabbits. The breeding small **blue petrel** of Macquarie is considered to be critically endangered.

The IUCN Red List of Threatened Species IUCN Red List

Decreasing	Stable	Increasing	Status Unknown
15 species	5 species	10 species	6 species

This is an incomplete table. It is just a sample of how we are losing our animals due to our callous disregard for them.

Some of the most endangered species in the world are:

Tiger – 5 species are extinct. Rest are critically endangered due to being hunted by man for its skin and body parts and as a sport. The remaining subspecies are all seriously endangered.

Leatherback turtle belong to the critically endangered species due to loss of habitat and choking on plastic which they often mistake for food

Chinese Giant Salamander: almost totally extinct due to its being a very popular food and due to the very high levels of pollution in its habitat in Southern and Southwestern China

Sumatran Elephant: is on the verge of extinction due to loss of habitat as a result of deforestation and due to hunting. The IUCN (International Union for Conservation) says it is protected

by legislation but that legislation does not extend to the bulk of
to its habitat

The Vaquita is a cetacean that lives in the Gulf of California. It
is mostly killed by indiscriminate trawling. It is also critically
endangered

The Saola is a bovine with prints on its face and very long horns.
It is often described as the Asian unicorn and for its rarity it is
hunted as a trophy. It is predominantly threatened by loss of its
habitat due to logging. It is also very critically endangered. Only
500 Saolas remain (2018).

The Polar Bear lives in the Arctic and has become endangered
due to loss of habitat by the melting of the Arctic ice caps. Its
food too has become scarce because of global warming which
has resulted in the ice caps melting.

The North Atlantic Right Whale: is the most endangered whale
species. There are less than 350 whales (2018). Though they
are a protected species they are still threatened by commercial
fishing. They also often drown when they get snagged in nets
and ropes.

The threat to its existence began in the 19th century when they
were hunted indiscriminately. Their population was reduced
by 90% and they have never recovered. Now there is a great
possibility that they may disappear forever.

The Monarch Butterfly is special among butterflies for the
migration of four generations together from Scotland to Mexico.
In the past 20 years their population has decreased by 90% due
to the loss of its food – the milkweed plant – and its habitat. This
had happened due to increased agriculture and the uncontrolled
use of chemical pesticides.

The Golden Eagle is among the top-most endangered species due to the loss of its habitat as a result of deforestation.

Giraffes are endangered because they are very vulnerable to poaching and due to deforestation. It has been estimated that in the last three decades 40% of the African giraffes have disappeared.

The giant panda was very critically endangered but due to conservation by the World Wildlife Fund for Nature that adopted the panda image it brought their plight into focus. They are still endangered but are in a much better place than they were.

The Iberian wolf has become extinct in some areas of the Iberian Peninsula. Where they are still to be found they are an endangered species.

The European mink in Spain is critically endangered due to a number of factors: loss of habitat, introduction and later release of the American mink, an invasive species (and they are prolific), on Spanish soil.

The Spanish imperial eagle, a really beautiful bird is now in serious danger of extinction. There are only 71 nesting pairs in Andalusia and 119 nesting pairs in Castilla La Mancha. This is due to deforestation and loss of their habitat, electrocution from power lines, poisons, pollution and spread of human populations. In North Africa, they have become extinct.

The Lesser Kestrel is also a very vulnerable species due to the destruction of their nesting sites, use of pesticides and change of land use.

The asp viper in Northeast of Spain is also considered endangered due to the intensification of agriculture, construction of tourist attraction spots and by being hunted by humans as they are poisonous.

The Iberian Midwife Toad is a separate species from other midwife toads. The males carry the fertilised eggs on their backs. They are endangered because they are threatened by fungal infection and the pollution of rivers.

The sturgeon used to be abundant in the Spanish rivers but in recent years none have been caught. It is believed that they have now become extinct in Spain due to over fishing, pollution of the waterways and dam construction.

Many other species are in danger of being extinct or have already become so. It is a sad and shocking indictment on our role as custodians of the land, air and seas.

Some shocking killings of hapless animals by humans

- A Cincinnati Zoo worker shot and killed Harambe a 17 year old gorilla at the zoo. This was because a three-year old boy climbed into the gorilla's enclosure and Harambe grabbed and dragged him. The child had no business getting into the cage. His parents or minder should have taken better care of the child.

- The Zimbabwe Conservation Task Force has named Walter James Palmer as the killer of Cecil a 13 year old Zimbabwean prized lion who was a protected subject of a study. Palmer is now wanted by the Hwange National Park Authorities in Zimbabwe for poaching and killing Cecil.

- 19-year old Texan Kendall Jones posted a picture of herself proudly showing off some animals that she killed for pleasure and sport. Among them were the following animals: a lion, a rhinoceros, an antelope, a leopard, an elephant, a zebra and a hippopotamus. It provoked world-wide condemnation of her cowardly killing acts.

- Rebecca Francis is a prolific killer of endangered species and other animals. She has a web site where she posts pictures of the animals she hunts across America and Africa. She also co-hosted the animal killing programme *The Eye of the Hunter.* Among the animals she has killed are buffaloes, bears, giraffes and zebras. She uses a bow and arrow.

- Copenhagen Zoo euthanized an 18-month old healthy giraffe and dissected it and fed pieces to the lions as zoo visitors watched. They compounded this by killing 4 healthy lions. A public outcry was raised at this meaningless slaughter.

- A Swiss zoo was sharply criticised for putting down a healthy brown bear cub that was being bullied by its father. It should not have been put down. It should have been separated from its father and rehabilitated. If the zoo keepers believed the cubs and mother should have been separated when the bullying began, why didn't they do it? Why did they kill the poor cub?. The bears Misha and Masha had been donated to the Berne zoo in 2009.
- Daniel Wayne Morton, a 19 year old Australian repeatedly bashed an injured kangaroo on the head. What a cruel act! He was fined $5000 and a 12-month CCO (Community Corrections Order).

If we cannot or do not want to protect animals in our care, we should not be having them in our zoos to be killed arbitrarily by a zoo worker. as happened to Harambe. Nor should be going after them to catch and/or torture and kill them. And people who hunt and kill for pleasure are bullies and cowards and they should be condemned for their actions – not commended for it. Or profit by it.

Animal Suicide

In recent times we have noticed a strange phenomenon – animals committing suicide. It might be that only now we are noticing it or it could be a totally new phenomenon. Whatever it is, it is happening these days around the world now. Here are some incidents that highlight this phenomenon:

- In 1845 A Newfoundland dog kept trying to drown himself by getting into the water and holding still. He was rescued but did the same thing any time he was not tied up (several times) and finally succeeded in drowning himself
- In the 1960's Kathy the dolphin in *Flipper* committed suicide by stopping her breathing. When the trainer removed his arm, she sank to the bottom – dead. This incident made him an animal rights activist. (Her story was featured in the 2009 documentary *The Cove*. She apparently grew tired of being in captivity
- In 1987 a paper appeared that pea aphids (*Acyrthosiphon pisum*) explode themselves to protect the group against ladybugs.
- Another example of such behaviour is that of the Malaysian worker ant (*Camponotus saundersi*) that too sacrifices itself for the greater good in the face of danger.
- In 2005 a group of 1,500 sheep jumped to their death from a cliff top. Some that jumped towards the end were saved because of cushioned impact.
- In 2009 a group of 28 cows and bulls jumped off a cliff in Switzerland over a span of 3 days and killed themselves. An accidental death can occur but not a deliberate mass suicide as happened in these incidents.
- In November 2011 a pod of 61 whales beached themselves at Farewell Spit in New Zealand. Only 18 survived.

- In 2012 a bear in a zoo – living in a small cell, stopped eating and starved himself to death. Animal Rights campaigners claim that this is a common occurrence with bears that are kept in confined spaces.
- The female octopus starves herself to death after the baby octopii are born. Female octopii lay eggs only once in their life time. They guard the eggs from predators. They do not eat during this time. When the eggs hatch, they die out of starvation.
- My father's dog, Jimmy, a Bull Mastiff starved himself to death when my father died. He died under my father's window.
- A mother bear, in 2011 smothered her cub and then killed herself on a Chinese farm to stop bile being extracted for human treatment as a supposed cure for liver and bladder problems. Taking bile from the bears causes a lot of pain to the animals.
- Male honeybees explode their own genitalia in order to pass on their genes and create more honeybees. They die but the group continues. They leave their sperm in the queen bee as they die.
- In *Psychology Today* Marc Bekoff A blogger wrote a post about a burro that walked into a lake and killed herself after the death of her infant.

Conclusion

Man's misuse and destruction of the natural world is eroding nature to the point when it will no longer be able to support the growing need for food and water. The decline in the earth's biodiversity is on a parallel with climatic change (UN-backed report by Medellin, Colombia 23.03.2018) and the two are interconnected.

Some important findings of the research related to the highly populated area of the Asia-Pacific region as well as around the world were the following:

- Freshwater has decreased by half since the 1950's
- In Europe the animal land species has decreased by 42% since 2010
- Both these are set to reach zero by 2048 (Medellin Colombia report)
- In France there has been a grim and frightening decimation of the bird population of the country
- The death of the very last white northern male rhinoceros is shocking as the burden of the existence of the species now centres on the only two remaining female white northern rhinoceros
- The EU instead of helping with the continued existence of cattle is ignoring the climate crisis and giving new subsidies for farm livestock in order for them to supply cheaper meat and meat products
- The damage to the land must be contained and reversed. A healthy land produces healthy food. Exhausted, leached land cannot do so. The quality and quantity of the produce is dependent on the quality of the soil. Our food system is broken and this is heading the planet itself to catastrophe with the populations being left either overfed (the

billionaires) or underfed and thus prone to disease and death (the average person) according to Jonathan Watts.

- Livestock reared mainly for consumption is also leading the land to overuse. 83% of farm land is used for livestock produce from which we get 18% of calories. Avoiding or sharply reducing the consumption of meat and dairy products will improve the environmental impact on the land (Damian Carrington)
- This view is also supported by Oppenheim who believes that transforming the land usage would make food supply more secure or within 20 years it could be much worse than it is today. This idea is also supported by many others like Caterina Ruggeri Laderchi research director at Folu who says saving the planet is important for business too. She says *"the shift in policy to sustainable production of healthy food could unlock $ 4.5 tn in new commercial opportunities each year by 2030"*.
- Benefits from subsidies have already been seen by higher yielding crops where such subsidies were given. Farmers in the EU given subsidies have reduced their greenhouse gas emissions from fertilizers by 17% while simultaneously yields rose.
- China is phasing out support for fertilizers.
- Another example where subsidy worked was in Costa Rica where eliminating the cattle subsidies in return for payment for improving the environment saw the *return of forests* there.

It is an unpalatable truth that humans have destroyed and are still destroying the earth and its inhabitants – the forests, the animals the birds, the sea creatures and our mineral wealth at an unprecedented rate. That is a fact that has been proven not just by various studies like UN reports but also by nature's rebellion in the form of melting ice caps, storms, hurricanes, earthquakes, volcanic eruptions, very strange weather and new viruses that keep mutating, like the Coronavirus. Many species are not just endangered but on the verge of disappearing. An IPBES (Intergovernmental Science Policy Platform on Biodiversity and Ecosystem Services) report says that the current rate of species extinction, globally, is ten to hundreds of times higher than it was over the past 10 million years. To me, this is plausible because we see, read and hear about the extinction of species – some put it at one million species that is on the verge of extinction from the earth. Some have lost and are losing their habitat. Out of the 5.9 million land-based species, 500,000 are in the process of losing their habitat for their long time survival. Scientists believe that this is the sixth mass extinction in the 4.5 billion-year history of the world.

Ecosystems, species, wild populations, local varieties and breeds of domesticated plants and animals are shrinking, deteriorating or vanishing," assessment co-chair Professor Josef Settele said.

The essential, interconnected web of life on Earth is getting smaller, weaker and at risk of becoming increasingly frayed.

Human life, human existence is now at risk unless we do something about this. The soil has been overexploited. We MUST once more make it healthy and fruitful.

PART V

GLOBAL WARMING

Over the past 50 years the average temperature around the globe has increased more than at any other time in recorded history. The trend is accelerating at an unprecedented rate. For example, according to experts 15 out of 16 hottest years in 134 years have occurred in the last 20 years.

Global warming is caused when carbon dioxide (CO_2) and other air pollutants and greenhouse gas collect in the atmosphere and they absorb sunlight and solar radiation. The atmosphere traps the heat and produces the greenhouse effect. The earth heats up. The main cause of this is the burning of fossil fuels and coal. As a result, the environment, health and economy are all impacted. Some of the trends that we have seen and will probably continue to see are:

o   Melting glaciers, (Greenland, Iceland, Arctic and Antarctic poles), and early snowmelt
o   Severe drought, water shortages,
o   Bushfires, forest fires…
o   Hurricanes, cyclones, tsunamis, tidal waves…
o   Increased earthquakes and volcanic eruptions
o   Rising sea levels leading to coastal flooding
o   New pests, heat waves, heavy downpours, floods
o   Strong negative impact on fisheries and agriculture
o   Extinction of species

o Dying of coral reefs
o Dying rainforests and cloud forests
o New infectious diseases like the SARs, MERs, Ebola, Bird flu and Coronavirus (COVID 19),
o Aggravated asthma and new mutated strains of flu
o Higher levels of air pollution (as happened in China and India in 2018 – 2019)
o The cryosphere is heating up. (These are the ice sheets, ice caps, permafrost floating ice seas, polar ice lakes, snow - all make up the cryosphere). If this melts it will be disastrous for the earth.

In order to counter this, the Paris Climate Agreement was signed by 195 countries pledging to cut pollution by 1.5°Celsius. The USA under President Obama was a signatory to the deal but in 2017 President Donald J Trump withdrew from the deal and opened up coal mines. America's pollution index is very high. It produces 1.7 billion tons of CO_2 annually.

Poul Christoffersen, a glaciologist at the Cambridge University's Scott Polar Research Institute had this to say: *Every year, there are many hundreds of large waterfalls providing water, but also large quantities of energy, down to the base of the ice sheet.* This water lubricates the bottom of the ice sheet, hastening its movement toward the sea, where it can contribute to sea level rise. This glacier mill as it is called is a well-like shaft that forms within a glacier or ice sheet. These holes are called moulins and they facilitate the meltwater to gather and travel to the bottom of the ice sheet underlining it and creating clusters of lakes under the ice. These then fracture and become waterfalls plunging into the ice and creating a domino effect.

The problem with the glaciers melt is its effect on the environment. Glaciers are melting at an alarming rate. And this is producing flooding and biodiversity loss. The effect of glacier melt on the environment is as follows:

- o **Global warming**: will increase. Glaciers play a major part in absorbing and reflecting heat. If they melt at this rate the earth will not be able to deflect the heat and so temperatures will increase.
- o **Shortage of electricity** because many countries depend on the melting waters to produce electricity. If this source is unavailable then some other source, causing much more pollution may be used.
- o **Extreme flooding**: the thawing glaciers cause abrupt water rise. This can lead to formation of and expansion of lakes and other bodies of water. Cities may get flooded leading to humanitarian crises. Cities like Venice are particularly at risk.
- o **Loss of biodiversity**: Arctic animals, birds and sea mammals need the ice to survive. If the ice melts they too might disappear.
- o **Disappearance of coral reefs**: If there is a sharp rise in water level, the reefs will not be able to get enough sunlight for photosynthesis to take place. Without photosynthesis the reefs cannot survive.
- o **Disappearance of fish** will also affect those who depend on fish as their staple diet.
- o **Effect on the Economy:** the glacier melt will lead to flooding and other glacier-related disasters which will require financial capital. Glacier melt would affect the world and not just one country. It would require large scale financial intervention.
- o **Reduced agricultural production:** due to lack of fresh glacier water during dry periods agricultural produce will be sharply reduced.
- o **Global warming** quite possibly would submerge small islands.

Environmental Pollution

Climate Change and the environment

Climate change affects every aspect of our lives including national security and the economy. It affects the way we live, what we eat, where we go. It affects our health and well-being. We are the products of our environment. Variability of climate affects not only our physical well-being but the economics and by extension the politics and cultural aspects of our lives. For example, in times of stress demagogues have a better chance of getting power than when life is smooth and easy. In times of pandemics the real character of the people becomes apparent – as is the case today with the COVID 19 pandemic. Take it to a lower, more basic level, the environment and the changes decide what we wear, eat, where we go, how we react.

Climate variability is an intrinsic part of our lives. But since the industrial revolutions the change is too great to ignore. The seasonal changes are a normal part of life but now everything has gone awry. We have floods followed by droughts followed by bush fire and cyclones and hurricanes. Nothing is stable anymore. Then we have new diseases that do not yet have a cure. Climate, it seems, affects not only the seasonal changes and weather and the environment but also national economy, national security, movements of people and so on. We shall look at the effects on the four primary impact points and then at the economy and national security.

The four primary points are the air, water, soil and habitat

Sophia Z. Kovachevich

Air Pollution

Air pollution is the excessive release of toxins into the air which affects human health and that of other living organisms. This pollution comes from the process of energy production. The burning of fossil fuel releases chemicals and gases into the air like ammonia, carbon monoxide, sulphur dioxide, nitrous oxides, methane, cfs (chlorofluorocarbons), organic and inorganic particulate matter and biological molecules that contaminate the air. Along with that it also generates smoke and other emissions into the atmosphere. It may cause diseases, allergies and even death. It plays a significant part in diseases like respiratory infections, heart disease COVID 19, COPD (Chronic Obstructive Pulmonary Disease), stroke, lung cancer and other pollution related diseases. It causes harm to other living organisms like animals and food crops. It may damage the natural or built environment. All living things generate some air pollution. This pollution is the most difficult to control. Air follows no boundary and air contamination in one country is bound to spread to others. Air pollution also leads to the proliferation of flu-like diseases. The US EPA had regulated more than 80 different toxins that are found in industrial pollution from asbestos and dioxin to lead and chromium. Even then, USA industries were among the worst polluters in the world. Under the Trump presidency, coal mines have been reopened, further exacerbating an already difficult situation. Some other pollutants are landfills, jet planes, airplanes, bombs and industries.

Air pollution is generally regarded as the biggest problem. It is caused by the burning of fossil fuels which generates smoke and other emissions into the atmosphere. Besides fossil fuels, the air is also polluted by the emissions from planes, jets, and testing and using of bombs and bombers especially in times of conflict (which is a constant in our modern world in some place or the other), and nuclear tests. There are no controls in place to monitor the impact on the air from these tests. They pollute the air and this ought to concern all who live on this planet. When the environment is contaminated and polluted so are we as we breathe that contaminated air. Our very survival depends on breathing. Even as late as 1972 (The Stockholm Conference) and 1992 (The Rio Conference), no provision was made to the relevance of weapons of war in atmospheric pollution. In the latter there was a reference in Principle 24 to the release of heat in relation to environmental purity.

Nuclear testing and use are lethal to us. Air quality is always affected by the chemicals that are released into the atmosphere and the heat that is released in the process. This heat is added to the planet's system and surely influences the streamlines of natural air flows over land and sea and so affects all life on earth.

Shells, nuclear weapons, chemical weapons are constantly being developed and tested with no care taken towards the impact on the air. These tests pollute the air by releasing high levels of toxins into the atmosphere. And they stay in the atmosphere for a very long time – ever spreading outwards. One of the worst is Depleted Uranium. It is a radioactive nuclear waste produced by industrial nuclear reactors. John Cattalinotto (*Metal of Dishonor*) says DU used by the Pentagon is a waste product *of the uranium enrichment process for making atomic bombs and nuclear fuel.* Because of its high density (1.7 times higher than lead) it easily penetrates tanks and armour. On impact it releases a highly radioactive aerosol of *uranium, unlike anything ever seen before. This is uranium oxide, a radioactive poison most dangerous when inhaled into the body, where it will release radiation during the lifetime of the person who inhaled it (ibid).*

> *This radioactive, poisonous product is produced due to the very high temperature created on impact that leads to combustion. It is then that at least 70%*

of the mass of the DU is released in aerosol form (i.e. particles below 5) and causes serious alpha radiation. That is why it is so highly toxic to humans, chemically and radiologically—because it is an alpha particle emitter. When these particles are inhaled into the body they contaminate the whole organism, spreading inexorably into every organ of the body (Betrayal a Political Documentary of our Times by Ashley Smith aka Sophia Z Kovachevich)

It is also very dangerous because it cannot be controlled within an area. Being lighter than uranium dust, it disperses very rapidly in the air, contaminating and polluting the whole atmosphere. And once in the atmosphere it is impossible not to breathe it in – gas masks, it seems, cannot keep it out. Everybody breathes it in – the babies, the old, the young, the armed, the unarmed – everybody. The victims and the victimisers are almost equally at risk. **DU is known to stay in the body once it enters, until the person dies.** There is no known cure for it as far as we all know and no one is searching for one. Once in the body, it penetrates into the lungs and can stay there forever. From there it irradiates to the tissues, contaminating them also with alpha particles, often causing emphysema and/or fibrosis. If swallowed, it enters the gastro-intestinal tract; it penetrates into the lungs from there and into the blood stream. It can be stored in the liver, kidney, bones and tissues for ages – always irradiating outwards into any organ not already contaminated. It affects the immune system, the renal system – in fact all systems of the human body. It causes congenital defects, cancer – in its most virulent form and other abnormalities and deformities. In brief, **it is a most inhumane weapon that affects the old, the young, the poor, the rich, the sick, the healthy and the unborn for generations to come** (Ibid).

Air pollution takes place in many ways. A **direct method** is the dropping of bombs containing *prohibited materials like DU, cluster bombs, graphite bombs etc. A more **indirect method** is by bombing factories, industrial plants for plastics, chemicals, oil, heating, fertilizers…. This can lead to major ecological and environmental catastrophe, besides the humanitarian aspect of the damage it can cause. For example, the destruction of so many chemical and industrial plants in Serbia like the fertilizer factories, plastics, petroleum derivatives among others has released thousands of tons of **highly toxic, tetra-toxigenic and carcinogenic chemicals into the air.** Some of these substances are chlorine, mercury, hydrocarbons, ammonia, nitrogen and sulphur oxides, phosphorous compounds and hydrogen halides* – says a report from the Serbian Chemical Society. *One terrible example of this was the bombing of the fertilizer factory in Pancevo, by NATO which caused the release of vast amounts of sulphur and nitrogen oxides. This resulted in **acid rain**, which fell on both sides of the agricultural areas of* the Danube (Ibid). So the crops were also contaminated. Today in 2020 people are still contracting and dying of cancer there which was a rare occurrence once. And it is not only Serbia. The same thing is happening in Afghanistan, Iraq, Syria, Yemen and so on – in all the hot spots of the world.

Another example was the bombing of the electric relay stations that released **a highly toxic substance – piralen.** The bombing of the petrochemical plant caused a **7000-fold increase in a concentration of the toxic vinyl chloride monomer (VCM)** in the neighbouring urban areas (report of the Serbian Chemical Society). Many people had to be treated for poisoning as a result.

A third more indirect way of polluting the environment and ecology is through the **transformation of the pollutants**. This may result in increased or decreased toxicity depending on other factors.

Sophia Z. Kovachevich

Bombing of chemical and other such factories, in war situations, leads to severe air pollution. It is the hardest one to control and the one that spreads the fastest and the fartherest in the shortest possible time. Air pollution depends, to a great extent on atmospheric conditions. For example, the bombing of the chemical factory in Pancevo that released vast quantities of VCM and other photogenes could have led to a really major catastrophe in Belgrade had the wind been an east-northeast one. Instead it was a westerly wind with the added bonus of unexpected rain and so Belgrade was saved. Prof.Polic (*Pollution and Conditions of This War – Danger of an Ecological Catastrophe*) says:

> *...it is almost impossible to evaluate the qualitative and quantitative aspects of downwind pollution because of rinsing (and the pollution of the soil, water and plant life) as well because of indirect influences caused by chloridisation and other chemical factors.*

After the bombing of the Pancevo chemical factory, the sunshine the next day caused photochemical reactions, especially in the upper layers of the atmosphere, like the troposphere and the stratosphere. Gas masks offer no kind of protection against such pollutants.

Another danger is from the incomplete combustion of materials which result in extremely toxic pollutants like Carbon Monoxide (CO), aldehydes (these participate in photochemical reactions), soot (absorbs highly toxic and dangerous polycyclic aromatic hydrocarbons etc.), heavy metals like mercury (especially in its methylated form), which are all highly toxic and can travel great distances in a short time. Then there is the use of the defoliant dioxin 2,3,7,8 (tetrachloro-dibenzo-p-dioxide) which was used in Vietnam (Agent Orange, resulting in the Agent Orange babies till today. Those who have ever seen them can never, ever forget those poor deformed babies). Then of course there is DU that pollutes everything it comes into contact with for generations to come. DU does not only have terrible direct effects but also indirect effects and has extremely high toxic qualities.

The burning of warehouse goods, plants, and refineries also adversely affected the ozone layer especially through the Greenhouse effect. In Pancevo the bombing of the Pancevo Industrial Complex released VCMs, chlorine, chlorine oxides, ammonia, nitrogen oxides, petrol, and petroleum products. These are all highly toxic gases and their level rose to 10,000 times higher than the permitted level when the bombs impacted. These formed black clouds, and the pall of smoke hung over the area for 10 days gradually spreading outwards to other neighbouring countries and areas, polluting and contaminating all in its path.

The constant and intensive flights of bombers, supersonic jets, planes and other aircrafts also adversely affect the already depleted ozone layer.

As we all know, the depletion of the ozone layer causes changes in living organisms. Rise in skin cancer due to the depleted ozone layer especially over New Zealand and Australia make it imperative to use sun block regularly and still skin cancer is a common manifestation often needing surgery or even leading to death. I have even seen fish with cancer at the Marine Laboratory in Wellington.

The depleted ozone layer also affects the nutrition chain world-wide. The gases that adversely affect the ozone layer travel far and know no boundaries and stay active over long periods of time. Since the ozone layers are thinnest over the northernmost and southernmost parts of the globe, those are the areas which will be affected the most in the long run.

Sophia Z. Kovachevich

Air Pollution Facts

➤ Air pollution represents a major public health challenge and has been linked to cancer, asthma, stroke and heart disease, diabetes, obesity, and dementia.
➤ Pollution from particulates cause over a quarter million deaths yearly only in the UK – according to a study.
➤ Heathrow, after Central London is a major hotspot for nitrogen dioxide (NO_2) pollution
➤ The poor quality of air is responsible for many deaths not just in the UK and Europe but around the world according to a report by the World Health Organisation (WHO).
➤ All EU states which are committed to air quality standards to protect public health have so far failed to achieve the required standards for NO_2 and PM_{10}. PM_{10} is particulate matter or atmospheric aerosol. This is a combination of PM (particulate matter) and SPM (suspended particulate matter) which is microscopic particles of solid and liquid matter suspended in the air. PM can be natural or anthropogenic. They impact both the atmosphere and precipitation which affects human health.
➤ A 2015 study by the MIT (Massachusetts Institute of Technology) revealed that ozone and PM_{10} contribute to many deaths and cost an estimated 21 billion US dollars yearly.

Possible solutions

➤ Replace fossil fuels with solar energy, wind power, hydro power
➤ Replace electric power generation with renewables and nuclear energy
➤ Replace fossil fuel motors with electric ones
➤ Reduce travel in vehicles with bikes or buses or some other alternative. It will make for much cleaner air as is seen in 2020 during the COVID 19 lockdowns.

Coronavirus or COVID 19

The Coronavirus belongs to a group of viruses that affect mammals, birds and humans. In humans it attacks:

- the respiratory system - lungs, throat respiratory tract
- Affects all systems of the body
- Causes fever
- Cough
- Shortness of breath
- Trouble breathing
- Fatigue
- Nausea
- Sore throat
- Pain in the ribs
- Chills and trembling
- Loss of smell
- Loss of taste
- Body aches
- Blood clots in the organs of the body
- It affects the brain
- More and more dangerous effects are being recorded regularly as studies advance

People most at risk are:

- Older people and the very young
- Those with underlying chronic health problems like heart disease,
- Poor immune system
- Diabetes,
- Kidney problems
- Sickle cell disease

❖ Pregnant women perhaps – not determined yet
❖ In the USA in July 2020, it was reported that a number of babies under 2 years of age tested positive for COVID 19

It can be mild or lethal depending on other factors like age, underlying health issues, social status and so on. No one is safe from this disease. The common cold belongs to the Coronavirus family but in its mild form. In its virulent form it caused the HIV, Ebola, Bird Flu, SARS, MERS and COVID 19 infections. It is an **airborne** virulent infection more aggressive than any other of its kind that we have ever seen before.

On June 25, 2020 there was an article by Sherry Groch and Liam Mannix trying to trace how the virus moves and infects and mutates as it travels.

It appears apparently that a tiger, Nadia in the Bronx Zoo in New York was the first to contract the virus from Wuhan China. How? The bats were in Wuhan, China and Nadia was in New York, USA. So how did this happen? Who was the unknown carrier? The virus could not have travelled without a host all that distance. Nadia's zoo went into lockdown.

A middle-aged woman in Melbourne, at the same time showed similar symptoms to the tiger. The sample of their virus was eerily similar. How? And then a woman in Taiwan showed the same genetic signature. Again – How in such faraway places was the same viral signature exhibited?

But unlike previous viruses, this virus does not spread in the same kind of way. This virus mutates with *tiny genetic tweaks* and spreads from one continent to another on board ships, airplanes and border crossings. It is the most perfect of globalised pandemics ever. Therein lies the greatest danger from it. It is extremely hard to contain this particular virus.

According to reports, the outbreak began in Wuhan, China and researchers published its genetic code. Now many other countries are publishing theirs. The little tweaks are visible and the more you study it, the worse it gets. Apparently, DNA experts have traced the distinct strand from the tiger to us, but who knows where it's going to end! It always seems to be a step ahead of us. Today I heard that it can and sometimes does, affect the functioning of the brain (June 2020).

Viruses are tiny particles, smaller than a small grain of sand and yet they drive forward evolution. Who knows what this virus will do?

Viruses abound in nature. There are myriads of viruses in the world around us, in the atmosphere, the oceans the seas, and the land. Most of these viruses are incapable of hurting us or leaping the barrier between man and other creatures. But sometimes, sometimes and no one knows how, when or why, they jump the barrier and infect us. We become their hosts. Unlike bacteria, they need hosts to survive and go forward. And once they find the host – they spread fast and inexorably – duplicating themselves thousands, millions of time as they go. The smart ones, like Covid 19, mutate as they go so it is difficult to keep up with them.

Our relationship with the Coronavirus began a long time ago with the flu viruses which in due course of time we could treat. Yes, it keeps mutating but we are able to produce vaccines to control the flu. This was not the case with the Spanish flu of 1918 that killed between 20 million and 50 million people worldwide and infected about 500 million people world-wide. COVID 19 is a mutation, I believe of the SARS-COV-2 in 2003 and the MERS COV in 2012. It found a host in us and jumped the barrier from a mammal to us and so here we are. **It has already infected 10,199,798+people worldwide and killed 502,947 people**

worldwide within the first half year according to CNN news (as of 29.06.2020).

Then 5.10.2020: Morning

<u>**Globally**</u>
Infected: 34,060,300   35,330,119
Dead: 1, 035,479   1,038,958

<u>**USA**</u>
Infected: 7,419,033   7,445,897
Dead: 209,811   210,013

Then 15.12.2020 Afternoon

<u>**Globally**</u>
Infected: 72,221,63 +571,758
Deaths: 1,612,014 +7,498

<u>**USA**</u>
Infected: 16,532,75 +192,041
Deaths: 303,482+1,341

In recent years the world has got more and more divided and xenophobic leaders have come to power in many countries. Right wing or extreme right wing parties have proliferated. The COVID 19 is a godsend for their purpose. It has been and is being used to whip up public fear of others. Populist leaders like Italy's Matteao Salvini, and France's Marine Le Pen, are trying to stoke up racial tensions by pushing the theory – which has not yet been proven for advocating the closure of borders to stop the COVID 19 from entering their countries. Germs do not respect borders. Yes, COVID 19 can be somewhat controlled with closed borders but one asymptomatic person can easily infect many others. America's Donald J Trump has been hysterically stoking fears of anyone who is not Christian white American. He is also trying to divide America. I would not be surprised if the Presidential Election, if as it appears Joe Biden is going to win, may lead to civil war and perhaps even the breakup of the United States of America.

Salvini, leader of the Lega party, believes that African immigrants brought COVID 19 to Italy and the borders with all EU countries should be closed to stop the **air-borne virus**. Italy got the infection long before Africa did and has had far more deaths and infections than Africa to date (June 2020). Many European nations like Italy (Lega), Austria (Freedom Party), Swiss People's Party, Spain's far-right VOX party led by Santiago Abascal would like to close their borders and want EU to do the same to all countries. Hungary's PM Viktor Orban says not so much COVID 19, as migration, is responsible for the real threat. In my opinion, that is not so. COVID 19 is a major threat. Not to any one country but to the world as a whole. And it is we who are responsible for that. We have abused and mistreated our world. Now has come the price that we have to pay. We can either let nature take its course and wipe us out or we can get our act together and care for our beautiful world the way we are meant to.

Germs happen. Was Spain responsible for the Spanish flu and asked to reimburse the world for having contracted it? No, it wasn't. Spain had as little control over the Spanish flu as China has over COVID19. Germs go where they can and do as they will. All they need are hosts.

COVID 19 is the cause for the 2019-2020 pandemic that has affected the whole world. It is a highly infectious, air-borne disease. The symptoms for this are a runny nose, fever, a dry cough, a sore throat, fatigue and shortness of breath. In very severe cases the fever is higher and there is a decrease in white blood cells. It may and often does cause death.

Some people may have the virus but they don't know that. However, they can spread it to others unknowingly. They are the asymptomatic carriers.

At first it was believed that the virus mostly affected the older population and people with underlying health issues especially chronic ones. But now it appears that it also affects the younger generation too. The virus doesn't care about age, race, religion, colour or anything else. It finds a host and attacks. The only thing to do is take precautions against it by following the guidelines that have been set by the medical profession. COVID 19 or the Coronavirus is, in my opinion, even worse than the Spanish flu. It is a result of our abuse and misuse of the earth; of our polluting our air, water and soil. It has affected 213 countries around the world. It has closed down the economies in many places and caused economic recession.

Most countries have been affected to a greater or lesser degree. The worst hit countries were the USA, Great Britain, Brazil, Italy, France, Russia, Spain, Colombia, Peru and India until now.

There is a strong connection between pollution and COVID 19. It appears countries that have more pollution have had more Coronavirus cases than countries with less pollution. It was also seen that when countries stopped using public transport due to the need to isolate themselves to stop the disease spreading, the air became cleaner. In the USA, parts of Europe and South America there were more cases due to higher pollution index whereas in Australia, New Zealand, and Scandinavian countries (except Sweden which did not isolate cases) there were relatively mild forms of the COVID 19 infection and fewer cases and deaths.

COVID 19, in a way, is Mother Nature's way of putting a stop to our abuse of the earth. We had many warnings – there was the HIV that first infected the primates and later us. Then there was the SARS that jumped from the civets to us. Following that was the Ebola from bats and now we have this terrible, terrible COVID 19. We have been abusing other living creatures. We use stun guns to train animals for the circus, we cage animals for our pleasure. It certainly is not for the animals' pleasure. So now we have been given notice to mend our ways. I believe there will be other corona viruses too – until and unless we stop our misuse and abuse of nature's gifts to us.

Following is a table of the most affected countries and Australia and New Zealand. We are proud of our government and medical profession.

Updated 03/12/2020 – last rows of figures in the following information chart

Country	No. of cases	deaths	recovered
USA	2,511,453 4,964,475 14,313, 941	126,924 161,436 279,865	771,155 8,462,347
UK	309,360 307,184 1,659,256	43,414 46,364 59,699	N/A
Brazil	1,280,054 2,858,872 6,436,650	56,109 97.288 174,531	697,526 5,698,353
Italy	239,961 248,824 1,641,610	34,708 35,181 57,045	187,615+890 823,335
France	162,936 194,029 2,244,635	29,778 30,305 53,816	75,351 165,563
Spain	247,905 352,847 1682,533	28,338 28, 499 45784	150,376 N/A
Australia**	7,595 19,444 27,939	104 247 908	6,958 25,614

New Zealand**	1,519 1,569 2,069	22 22 25	1,484 1,974
Russia	620,794 866,627 2,347,401	8781 14,490 41,053	384,152 1,830,349
China	83,483 84,491 86,130	4,634 4,634 1,484	78,444+11 81,667
India	9,534,964	138,657	8,973,373

**low pollution index 27/06/2020
Information from CNN News on 27.06.2020
https://www.worldometers.info/coronavirus/countries-where-coronavirus-has-spread/03/12/2020

Being a pandemic it has affected countries around the world. The chart above shows how pollution affects the presence of the Coronavirus. Countries with a high pollution index among other reasons have had more severe outbreaks than countries with a low pollution index

Percentagewise

24.08.2020.	population	infected no.	%	fatalities no.	%
Country					
China	1,440,000,000	84,967	0.0059%	4,634	0.0003%
USA	**332,500,000**	**5,793,461**	**1.7424%**	**179,329**	**0.0539%**
England	55,500,000	325,642	0.5867%	41,429	0.0746%
Australia	25,500,000	24,812	0.0973%	502	0.0003%
Victoria	6,490,000	18,231	0.2809%	415	0.0064%
NZ	4,676,000	1,683	0.0360%	22	0.0005%

By Sophia Kovachevich

Bombs and Aviation

The earth was a much healthier place and the air better and purer not because there was less war – there wasn't but because people as I mentioned earlier used spears and bows and arrows. And even when they used the fire throwers it still was not as bad as since the invention of bombs and aircrafts and bombers. The carpet bombing being the worst as it leads to fire being ignited which brings its own short and long term effects.

War today is very different to what it was pre-industrial times and even post-industrial times. The weapons are very advanced and mechanised. The effects are not felt by the target alone but even by the victimisers. The quality of the environment is negatively affected for generations to come. The non-combatants suffer even more than the combatants.

Then there is the noise pollution that modern wars bring with them whether it is the noise of bombs falling or the rain of bullets or missiles. Or, bombers streaming across the sky in search of fresh victims and targets. The victimisers are safely ensconced in their planes, fighter jets or homes far, far away. Death is not taken to them. Death is sent to countries and peoples who cannot protect themselves. Such is modern warfare.

When a bullet is fired there is the noise of it being fired, the impact when the target is hit. But along with this there are also the particles that the bullet releases into the air which settle all over the place to become part of the air. In our times millions of bullets are fired in war-torn places every day. Their effect on the air – especially wars that keep going on for generations as in Afghanistan, Yemen, Iraq Lebanon, and other places – contaminate the atmosphere over very long periods of time.

Hand grenades, bombs incendiary bombs (filled with napalm and white phosphorus to cause fire) cluster bombs, DU bombs get worse and worse. World War II saw the carpet bombing of Dresden, Hamburg, Warsaw and other European and Japanese cities for well... *strategic reasons*. Those lit fires throughout the city. In 1937 during the Spanish Civil War, the Spanish Air force and its allies bombed the city of Guernica non-stop for 48 hours which created a firestorm. Everything that stood in the way of the fire was incinerated. The same happened in a number of cities in Germany, Poland and in Japan. The effects of the atomic bombs dropped on Hiroshima and Nagasaki can still be seen. The napalm and Agent Orange bombs on the Mekong Delta still show the after-effects on that area. The trees are still stunted, the children are still born deformed even though peace was declared in 1975 – 45 years ago

World War Two also saw the extensive and intensive bombing of the Western Front.

In World War I chemical weapons were widely used which caused a lot of injuries which often affected the lungs and caused slow, horrifying deaths. Chemical weapons were also widely used in Iraq and other war-torn areas in the Middle-East.

The point is not only did the weapons cause instantaneous damage, but the by-products of intense fire on the air had toxic metals, asbestos, dioxins, polycyclic aromatic hydrocarbons, polychlorinated biphenyls and hydrochloric acids which polluted the air.

Wilfrid Owen World War I poet and soldier captured the effect of such usage of chemicals very tellingly in his poem *DULCE ET DECORUM EST PRO PATRI MORI:*

> *Gas! GAS! Quick, boys!—An ecstasy of fumbling*
> *Fitting the clumsy helmets just in time,*

But someone still was yelling out and stumbling
And flound'ring like a man in fire or lime.—
Dim through the misty panes and thick green light,
As under a green sea, I saw him drowning.

In all my dreams before my helpless sight,
He plunges at me, guttering, choking, drowning.

Now in the 20 and 21st century the bomb we have is the nuclear bombs. These are lethal and cause immense damage. They are made by splitting uranium or plutonium. The same process is applied by splitting hydrogen atoms in hydrogen bombs When detonated they cause a fireball effect and intense radiation They always cause intense and far-reaching environmental damage and destruction.

This type of bomb brings instantaneous death and annihilation with it as the bombing of Hiroshima followed three days later by that of Nagasaki showed. In 1945-1946 the bomb was in its rudimentary stages and it was absolutely lethal. Such bombs, detonated above ground, release severe radiation, poisoning, burning and death. Radioactive particles are released into the stratosphere leading to global fallout. The tragedy at Chernobyl in 1986 contaminated five million acres of cropland in the Ukraine. Radiation levels following this in vegetables and milk was extremely high. When detonated underground the result is even worse.

Exposure to nuclear bombs besides causing severe burns and extremely high radiation levels also cause alterations in the DNA of humans, animals, and plants causing mutations, cancerous tumours, extra limbs, two heads and so on.

Aviation is a major source of air pollution and seriously impacts health. It can cause lung, throat, nasal, larynx and brain cancers;

lymphoma, asthma, leukaemia and birth defects. The highly carcinogenic benzpyrene, which is a by- product of jet fuel combustion attaches to soot and can cause cancers and tumours in humans through lung and skin absorption.

Jet and airplane emissions affect a 25 mile area around its runway. Crops dusted by jet emissions affect living things including people with the toxic emissions. Commercial planes let off hundreds of tons of toxic pollutant into the atmosphere which then land on the earth and on living things causing all sorts of cancers.

It is estimated the number of early deaths caused by air pollution is double that caused by tobacco. In Europe the dirty, contaminated air causes more deaths than the global average.

Toxic air not only affects the lungs but new research has shown that it also impacts the heart and causes strokes entering via the blood stream.

Water Pollution

Water pollution is less acute than air but just as potentially dangerous. Water pollution is when bodies of water become contaminated usually due to human activities. These bodies are lakes, rivers, oceans, seas, aquifers and groundwater. This happens when contaminants are introduced into bodies of water either directly or indirectly. For example, releasing improperly treated wastewater into natural bodies of water will contaminate all the water. This can lead to contamination of the natural aquatic ecosystems. When this occurs, it can lead to diseases and even death because the water is accessed for drinking, cooking, irrigational purposes and so contaminates everything it comes into contact with.

There are two main ways to classify water pollution – that of the surface water and of the groundwater. Marine pollution and nutrient pollution are sub-divisions of the two main categories. Water can be contaminated by storm drain or waste-water treatment plant systems. This would be direct contamination. Or it could be indirect through the contamination of agricultural run-offs. This contamination takes place over time. Whatever the case, it affects the environment and all living creatures and organisms. And it is caused by the release of pathogens and chemicals into the water as well as by natural processes like earthquakes, volcanic eruptions, formation of algae and other natural phenomena. These also cause changes in the water composition.

Water pollution is a major environmental, global problem. It has caused and is causing deaths and infections and new diseases worldwide. In developing countries it causes a huge number of infections and diseases and to a somewhat lesser extent in developed countries.

The first type of surface water pollution refers to rivers, oceans, seas and lakes. A subset of this would be marine pollution. One – very direct way is by emptying sewage and industrial waste into the ocean. This generally happens in developing nations. Plastic is another problem. 90% of the total plastic in oceans comes from these sources. The plastic debris floating in the oceans is trapped by the vortexes in the ocean and the toxic chemicals are absorbed into them. Anything that feeds on it gets contaminated and passes it on to whatever eats it in turn. Many plastic containers are long lasting and sometimes when a large fish or bird eats that, it blocks the creature's digestive system causing starvation and death.

Then there is the silted runoff which can block out sunlight making it impossible for water and ocean plants to carry out photosynthesis.

Ground water pollution refers to the interaction between the surface and ground water which is a complex process.

In war the bombing of industrial facilities, oil and oil processing plants, chemical plants, and transformers all cause spills that are extremely harmful. This may lead to ecocide on a major scale.

The pollution of waterways with its oil and derivatives and the potential pollution with acids, alkalis, ohenoles etc. are just as frightening. On the surface level, oil flows away, acid and alkalis are diluted and phenols are hydrolysed. But under the surface level is where the danger lies. Underground water has a much more limited capacity to purify itself. Wells like *Makiš* (in Serbia) are in great danger and are a danger because pollutants reach it from surface water after they are filtered with the pollutants seeping underground leaving the cleaner water on the surface. These do self-purify underground but allow all the toxins to accumulate. A report by the Chemical Faculty of the University of Belgrade (**Prof Predrag Polic**) says that if these pollutants are not degraded they can be mobilised through changes in the physical and chemical properties of the water – ionic forces, pH redox potentials, the presence of complexing agents (including natural ones like humic substances) – all of which increase or decrease the mobility and toxicity of the pollutants. Water pollution is especially serious in artificial reservoirs and dams because the sluggish movement of the water within enclosed spaces, makes the water more toxic as the sedimentation process is that much slower.

The presence of warships, submarines, battleships in the area also add to the pollution - as it always does in such situations.

Another way of polluting the water is through accidental oil spills which contaminate the water and trap birds and animals. It is very hard to clean up.

The pollution and contamination of any body of water in Europe is bound to affect other European countries over time, as water like air does not know man-made boundaries. As we have already seen, the contamination of the Danube and Adriatic within the Yugoslav boundaries had an immediate impact on the neighbouring European countries. Fish have died in vast numbers in Yugoslavia and elsewhere. In Italy, quite early in the NATO bombing campaign, many Italian fishermen complained that most of the catch in their net were dead fish; sometimes they even caught unexploded bombs that were dropped over the Adriatic by NATO planes on unsuccessful missions. **In the Danube many species of fish have died out** since the contamination and clogging of the river. Many neighbouring countries – since the Danube is the lifeline of Europe - have also felt the negative after-effects of the pollution of the Danube.

The destruction of Yugoslav industries and technology by NATO will make the cleansing of these polluted bodies almost impossible. This in turn is bound to have catastrophic effect on the health of the population, since both surface and underground water will be carrying impurities. The bombing of the transformer stations released large quantities of PCB (polychlorinated biphenyles) that cause cancer. The bombing of the oil refineries, the transformer stations, industrial plants, transmitting towers, especially the huge one on Mt. Avala, Belgrade have all released vast amounts of PCB. It is a known fact that one litre of PCB contaminates one billion litres of water. Europe shares its waterways. Most of those rivers that flow through Yugoslavia, also flow through other European NATO countries.

It is no wonder that so many species of fish in these waterways are endangered, vulnerable or even more tragic – extinct.

Soil Pollution

Soil pollution is defined as the presence of toxic chemicals (pollutants or contaminants) in the soil, in concentrations that pose a risk to human health and/or the ecosystem. In the case of contaminants which occur naturally in soil, even when their levels are not high enough to pose a risk, soil pollution is still said to occur if the levels of the contaminants in soil exceed the levels that should naturally be present. It is caused by xenobiotica (man-made) chemical formulations. Soil contamination is mainly due to man-made waste. The waste produced by nature like dead plants, animals, rotting fruit and vegetables only help by making the soil more fertile.

Pollution is mostly due to industrial action, agricultural chemicals and improper disposal of waste products. The most common chemicals are: PAHS (petroleum hydrocarbons), polynuclear aromatic hydrocarbons (such as naphthalene and benzo(a) pyrene, solvents, pesticides, lead, and other heavy metals.

The more industrialised a country is, the higher is the contamination and the greater the health risk. These risks are of two kinds – primary by vapours from the contaminants or secondary from the contamination of water supplies and underlying soil.

Types of soil pollution

Radiation: Bombs and nuclear explosions are high-level, very serious types of radiation but there is also the low-level insidious type, which generates low-level radiation like the cellular phone, cordless phone, cell-phone towers, TVs, ovens, microwaves, broadcast antennas, military and aviation radars, satellites, wireless internet, and X-Rays and so on.

Chemical pollution is increased presence of chemical pollutants in the soil. Chemicals that pollute are generally man-made and they are generally toxic. Then there is chemical intoxication which is caused by exposure to chemical pollutants. The results may be immediately visible or appear weeks, months or even years later. Severe chemical exposure may result in death. Then there are the chemical compounds which may be organic or inorganic. These are the main chemical pollutants. The commonest compounds are those used most widely and which do not degrade easily. These are the herbicides, pesticides, insecticides – used in agriculture as well as the chlorinated solvents used in many industrial processes and in dry cleaning.

Chemical pollutants result from activities like manufacturing, handling, storing and disposing of chemicals in industrial places like oil refineries, coal power plants, construction, mining & smelting, transportation, agriculture and household activities.

Oil spills: These include any spill of crude oil or distilled products like gasoline, petrol, diesel oil, jet oil, kerosene, Stoddard solvent, hydraulic oils, lubricating oils and so on. These can pollute the land, air and water surfaces. One spill may have more than one solvent in it and the spills are usually in large quantities. **A lot of oil spills occur in the water and kill fish and birds.** Oil spill pollution is the negative effect that oil spills have on living organisms including humans because of its composition. It has organic components as in crude oil and oil distillate products. Hydrocarbons are made exclusively from carbon and hydrogen atoms which are bound together in various ways to produce end products like paraffin, isoparaffin, aromatics (like benezene and PAHs), unsaturated alkanes etc. Other compounds in crude oil besides carbon and hydrogen are sulphur, nitrogen and/or oxygen atoms.

Causes: All soil polluted or not, contains contaminants like metals, inorganic ions and salts like phosphates, nitrates, sulphates, carbonates and many organic compounds like lipids, fatty acids, DNA, PAHs, alcohol, proteins etc. These compounds are formed by soil microbial activity and decomposition. The main causes of soil pollution are the biological agents and human activities, like the use of pesticides to stop crop infestation, urban or industrial waste, radioactive emissions and other toxic substances. These could be:

- Biological agents like manure, digested sludge in the form of human, animal or bird excreta.
- Agriculture: use of pesticides, fertilizers, herbicides, debris, manure.
- Radioactive pollutants: like radium, thorium, uranium, nitrogen etc. which can infiltrate the soil and create toxicity.
- Urban waste: like garbage, sludge, rubbish, domestic and commercial sewage and commercial waste.
- Industrial waste: like pesticides, steel, cement, glass, textiles, medicines, petroleum etc. produced by paper mills, oil refineries, sugar factories, petroleum industries and other similar products
- Contaminants: like lead (PB); Mercury (HG); Arsenic (AS); Copper (CU); Zinc (ZN); Nickel (NI); PAHS (polyaromatic hydrocarbons); Herbicides/insecticides (as in agricultural activities/gardening).
- Besides this in war-torn areas many of the countries were mined in unmarked place. These pollute the soil, kill or injure people and to a lesser extent contaminate the air.

Effects: Soil pollution affects humans, plants and animals. The health, age and susceptibility are factors in the degree of effect the pollutant will have and the type of pollutant it is. In general children and the old are more susceptible. Children come in maximum contact in the playground and so are most at risk from pollution and in war-torn countries also from mines.

Soil pollution can affect people through inhalation of gases either directly or through the movement of pollutants by the wind or during transportation. Some common symptoms are headaches, skin rash, fatigue, eye irritation, neuromuscular blockage, kidney and liver damage and various forms of cancer.

The other way the soil can affect people and animals is through the food that is grown in contaminated or polluted soil.

As the water and air are polluted by the release of toxins so is the land, and the soil. The pollution of the soil is perhaps even worse because the whole food chain is contaminated for generations to come. The crops grown are poisoned, the cattle feeding on the grass and plants imbibe the poison and themselves become contaminated – their meat and milk. We saw the effects of soil pollution in the previous bombings of Hiroshima, Nagasaki and to a much greater and more graphic sense, of Vietnam, where until now large areas of once fertile land will not grow anything at all. Even the trees are crooked and stunted. It looks like blighted land. The poisoning of the soil and the food chain in Yugoslavia will directly or indirectly seriously affect the rest of Europe.

In conclusion I can only say that man's inhumanity, man's baseness to man far surpasses anything any other species can do to us. And we are supposed to be the crown of creation, the epitome of perfection of God's creation. I can see why USA would want to contaminate Yugoslavia, as it did Japan, Cambodia, Vietnam, etc. etc. **It is in US interests to have a weak, divided,**

sick and incapable Europe and Asia. The only threat to US domination can come from Europe (China is too far away, not interested in Europe and less aggressively imperialistic). If one carefully considers US policy towards Europe since the World Wars, it becomes obvious that the US has consistently tried (and generally succeeded) in undermining Europe. The Yugoslav debacle was no exception.

What is hard to understand or reconcile is why the NATO states bordering Yugoslavia agreed to their own territories being contaminated - simply to boost the US ego and economy. Germany, Austria, Italy, Bulgaria, Romania, Greece[1] – and all others have suffered and will suffer due to the severe pollution caused by the NATO bombs. Britain being an island and much further away will suffer much, much less. So, for Britain to agree to the bombing, (in fact Blair was louder than anyone else), is more understandable – though not forgivable. Britain, especially under Blair was incapable of charting its own course and was desperately holding on to the US coattails. US will never consider Britain its equal, but will treat it as a poor relation, to be used and then abused. Where now is the British pride? Blair sold it for – what?? In unity lies strength. In disunity, and discord lies destruction. Perhaps it is only a united Europe which can stem the tide of this modern day version of megalomania which has become much worse under President Trump and his weak-kneed sidekick Pompeo and his YES SIR cohort.

---

[1] Greece was the only NATO member to strongly condemn the bombing from the beginning.

Landmines

Explosive land mines were first used in 1277 AD by the Chinese Song Dynasty against an attack by the Mongols, who were besieging a city in southern China. The invention of this detonated "enormous bomb" was credited to Lou Qianxia in the 13th century. But mines really came into their own with the Great Wars. There are still hundreds and hundreds of them scattered in many countries around the world.

Landmines when detonated, contaminate the very air around the vicinity besides killing, mutilating and injuring all living creatures that they come in contact with. They contaminate the air with the toxins in them.

According to (https://medicadictionary.thefreedictionary. com/land+mines) a land mine is described as *a victim-triggered antipersonnel device, buried in a road or field and intended to— when trod upon or run over by a vehicle—explode and kill/maim the enemy. These are explosive devices placed in or on the ground to injure, kill, or destroy humans, animals, or equipment passing over or near them.*

Injury from such mines was and is a serious threat for the civilians and the military. In 1996 a study estimated that there were about 100 million anti-personnel mines laid around the world and most in unmarked areas.

The Ottawa Convention of 1997 was a convention *on the Prohibition of the Use, Stockpiling, Production and Transfer of Anti-personnel Mines and their Destruction.* It describes land mines or anti-personnel mines as: *"...a mine designed to be exploded by the presence, proximity or contact of a person and that will incapacitate, injure or kill one or more persons..."* Land mines are containers filled with explosive material and triggers that will detonate it on contact with a person or vehicle. The damage is caused by an explosive blast, fragments or a jet of molten metal when used against tanks that incapacitate the contact person or vehicle. They are usually buried under 15 cm of the ground.

Mines are of 4 kinds:

Anti-personnel and anti-tank mines, Anti-helicopter mines, and nuclear land mines.

All, besides being toxic and dangerous land-mines also contaminate the air and so negatively affect human health and welfare. They also contaminate the environment and also kill, maim and injure unsuspecting animals that may accidentally step on them.

Anti-personnel: (AP) mines are small explosive devices between 5-15 cm in diameter that can be laid by hand or that can be scattered just beneath the surface from dispensers, or by helicopters. They not only seriously injure the person but also are a psychological deterrent. They also increase the risks (both medical and the evacuation process) to the injured of all combatants affected by it, thereby slowing down the enemy force. They can be activated by direct contact or by trip wires. When activated, the blast can have metal pieces and shrapnel and extremely hot gases exiting with a huge force. Besides causing physical harm these gases also contaminate and toxify the atmosphere and poison the soil. It can, in this way contaminate whatever comes in contact with it man or animals or any other living creature

Among the anti-personnel mines there are:

- Fragmentation and stake mines: these have metal casings designed to rupture into fragments upon detonation.

They can cause severe damage to the legs, stomach and chest as they detonate. They can shoot the fragments which are usually stuffed with ball bearings, flechettes (tiny metal darts) or metal fragments which are lethal and do horrible damage on being detonated as they exit out in an horizontal arc of 60° and a vertical height of 2 metres. It can kill from 50 metres away.

- Bounding mines: is probably the deadliest of the AP mines. It was German made. *They called it Schrapnellmine, Springmine or Splittermine.* It was generally referred to as the *'Bouncing Betty'.* These can be triggered by as little as 1.5 kg of weight or by using trip wires. Once it explodes, it goes waist high and then detonates fully in a 360° arc. The fragments can kill as far away as 35 metres and cause damage from 100 metres away

- Explosive blast: these are the commonest and cheapest (about US $ 3.00) of AP mines. They are designed to rip off the lower part of the legs. They insert dirt and rip off bone from the upper leg, often leading to serious infection and needing amputation. They cause very severe injury rather than death. One type of AP mine, commonly found in Afghanistan, is the attractive and colourful **'butterfly'** mine which children can't resist. So a lot of victims of this type of mine are children.

- Shaped charge mines: There are several forms of shaped charge. A typical modern lined shaped charge can penetrate steel armour up to a depth of 7 or more times the diameter of the charge. It does not depend in any way on heating or melting for its effectiveness. For example, a linear shaped charge (LSC) has a lining with V-shaped profile and varying length. The lining is surrounded with explosives. The explosive is then encased within a suitable material that serves to protect the explosive and to confine (tamp) it on detonation. These mines can cut through metal, armour and form 'wells.'

- Directional mines (Claymores) shoot out steel balls at a very high speed in one direction. They are triggered by trip wires and can kill as far as 200 metres.

- Flame mines: During World War II, flame mines known as the *flame fougasse* were produced by the British during the crisis of 1940. Later, the Russians produced a flame-mine, called the FOG-1. This was copied by the Germans to produce the *Abwehrflammenwerfer 42*. They were effectively disposable, trip-wire triggered flamethrowers that caused severe damage.

- Scatterable mines: these are dropped by aircrafts or by the artillery. They land without exploding. But when they are picked up, they detonate. These are also called butterfly mines because of their bright colours and gently floating down without going off. That happens when some innocent child or adult picks it up. It was (and is?) widely used in Afghanistan and children there are still becoming its victims.

- Chemical mines were made by the USA, Britain and the Soviet Union. In this a number of explosive lens are used to change a number of different detonation waves into a single converging one. This wave collapses the various shells (tamper. Reflector, pusher etc.) and then compresses the fissionable core into critical matter.

- Anti-tank mines (AT): These are also called *The Big Killers*. These are designed to destroy or incapacitate tanks and other armoured vehicles. They have much heavier charges than the APs – of up to 14 kg. When they hit a lightly armoured vehicle like pick-up trucks, utes, sedans, jeeps etc. the result is catastrophic. ATs also prevent the injured being taken for treatment. They also make travelling on roads dangerous for all army or civilians or medical supplies vehicles from operating. Most injuries to UN and NGO personnel have been due to ATs.

- Shaped charge mines
- Full width mines
- Side attack mines
- Wide area mines

In the conflicts of the 21st century, anti-personnel improvised explosive devices (IED) have replaced conventional or military landmines as the source of injury to soldiers on the ground and civilians. The reported injuries were far worse than landmines of earlier times, and they resulted in multiple limb amputations and lower body mutilation. This combination of injuries has been given the name "**Dismounted Complex Blast Injury**" and is thought to be the worst survivable injury ever seen in any war. Two mines developed by The USA post World War II are the M14 – a pressure operated blast mine that can do much more serious damage than the older blast mines and the M16 which is a bounding/ fragmentation mine combining characteristics of both. There are at least 600 different types of anti-personnel land mines.

The worst mine affected areas are: Afghanistan, Cambodia, Ukraine, Iraq, Syria, Laos, Bosnia, Georgia, Mozambique, Angola, Myanmar, Nicaragua and Somalia.

Mines contaminate the soil, cause destruction and are a hazard for humans and animals.

These mines besides the physical damage done to the people, also affects the atmosphere and the air we breathe. They also affect people psychologically.

Habitat pollution

Habitat pollution encompasses the air, land, and water. It is carried out on many fronts. There is of course the chemical destruction but there is also the noise pollution. Ecosystems left alone do well and act as a balance. Any change upsets the balance. Humans impact the ecosystems in many ways. For example, by deforestation and pollution of the earth– land, sea, air, water – and so rendering many species extinct.

> ➤ Habitat fragmentation – the clearing of land to build roads, houses, farmland etc. What occurs then is that many species lose their habitats and their food supply and so become extinct in due course.
> ➤ Fire suppression – There are 4 areas of tropical moist forests –California Floristic Province (USA), Cape Floristic Province (South Africa), Mediterranean Basin and Southwest Australia. All these are scrublands that have been converted to wine land and cropland. This alteration interferes with the natural balance. Native vegetation has been lost and/or has become extinct in these areas.
> ➤ Anthropogenic Pollution – the burning of the non-renewable fossil fuels, too much garbage in landfills, landfills themselves with all the toxins that they release, and polluted farm run-offs all contribute to the extinction crises on the earth today and the appearance of new diseases.
> ➤ Oceans – two-thirds of the Earth's surface is covered with water. But we only know about a quarter of the marine life, plant life, algae and other inhabitants of the ocean. Only in this century scientists have added 13,000 until now, unknown marine species to our list. The peak marine biodiversity is to be found in the Tropics. The Coral reefs account for about 100,000 species but the total Coral

reefs cover only 0.2 area of the planet. About a third of the known fish species live in the Coral reefs. 99.8% of the water cover is still unexplored and unknown. What the rainforests are to the land the coral reefs are to the water.

With population explosion and the accompanying poverty, the reefs are getting overfished. Sometimes the fishermen use dynamite or poison on the fish. Besides, the reefs are also threatened by coastal development, pollution, ocean acidification and global warming.

About ¾ of our coral reefs are threatened with deforestation making sediments wash into the reefs and runoff from the land. Another major problem is bottom trawling that seriously upsets the balance in the underwater world.

Then there is the problem with freshwater ecosystems. These ecosystems are of two kinds: flowing water (seas and rivers) and static water (lakes, ponds...). Problems here are about damming and channelization. Enroute these waters are also used for agriculture or lost in evaporation. And there is the major problem of pollution (see Part V Water pollution).

Habitat destruction/reduction

Along with habitat pollution there is also habitat destruction. This is the process by which natural habitats become unable to support its native species. They are displaced or die thus reducing or destroying the biodiversity of the place. Habitat destruction is currently ranked as the main cause of species extinction worldwide. Besides that, it can also be because of environmental change, climatic conditions, earth movements, and invasive species that help deplete ecosystem nutrient. A lot of habitat destruction is caused directly by humans.

Habitat destruction takes place for many reasons. Some of them are:

- Clearing areas for urban sprawl
- Clearing for roads and other structures
- Clearing for agriculture
- Mining
- Logging
- Trawling
- For harvesting the natural resources
- For industrial production

When habitats are destroyed there are also indirect consequences like climate change, introduction of invasive species, nutrient depletion in the ecosystem, and water and noise pollution.

Pollution, very common since the Industrial revolutions, causes chemical rather than physical destruction of a habitat. It occurs on land, in the sea, river, and fresh water sources. It affects all animals and living creatures within the area – poisoning them, forcing them to migrate, or causing diseases. Pollution can destroy habitats in a number of ways:

(a) **Environmental pollution** is the adding of any substance – solid, liquid or gas, or any form of energy like heat, sound or radioactive materials to the environment at a faster rate than they can be processed, absorbed, dispersed, diluted, decomposed, recycled or stored in a safe form. Pollution of all kinds can have negative effects on the environment and wildlife and often impacts human health and well-being too.

(b) **Habitat destruction** is generally preceded by habitat fragmentation. And when the habitat is destroyed the indigenous plants, animals, insects and all other organisms of that area decline and in due course become extinct. This ends up threatening the biodiversity of the area. Temple pp 453-485 discovered that 82% endangered bird species was seriously threatened by habitat loss. Most of the amphibians were also threatened by habitat loss. They could only breed in modified habitats. Endemic organisms are most at risk because this is their only habitat and they do not really have a chance of recovering in a foreign habitat. Then also many endemic organisms require specific circumstances for their survival in specific ecosystems. They cannot survive in a foreign environment and so become extinct. Habitat destruction also leads to loss of genetic diversity as their range is curtailed and the young produced may be unable to breed. For example, the Giant Panda of China once flourishing all over China is now found in sharply reduced numbers in fragmented places. They are on the endangered list.

Noise pollution, water pollution and environmental pollution all have a strong impact on the living organisms in their sphere of influence. As the habitat is destroyed, the living organisms including the plants and animals all have a reduced carrying capacity – i.e. their populations decrease and extinction is more likely to occur. Endemic organisms are much more at risk under such circumstances because they survive only in certain ecosystems. Another problem with endemic organisms is that when their habitat is reduced, there is also reduced space. Many become infertile. One example of this is the giant panda of China. Many of the young ones were born infertile and from being a common sight it is now a rare sight to see them. Extinction starts to take place reducing biodiversity. This infertility can also be seen in the tropical regions that have high concentrations of endemic populations. This is also visible in island populations like in New Zealand, Madagascar, the Philippines, Japan,

Malaysia, Indonesia and parts of South-East Asia among others. Coral reefs including the Great Barrier Reef, eastern coasts of Asia and Africa, South America and the Caribbean are affected due to various types of pollution.

Regions with unsustainable agriculture or unstable governments like those of Central America, Sub-Saharan Africa and South America see much more habitat destruction and thus more loss of biodiversity.

Like the tropical forests, many forest ecosystems have suffered destruction through farming and logging which has severely impacted 94% of temperate broadleaf forests and old growth forests which have lost 98% of their previous area. Tropical, dry deciduous forests are easier to clear and so less than 1% of Central America's Pacific Coast dry forests remain and less than 8% of those in Madagascar remain.

Wetlands too, have been severely impacted with more than 50% of their areas destroyed in the United States and between 60-70 % of wetlands in Europe has been totally destroyed. In part, it was due to the greater demand for housing and tourism.

Plains and deserts have been less impacted. Only 10% to 20% of drylands, including temperate grassland, savannahs, shrub-land and scrub have been impacted.

Conclusion

Tanks, armoured vehicles, mines, heavy vehicles and cars all release toxins into the air that pollute it. Large trucks are among the daily contributors to black carbon emissions. Research has shown that air pollution causes cancer, respiratory problems, cardiac problems, neurodegenerative problems among a host of other health problems. Cars alone cause about 73% of air pollution, leaving behind a carbon monoxide (CO) and a nitrogen oxide footprint. When the pollutants combine with sunlight and heat, smog is formed. In India for example smog becomes so thick that normal breathing becomes very difficult and a grey pall hangs over the areas. US has only 30% of the world's vehicles but it produces 50% of the automotive air pollution. Particulate matter is singlehandedly responsible for about 30,000 premature deaths every year around the world. In 2013, transport vehicles contributed more than half of the carbon monoxide and nitrogen oxides, and almost a quarter of the hydrocarbons emitted into the air.

Or take the case of Canada. About 30% of Canadians live within 500 metres of a major roadway and they are assaulted by the noise pollution of vehicles.

Added to this is also the emission of toxic gases into the atmosphere from the burning oil wells for example in Iraq which makes breathing extremely difficult.

Large heavy trucks are among the greatest polluters and contributors of CO_2 emissions around highways and by-ways. Testing of this was carried out in Ontario, Canada and near roads from Vancouver to Toronto in 2018. Their survey results bore out the facts that large, heavy older trucks emit more black carbon than a few cars. They also noticed that weekend emissions were much less as there were mainly cars on the same roads. And now in early 2020 all countries that imposed isolation policy due to COVID 19 had a much better pollution index as there was less traffic on the roads.

Climate Change and national Security

Climate security is the security risks inherent to the security that directly or indirectly relates to climate change. In the Global Risks Report 2019 published by the World Economic Forum, they cite climate change as among the major issues concerning nations. Climate change has extreme weather conditions, droughts, floods, hurricanes, forest or bush fires, earthquakes and other natural disasters that upset the natural balance.

In 2017 the Global Challenge Foundation discussed a broad range of security related issues, climate change among them and concluded that global warming would have a disastrous effect on the climate of the whole world as is already happening these days.

Climate change affects governmental policies e.g. famine leads to mass refugee problems as people leave a country to survive or need help on a massive scale. Hurricanes and other natural disasters need economically viable countries to send aid to the affected countries. And the list goes on. Once we recognise and accept that not all countries have the same capacity or are economically viable, it becomes clear that it is a global challenge that affects all to a lesser or greater degree. There are many concerning issues here, but the most important ones are extreme weather, lack of climate action and natural disasters. Climate change is now a case of national security.

The past 115 years have shown a steady warming period globally in modern history and the past few years have been the worst on record. It has also seen a lot of unexpected, extreme and rough weather patterns. These have led to some catastrophes and humanitarian crises – famine, drought, forest and bush fires, mass migrations, etc. etc. All this suggests abrupt and sharp climate changes.

Global warming is not just the government's responsibility, but also the responsibility of all human beings who inhabit the world. It is time to do something but action is not easy, many kinds of industries spread dangerous myths about climate change. First of all we need to reduce the dangerous gas emissions, then how to change the polluted air to clean air.

Building on two previous studies, a landmark 2013 peer-reviewed study evaluated 10,306 scientists to confirm that over 97 percent climate scientists agree, and over 97 percent of scientific articles find that global warming is real and largely caused by humans.

This shows that global warming is real and humans have their responsibility and cannot back away. People should not eat so much beef because a cow on an average, releases between 70kg and 120 kg of Methane per year. Methane is a greenhouse gas like carbon dioxide (CO_2). The release of about 100kg of Methane per year for each cow is equivalent to about 200-300 kg of CO_2 per year. Therefore, governments have to act fast or else, people might get sick or people might die faster and there may be many more different kinds of diseases. As we have already seen the flu virus mutates each year and new vaccines are needed. And now we have the extremely dangerous COVID 19 pandemic that seems very hard to control.

Since 1850, almost all the greenhouse gas emissions and other human activities can be explained. If greenhouse gas emissions alone were warming the planet, we would expect to see the seasons adjust to the temperature drop and cool down the planet.

These conclusions have led to more than 100% of observed warming and could be attributable to human activity. A human contribution of greater than 100% is possible because natural climate change associated with volcanoes and solar activity would most likely have resulted in a slight cooling over the past 50 years, recovering some of the warming associated with human activities.

Global warming is a fact and not a myth and human beings should begin to take positive steps to control it, if we want the earth as we know it, to exist.

Climate change and economy

Climate is the long-term average of the weather in a specific area, typically averaged over a period of 30 years. Some of the meteorological variables that are commonly measured are temperature, humidity, atmospheric pressure, wind, and precipitation. In recent years global warming has affected the climate systems.

Climate change as everyone knows, is affecting the world very negatively. It includes long-term shifts in temperature, droughts, bush fires, hurricanes, floods, tsunamis, typhoons and other natural disasters. It leads to long term shifts in temperature, winds, precipitation, disruption in weather patterns etc. It has caused global warming. As we are all aware, the average temperature has gone up by 1° Celsius. This has led to the ice caps melting and many other associated phenomena. Temperatures in the Arctic and Antarctic are rising faster. The ice is melting, seas are rising, animals and birds in the Arctic and Antarctic are more and more at risk.

Climate destabilisation has caused a lot of unseasonal weather conditions. Some areas are getting colder and some are getting warmer. There are more frequent blizzards, heat waves, droughts followed by flooding as has happened in Australia. The weather has become unpredictable. Extreme weather has manifested itself in recent times not just through blizzards and droughts but also includes hurricanes, bush fires, floods, heavy rainfall, snowstorms, hailstorms, ice melts etc. All these lead to greater economic investments to manage the problems.

It has been estimated that human productivity is at its peak when temperatures are around 13° Celsius and productivity is at its lowest when it is very hot. This means that productivity is better in colder countries that already have better economies than in the hotter tropical countries. Viruses too are generally more virulent in hotter areas except for the COVID 19 which seems to flourish in colder weather. This makes me stop and think what if all future viruses behave in the same way? The global economy may be in deep trouble when life comes to a standstill as has happened with COVID 19 pandemic.

Temperature increase or decrease affects the productivity in the non-agricultural field as well as agricultural fields. Accumulated temperature in the agricultural field is a weather parameter that directly influences the productivity of agricultural plants. All biological and chemical processes taking place in the soil are connected to air temperature. The heat supply of crops is characterised by a sum of average daily air temperatures that are higher than a biological minimum during a vegetation period. Both too-high and too-low temperatures spoil the course of biochemical processes in cells, and irreversible changes can be caused that lead to a stoppage of growth and the death of plants.

The growth of plants is possible within comparatively broad temperature limits. There are three distinct fundamental temperature points of growth: minimal temperature, which is enough for growth to start; the optimal one, which is the most advantageous for growth processes; and the maximum one, where growth stops.

Climate change can cause the temperature to rise causing sea levels to rise that can critically impact the infrastructure – damaging property. It causes bush and forest fires or hurricanes or earthquakes. It also negatively affects agriculture, forestry, fisheries and tourism. Agriculture is especially vulnerable to climate change. Drought, floods and fires severely affect the economy as we have seen in Australia in 2019-2020. Extreme rainfall causes flooding and fields can get washed away; livestock can drown, feed can get spoiled. This would lead to rise in prices and decrease in supplies. Many crops like corn, wheat, soybean, rice, cotton, oats do not grow well above certain temperatures. Temperature change affects them adversely. In drought situations water lack affects crop as it also does when there is too much water. Then crops rot. Then in such situations (drought and excessive water) there is the problem of increased pests, weeds, and fires. Farmers struggle to stay afloat. Food prices shoot up. People suffer.

Infrastructure too, is at risk from flooding when sea levels rise due to ice melt or there are floods. Then there are also fires, that impact on infrastructures. That can lead to loss of property and installations, roads and railway lines and of course equipment. Communication systems can also be affected as cables can lose function.

Climate Change and Natural disasters

Climate change contributes greatly to natural disasters. In Australia drought conditions, in recent years most especially, have led to bush fires that have devastated the land and greatly hurt the economy. Then there were severe floods that also impacted on parts of Australia especially Queensland. It has also had a profound effect on the Australian economy in the sphere of exports by undermining its export value, by dragging down production and affecting the consumers' confidence. Even the Australian Reserve Bank has voiced its concerns about the effect of climate change on the national economy. The head of the bank has commented: *The economic implications are profound. As the world is getting hotter, and the climates more variable, and we're seeing already in Australia, perhaps more than anywhere else in the world, the effects of that, right now, we've got a drought that's detracting this year a quarter of a per cent from GDP as it has for the last year."*

Climate change has led to long-term disruption of seasonal weather patterns. It has caused global warming that has had and is having a drastic effect on the world. It has led to uneven temperature rise. It has led to ice caps in the Arctic and Antarctic melting rebounding negatively on the lives of Arctic and Antarctic animals and their habitat. Animals in these places are on the path to lose their habitat and food supply. The polar vortex, as a consequence has split and blocked the jet stream.

We now have very unstable weather conditions. Blizzards, hurricanes, heat waves, tornadoes, wildfires, bushfires, floods, droughts have all become common occurrences. There are also violent hail storms, snow storms, dust storms around the world. Extreme weather is another consequence of how climate change affects the economy.

Around the world too climate change has had a lot of immediate and long term effect on the economy. In some areas that have been impacted by climate warming e.g. flooded coastlines, drought-stricken farmlands, areas where natural disasters like hurricane have hit, there is mass movements of people to 'safer' countries. Many target countries cannot handle such large mass emigrations.

In places there have been droughts that have led to movements of population where food is more readily available. But the target countries like Italy could not handle the huge influx of refugees from Asia and Africa. That affected its economy. It caused food prices to rise, for example corn and soybean yields were very low. Cattle and other meat sources were stretched. This led to a spike in beef, milk and poultry prices. Worker productivity declined sharply especially outdoor workers. Cost of food rose. In 2020 the warming oceans pushed the price of fish to fall. The yield was 4% less than in 2019 especially of cod, haddock and herring. In Japan it went down by 35%. This negatively affects those whose primary diet is fish. It also impacts on the workers in the Fisheries industry.

Global warming is the direct impact from the huge amount of greenhouse gas and CO_2 (Carbon Dioxide) that we produce. This gas is the result, to a great extent, of burning fossil fuels. The gas blocks off the heat rays from dispersing and instead redirects it back to the earth. Therefore, the earth's temperature rises and this causes a lot of economic fallout besides environmental and others as discussed earlier.

And it is not just the land that is affected. The oceans have warmed because they have absorbed a lot of CO_2 and so become more acidic. This is causing fish and corals to die. It also presages that the waters will rise and cause coastal flooding. The industries most at risk from global warming, according to reports are:

agriculture, fisheries and forestry. To add to this President Donald J Trump reopened coal mining and also withdrew from the Paris Climate Accord which is aimed at containing global warming.

Climate change also greatly contributes to hurricane impact. For example its impact on Hurricane Irma was threefold. First, the rising sea levels worsened the hurricane and there were more than usual surges and flooding. Second, South Florida's average August 2017 temperature was four-tenths of a degree above normal. Florida's average temperature from January through April 2017 was the warmest during that period on record. And finally, global warming slows weather patterns. It allows hurricanes to hover over an area longer thus causing more damage.

Increase in warmth and precipitation also leads to proliferation of waterborne and food borne diseases and allergies. It also leads to infestations and proliferation of disease-spreading insects like those that cause Zika (a type of mosquito-bearing disease), West Nile, Dengue, Lyme (a tick borne disease) and COVID 19 (Droplet borne disease). Besides bearing diseases and infecting people climate change and disease can lead to mental health issues e.g. isolation of the patient, its effect on the elderly, children and low-income families as these groups are the most affected and at risk. Lockdown e.g. from COVID 19 lockdowns around the world can and has led to psychological problems.

Tourism is also affected due to natural disasters. For example when there are fires, the atmosphere can become toxic due to smoke, tourism will be curtailed. E.G. COVID 19 has resulted in a shutdown of the tourism industry as countries have closed their borders. That leads to loss of income and affects the economy. Or when the water quality suffers for whatever reason – pollution, excessive algae production or whatever, water-related sports are affected, thereby also affecting tourism. It would also lead to loss of biodiversity as we saw in Australia after the bush fires of 2019-2020.

Rising sea water can also inundate and perhaps even submerge small islands.

In 2017 altogether 146 tropical cyclones had formed over the Atlantic, Pacific and Indian oceans. Australia saw a number of cyclones some reaching tropical storm intensity.

The most powerful hurricane in history over the Atlantic was Maria (Puerto Rico & Dominica, Barbados, Haiti) which killed 3000 people. It hit Puerto Rico the hardest on September 5, 2017.

The costliest was Hurricane Harvey over the Atlantic. It hit Houston in August 2017 joining with Hurricane Katrina as the costliest worldwide. It was a Category 4 hurricane.

They led to economic downturn for the countries affected and richer countries were also affected as they had to bail out the affected ones.

Scientists have pointed out that the increase of CO_2 emissions contributes to warmer ocean waters and more moist air which leads to more rainfall. This was borne out by Hurricane Irma that caused more flooding to vulnerable areas.

After Irma's landfall, Donald Trump was asked about the connection between hurricanes and climate change, and he said: *"We've had bigger storms than this."* Richard Branson who was directly impacted by hurricane Irma said: *"hurricanes are the start of things to come. Look, climate change is real. Ninety-nine per cent of scientists know it's real. The whole world knows it's real except for maybe one person in the White House."*

Climate change also causes viruses to mutate and affect populations extensively as the Corona Virus - COVID 19 has demonstrated. It is a pandemic that has affected the whole world. People say it has already caused more deaths than in World War II and the only comparison is with the Spanish Flu of 1918, which too, was a pandemic. It had infected 500 million people world-wide and killed between 17/20 to 50 million people at that time. It was the deadliest until this Corona Virus or COVID 19.

Every problem has a solution. It is time for us to deal with the problem connected with greenhouse gas and climate change. This problem with greenhouse emissions and global warming can be redressed in the following ways:

We can (and should):

- ❖ reduce CO_2 emissions by at least 40%
- ❖ Increase use of renewable energy
- ❖ Increase the forest stock
- ❖ Increase forest coverage
- ❖ Decrease waste in whichever way we can
- ❖ Be more conscious/aware of what we put/throw/dispose into our environment
- ❖ Become more environment conscious
- ❖ Reduce plastic/artificial fibre use

We can help to reverse or stop climate change in the following ways:

- ✓ By becoming carbon neutral – by planting mangrove trees that absorb CO_2
- ✓ By planting trees and other plants to stop deforestation.
- ✓ By trying for a vegetarian based diet over a meat-based diet – as animals cause deforestation and release a lot of CO_2 and greenhouse gases

- ✓ Avoid using palm oil that comes from tropical and carbon-rich swamps
- ✓ Fund/use green energy when and where possible like solar panels or wind turbines
- ✓ Avoid products with generic vegetable oil
- ✓ Reduce waste food as they too produce a lot of CO_2
- ✓ Cut down and try to stop fossil-fuel usage

Climate change is a fact. But we have only one earth. It is up to us to protect our heritage. Decisive action today will make a better earth for our descendants tomorrow!

PART VI

RIGHT WING PARTIES AND THE ENVIRONMENT

Ernst Haeckel, a German zoologist apparently invented the term ecology in the 19th century to show man's symbiotic relationship with the natural world. He believed in respect for nature. However he also believed in the survival of the fittest – like Social Darwinism and that the weak and those that (didn't adhere to his view) were dispensable. He divided nations, cultures and races into superior – meant to survive and inferior – expendable. His views were very similar to those of Adolf Hitler. Haeckel was also one of the founders of eugenics and euthanasia, all of which had a profound impact on the Nazi world view. Neo Nazis today claim to follow the same trends but that is not really the case.

Since World War II, the Green movements that have sprung up all over the world are largely democratic in nature and are as concerned about the well-being of humanity as they are about the health of the planet as a whole (worldfuturefund.org).

The Greens are the most concerned with the saving of the planet, controlling pollution and protecting the ecology. The extreme Right is not. But here is the conundrum:

The Nazi government passed a law protecting the natural environment of **their country** – its flora and fauna. But they didn't follow through as their actions showed. They frowned upon experimenting on animals but used humans – young and old, pregnant women and others for their most horrific experiments. They passed laws safeguarding animals but not people of other races or German socialists and educationists. They passed laws safeguarding the environment but in actual practice they destroyed the environment as the gas chambers demonstrated – cremating helpless people and polluting the environment with noxious gases. As Neumann says: the *Nazis, "were always racists and militarists and were 'red' in terms of the blood they spilled rather than 'green'* – Dr, Boaz Neumann Teoria Uvikoret vol 40.

Neumann also believes that it is quite possible to understand the connection between the Holocaust and ecocide – the murder of an entire world where the Jews among many other races – Gypsies, Russians, part-Germans and so on were regarded as an inferior race(s) with no right to the same world. Today we, too, are destroying the environment with our selfishness and callous disregard of the natural world. We are committing ecocide. With President J Trump leading the way.

The modern day right wing parties share similar views and it seems the world is heading towards another major confrontation. They believe in White supremacy and have it spread world-wide. In the United States, the Blacks, the Hispanic and the immigrants are regarded by the Right wing as inferior. In many countries around the world where there is a substantial Right wing, immigrants are unwanted. And now many are using the COVID 19 to push back against immigration. Xenophobia and racism have taken a turn for the worse. Trump has not only withdrawn all protection of the environment but has reopened coal mines to further pollute the air. His rants against many races and religions is public knowledge and clearly demonstrates his xenophobia.

Our earth is being raped by us. Our fauna and flora is becoming extinct at a faster rate. And if we go into another war, the poor earth will suffer terribly with the much more advanced weapons of war. If the right come to power around the world, then there is very little hope for mankind. At present the situation in the USA bodes a civil war in the making or even a break-up of the country all thanks to the ego of President Donald J Trump who cannot see the flowers for the slime at his feet.

AUSTRALIA

A brief introduction

Australia is often referred to as the island continent. It lies in the Southern Hemisphere. It is separated from the Asian continent by the Arafura and Timor seas. The Coral Sea lies off the coast of Queensland and the Tasman Sea lies between Australia and New Zealand. It is the world's smallest continent with an area that is the sixth largest in the world. It is also called the island continent due to its isolation and size. By size, it is the sixth largest country in the world having an area of 7,692 million square kilometres. It lies on the Indo-Australian plate. Mainland Australia is the lowest and most primordial landmass in the world. It used to be part of Gondwana but when that land mass broke up Australia was separated. Then between 8,000 and 6,500 BCE the northern part was flooded and Australia also separated from New Guinea and became an independent continent. Currently it is moving towards Eurasia.

Australia is very much influenced by the currents of the Indian Ocean and the El Niño-Southern Oscillation. These coincide with the drought periods that Australia is prone to and to the seasonal cyclones in northern Australia.

The first inhabitants of this continent were the Aborigines and the Torres Strait Islanders. They came to Australia about 55,000 years ago most probably from Asia.

The first Europeans to land in Australia were the Dutch under Willem Janszoon in 1606. Later in the same year the Spanish explorer Luis Vaz de Torres came to Australia and navigated the Torres Island and other islands in the Torres Straits. Then Captain Cook came to Australia on April 29th 1770 and on his return to Britain, suggested Australia as a British penal colony. British jails at that time were overflowing. So, Captain Cook set out to claim Australia for the British Crown as a colony.

In 1788 Australia was established as a British penal Crown Colony of New South Wales with the first settlement being at Port Jackson. The native Aborigines had a hard time and lost their freedom. After this many native species of mammals, birds and amphibians started to disappear due to excessive hunting by the British Europeans.

At that time Australia was not one federation but different states with different rules, currency, passports.... In 1901 they came together and formed a federation and that was a smart thing to do. The federal government is responsible for the whole country with a Prime minister at the head while each state has their own premiers with their independent powers.

Australia is divided into States and Territories. The federal capital is Canberra located in the Australian Capital Territory or ACT. The other territory is the Northern Territory (NT). The states are New South Wales (NSW), Victoria (VIC), South Australia (SA), Tasmania (TAS), Queensland (QLD) and Western Australia (WA). The largest city is Sydney but the cultural capital is Melbourne in the state of Victoria. The other major metropolitan cites are Brisbane (QLD), Perth, (WA), Adelaide

(SA) Hobart (TAS) and Darwin (NT). Queen, Elizabeth II of Britain is the official head of the country. Australia is officially known as the Commonwealth of Australia. It is a constitutional democracy. At important functions the Queen is represented by the Governor-General who is appointed by the Queen with advice from the Australian Prime Minister. There is the Prime Minister and his Cabinet. Then there are the state premiers for each state.

Extinct and endangered animals

Recent research shows that Australia is losing species at an alarming rate. This should give us pause. We have a unique biodiversity but it is endangered when our fauna and flora are endangered. Ecosystems are highly susceptible to change, and the constant and consistent alteration of the ecosystem upsets the balance and threatens the biodiversity. According to many reports we are losing or endangering the species at an alarming rate. We have a lot of kangaroos but there have been times when mature kangaroos have been shot to reduce the population and the Joey murdered in very graphic ways e.g. by swinging their heads into hard surfaces or so I've read. I have not seen that with my own eyes. That is cruel, morally wrong and an indictment on us.

Koala & Baby – always time to rest | Photo by Miroslav Jokic

Extinct Australian animals 1788 to 2020

Extinct species are those that are no longer found in our world. Some have been hunted to extinction while others became extinct due to loss of habitat, disease or introduced species. Australia has one of the highest extinction rates in the world according to some reports. The following chart shows some of the extinct species:

Birds

Common name/species	location	comment
Orange bellied Parrot (*Neophema chrysogaster*)	VIC & TAS	Critically endangered since 1900"s. Threat from clearing of farmland, planting foreign plants
Regent Honeyeater	NSW	Endangered due to the 2020 fires. Many habitats wiped out
Western Ground Parrot	Cape Arid National Park (WA)	Critically endangered especially due to 2020 fires. Only 150 parrots remain
Glossy Black Cockatoo	Kangaroo Island (SA)	Critically endangered due to burning of habitat – 50% to 60%. 400 cockatoos left before the latest fire. Present numbers unknown
Tasman starling/Aplonis Fusca	Norfolk Island, (external territory) Lord Howe Island NSW	Last seen in 1923. Predation from introduced species including black rats
White-throated pigeon/ Columba vitiensis godmanae	Lord Howe Island (NSW)	Last recorded in 1853. Extinct due to over hunting
Red crowned parakeet (Cyanoramphus Novaezelandiae subflavescens)	Lord Howe Island	1869 last recorded. Persecuted for garden & crop predation. Extinct

Common name/species	location	comment
Rufous bristlebird/ Dasyornisbroadbenti litoralis	Western Australia	Western one extinct though the eastern one is vulnerable & rarely glimpsed
King Island Emu/ dwarf emu/Dromaius Novaehollandiae minor	King Island (TAS)	Extinct due to overhunting & deliberate brush fires. (Last 2 died 1822 in captivity).
Kangaroo Island emu/ Dromaius Novaehollandiae baudinianus	Kangaroo Island (SA)	1827 Extinct due to over-hunting and deliberate brush fires
Tasmanian emu/ Dromaius Novaehollandiae diemenensis	Tasmania	1850. Extinct due to over-hunting and deliberate brush fires
Roper river scrub-robin/ (Drymodes superciliaris colcloughi)	Northern Territory	last recorded 1910
Norfolk ground dove/ (Gallicolumba norfolciensis)	Norfolk Island	1850's Extinct due to introduced predators
Lord Howe gerygone/ Gerygone insularis	Lord Howe Island	Last recorded in 1928. Extinct due to introduction of black rats on ship *SS Makambo* in June 1918
New Zealand pigeon (Hemiphaga novaeseelandiae spadicea)	Norfolk Island	By 1850 was already scarce Last seen in 1900. Extinct due to overhunting. A very tame bird.
Norfolk Island long-tailed triller/Lalage leucopyga	Norfolk Island	Last recorded in 1942. Extinct due to predation by Black Rats & loss of habitat
Norfolk Island Kaka/ Nestor productus	Norfolk Island	last seen in 1851
Southern Boobook/ Ninox novaeseelandiae albaria	Lord Howe Island	extinct in the 1950's

Sophia Z. Kovachevich

Common name/species	location	comment
Northeastern Bristlebird	NSW & QLD	50 birds were left. Critically endangered. 2020 fire destroyed some of its habitat in QLD
Norfolk Island Boobook/ Ninox novaeseelandiae undulata	Norfolk Island	Last seen in 1996
White Gallinule/ Porphyrio albus	Lord Howe Island	First seen by the British sailors in 1788 & 1790. Extinct
Lewin's Water Rail/ Rallus pectoralis clelandi	WA	Last recorded 1932
Paradise Parrot/ Psephotus pulcherrimus	NSW, QLD	Extinct around 1927. Starvation: lack of grass seed after drought; introduction of the prickly pear, brushfires, overgrazing,
Macquarie Island Rail/ Gallirallus philippensis Macquariensis	Macquarie Island (TAS)	last recorded 1932
Lord Howe Fantail/ Rhipidura cervina	Lord Howe Island	Last recorded in 1924. Extinct due to introduction of black rats on ship *SS Makambo* in June 1918
Norfolk Island Thrush/ Grey-headed Blackbird/ Turdus poliocephalus	Norfolk Island	Last recorded in 1924. Due to introduction of black rats on ship *SS Makambo* in June 1918
White Chested, White-Eye Norfolk Island Silvereye (Zosterops albogularis)	Norfolk Island	IUCN considers them endangered. Not seen 30+ years. Perhaps extinct
Robust White-eye/ Zosterops strennus	Lord Howe Island	Last recorded in 1923. Extinct due to introduction of black rats on ship *SS Makambo* in June 1918

Common name/species	location	comment
Spectacled Flying Bat	QLD	Seriously endangered since 2018 bush fire
Greater Glider	VIC & NSW	Critically endangered due to 2020 fires

Amphibians

Common name/species	location	comment
Southern Corroboree Frog	VIC & NSW	A tiny frog. Less than 150 left; Critically endangered; edge of extinction Threatened by the Chytrid fungi. Captive-breeding programme has begun
Armoured Mist-Frog	QLD	Critically endangered. Not seen since 2008 Chytrid fungal disease killed many
Gastric-Brooding Frog/ Rheobactrichus silus	Qld	Last wild specimen recorded in 1981 Extinct?
Eungella Gastric-Brooding Frog/ Rheobactrichus vitellinus	Qld	Last wild specimen recorded in 1985 Extinct
Sharp-Snouted Day Frog/Torrent-Frog/ Taudactylus acutirostris	Qld	Last wild specimen recorded in 1997
Southern-day frog or Mt Glorious Day Frog/ Taudactylus diurnus	South-east Qld	Last wild specimen recorded in 1979

Reptiles

Common name/species	location	comment
Christmas Island Forest Skink/Emoia Nativitatis	Christmas Island	Last captive specimen died May 31, 2014. Extinct
Victorian Grassland Earless Dragon/ Tympanocryptis pinguicolla	VIC	Last wild specimen died 1969. Possibly first recorded extinct reptile on the mainland
Short-Nosed Sea Snake	WA (Ningaloo Reef)	Critically endangered. Not seen since 2005. Threat due to climate change, mining & bleaching of reef
Leaf-Scaled Sea Snake	WA (Shark Bay)	Critically endangered. Not seen since 2005. Threat due to climate change
Blue Mountain Water Skink	Blue Mountains (NSW)	Endangered. Many habitats wiped out in 2020 fires

Mammals

common name/species	location	comment
Boodie burrowing bettong (Bettongia lesueur graii)	WA (inland)	once abundant, now extinct
Brush-tailed Rock Wallaby	NSW	Was vulnerable, now endangered due to 2020 fires. Habitat & native vegetation (staple food) loss
Quokka	WA	Endangered. 2020 fire destroyed main habitat. In danger from foxes & cats

common name/species	location	comment
Southern Bent-wing Bat (*Miniopterus schreibersii bassanii*)	VIC & SA	Critically endangered. In decline for 2 decades by 67%. Threatened by habitat loss, pesticides & disruption of breeding habits by humans
Brush tailed bettong/ Bettongia pencillata	NSW, NT, SA, VIC, WA (southeast mainland)	Critically endangered
Kangraoo Island Dunnart	Kangaroo Island	Critically endangered. May have been wiped out by fire 2019
Koalas	NSW & VIC	Endangered. Thousands died in the 2020 fires. Many affected & infected with chlamydia.
Desert rat kangaroo / Caloprymnus campestris	Qld, SA, NT	last recorded 1935
Hastings River Mouse	NSW	Endangered. Many died in the 2020 fires
Pig-footed bandicoot/ chaeropus ecaudatus	NSW, NT, SA, VIC, WA	last recorded 1950's
White-footed rabbit rat/ Conilurus albipes	NSW, Qld, SA, VIC	last recorded 1857
Central Hare wallaby Lagorchestes asomatus	NT	last recorded 1935
Rufous hare-wallaby/ Lagorchestes hirsutus	NT, SA, WA (southwest mainland)	vulnerable
Eastern hare wallaby/ Lagorchestes leporides	NSW, Qld, SA VIC	last recorded 1890
Banded hare wallaby lagostrophus fasciatus albipilis	WA (mainland)	Highly vulnerable to predation by cats & foxes
Tammar wallaby/Macropus eugenii	SA	population rediscovered in New Zealand, reintroduced in parts of Australia
Toolache wallaby/Macropus greyi	SA, VIC	last recorded 1932

common name/species	location	comment
Lesser wallaby/Macrotis leucura	NT, Qld, SA	last recorded 1931
Bramble Cay melomys/ Melomys rubicola	Bramble Cay Qld	last recorded 2016
Long-tailed hopping mouse/ Notomys longicaudatus	NT, SA, WA	last recorded 1901
Big-eared hopping mouse/ Notomys macrotis	WA	last recorded 1843
Darling Downs hopping-mouse/Notomys Mordax	NSW, Qld	last recorded 1846
Crescent nail-tail wallaby (Onychogalea lunata)	SA, WA	last recorded 1956
Western barred bandicoot (peramelesbougainville,)	NSW, Extinct; VIC (mainland) vulnerable	extinct in NSW due to predation by foxes and feral cats
Desert bandicoot/ Perameles eremiana	NT, SA, WA	Last recorded before 1960. Extinct due to predation by cats, foxes, habitat alternation, introduction of exotic herbivores, & changed fire regime
Christmas Island pipistrelle/ Pipistrellus murray	Christmas Island (external Australia Territory)	last recorded 2009
Broad-faced potoroo/ Potorous playtops	WA	last recorded 1865
Blue-grey mouse/Pseudomys glaucus	NSW, Qld	last recorded 1956
Gould's mouse/Pseudomys gouldii	NSW, Qld, SA, VIC, WA	last recorded 1857
Dusky flying fox/Pteropus brunneus	Qld	last recorded in late 1800's
Maclear's rat/Rattus Maclear	Christmas Island	last recorded 1908
common name/species	**location**	**comment**
Bulldog rat/Rattus navtivitatis	Christmas Island	last recorded 1903
Thylacine Tasmanian tiger or wolf (Thylacineus cynocephalus)	Tasmania	last recorded in 1936

common name/species	location	comment
Christmas Island shrew (Crocidura trichura)	Christmas Island	last recorded 1985
Lesser stick-neck rat/ Leporillus apicalis	NSW, NT, SA, VIC, WA	last recorded 1933
Lord Howe long-eared bat/ Nyctophilus howensis	Lord Howe Island	skull found on Island in 1972 - extinct
Christmas Island pipistrelle (Pipistrellus murrayi)	Christmas Island	last recorded August 2009

Invertebrates

A number of Australian invertebrates have been listed as extinct by the World Conservation Union.

common name/species	location	comment
Lake Peddar Worm/ Hypolimnuspedderenis	Tasmania	Last recorded in 1972. Extinct status in 2000
Campbell's Island snail/ Advena campbelli	Norfolk Island	Assumed extinct but reintroduced. Predation by rats & chickens
Norfolk snail/ Nancibella quintelia	Norfolk Island	Critically endangered predation by rats & feral fowl
Lord Howe snail/ Tornelasmias capriconi	Lord Howe Island	critically endangered due to predation by rats & feral fowl
Macquarie slug/Angrobia dulvertonensis	Port Macquarie	last recorded 1996 assumed extinct
Lord Howe Slug/ Placostylus bivaricosus etheridgei	Lord Howe island	critically endangered due to predation by rats & feral fowl

Sophia Z. Kovachevich

Fish - Recently extinct/endangered

Common name/species	location	Comment
Derwent River Sea Star (*Marginaster littoralis*)	Derwent River estuary, Hobart	Critically endangered. Only 5 known populations left due to introduction of NZ Sea-Star
Kangroo River Perch	Shoal Haven River	Small silver-grey fish. Last seen 20 years ago (in 2000)
Macquarie River Perch	Macquarie River	Silvery dark grey often mottled Endangered – catch & release
Blobfish (Psychrolutes marcidus)	Mainland Australia & Tasmania	vulnerable
Pygmy Perch	Murray-Darling Basin	Recovered from near extinction
Lord Howe Island Phasmid (Dryococelus Australis)	Lord Howe Island (Balls Pyramid)	Since 1918 threat from black rats. Now threats from rodents & loss of adequate food source
Margaret River Burrowing crayfish (*Engaewa pseudoreducta*)	Margaret River	Critically endangered. None seen since 1985. Greatest danger was / is from land clearing, farming & mining. Feral pigs also damage their habitat

The **Platypus** is an Australian icon. They evolved 120 million years ago and offer an insight into the link between mammals and reptiles. The UCIN listed them as near-threatened. In 50 years they have declined by 73%. Some scientists at the University of Melbourne published a report in 2019 showing that since the last decade there have been no sightings of platypus in 41% of their erstwhile habitats. These very unusual creatures are threatened by pollution, land clearing, and predation from invasive species like the introduced foxes, feral dogs and cats – especially when they travel overland. Then there are the yabby traps (Opera House traps) which disable them from coming up for air. So they drown. These traps are now banned in parts of NSW and in ACT. Besides these there is also the problem of ingesting huge doses of human antidepressants from aquatic insects in streams near Melbourne. Other drugs from similar sources have shown up in the dead platypus' systems according to a 2018 study.

In the 19th century, tens of thousands of platypuses were killed for their thick pelts, which were turned into slippers or rugs.

Australia has the worst mammal extinction rate in the world

Marine animals
Numbers of species in each list

	Critical	Endangered	Vulnerable	Extinct
Fish	7	16	24	10
Frogs	5	14	10	4
Reptiles	8	17	34	1
Birds	9	47	62	24
Mammals	5	34	55+	27
Other	23	17	11+	6
Total	**57**	**161**	**196**	**62+**

Since the arrival of European settlers in 1788 Australia has lost numerous native animals and plants, sea creatures, birds, reptiles, amphibians and insects. The Tasmanian tiger is a prominent example of a recently extinct Australian animal. The last died in captivity in 1936.

Australian vulnerable animals and sea animals

Koala	Blobfish	Giant clam
Quokka	Possum	Wallaby
Antechinus	Numbat	Eastern Bettong
Tree kangaroo	Australian Sea Lion	Snubfin dolphins (critical)
Australian Sea Lions	Dugongs	Dolphins (There were 15 varieties. Some endangered now)

Hammerhead Sharks. (iconic species)	Cassowary	Tasmanian Devil
Wombat	Gouldian Finch	Spotted Quoll
Night Parrot	Bandicoot	Greater Bilby
Southern Bluefin tuna (critically endangered)	Southern Right Whale Eubalaena australis (Desmoulins, 1822)	Dugongs
Koala (especially after the fire of 2019-2020)	White-throated snapping turtle	Blue Whale (international waters too)
Sei whale	Fin whale	Humpback whale

Decreasing	Stable	Increasing	Status Unknown
15 species	5 species	10 species	6 species

This is an incomplete table. A lot of the above information is from the Environment Protection and Biodiversity Conservation Act 1999 and the IUCN Red List

According to the AMCS (Australian Marine Conservation Society), tiger sharks should be listed as endangered and Humane Society International (HSI), after a study reported a shocking 71 per cent decline of the tiger shark in only three decades.

The authors of the study, in the journal Biological Conservation, commented that commercial fishing was likely a major cause of the plummeting numbers over the last 33 years. Queensland's lethal Shark Control Program (SCP) was another significant cause of the crash in numbers. This decline would qualify tiger sharks on the east coast of Australia for an endangered listing, they said.

Dr Leonardo Guida, shark scientist at AMCS (Australian Marine Conservation Society) said: *"This research is yet another sign that Australia isn't doing enough to protect the tiger shark from heading to extinction. It was only a few months ago a major study revealed that the east coast of Australia was one of the few places in the world where tiger sharks experienced the greatest threat from commercial fishing."*

The Queensland Shark Control Program (SCP) catches and kills marine wildlife throughout the state, including within the Great Barrier Reef Marine Park. Tiger sharks are one of 19 target shark species in the SCP and are shot dead if caught alive. Since 2001, the SCP has killed over 10,000 animals, including more than 2,500 tiger sharks[1].

Lawrence Chlebeck, Marine Campaigner at HSI said: *"Tiger sharks science tells us that killing sharks does not improve beach safety. To protect the Reef the Queensland Government needs to protect sharks and implement more modern and effective strategies to protect swimmers."*

HSI has challenged the impact of the SCP on the reef ecosystem, and its inability to protect ocean users. The Administrative Appeals Tribunal in Brisbane ruled in favour of HSI and ordered an end to the shooting of tiger sharks, but the Queensland Government has sought to overturn the decision in the Federal Court.

In response to HSI's initial challenge of the SCP earlier this year, the Queensland Administrative Appeals Tribunal stated, *"...there is a significant decline in tiger shark population and that the SCP makes a significant contribution to that decline."* The Tribunal concluded that the lethal component of the SCP *"...does not reduce the risk of unprovoked shark attacks... the scientific evidence before us is overwhelming in this regard."*

HSI and AMCS are actively investigating possibilities for a tiger shark nomination as an endangered species to improve its protection as part of their national "Shark Champions" campaign.

Threatened Species in Australian waters are the following:

Great Barrier Reef,

- Australian Sea Lions. Australian sea lions are a type of seal that are native only to Australian shores. They were listed as vulnerable under the Commonwealth Environment Protection and Biodiversity Act 1999 and 2005. They are listed as threatened in their habitats of South Australia and Western Australia.
- Dugongs. Dugongs are shy, elusive marine mammals that depend on healthy seagrass meadows and so inhabit coastal waters. They are threatened due to coastal development and industrial activities. Plastic in the water pose a threat to them. They are very gentle creatures. Their closest relative the Steller cow was hunted to extinction. Dugongs are listed as vulnerable.
- Dolphins. 15 species of dolphins and one species of porpoise live in Australian waters.
- Hammerhead Sharks. Hammerhead sharks are an iconic species inhabiting Australia's waters but are now endangered.

Endangered Species among a host of others

cassowary	Tasmanian Devil	wombat
Gouldian Finch	Spotted Quoll	Night Parrot
Bandicoot	Greater Bilby	Orange bellied parrot
pygmy possum	eagle ray	7 species of turtles
Dugong	hammerhead shark	Sea lions

Australia is home to the most incredible ocean wildlife on earth, but many of our species are threatened or endangered. Our threatened marine life like our turtles, whales and sharks includes the tiger shark 71% which has shown a decline in last 3 decades along Australia's east coast.

Critical list

Snapping Turtle	Leadbeater's Possum	
Plains Wanderer	Handfish	

Extinct

Tasmanian Tiger	Red-Fronted Parakeet	Gastric –brooding Frog
Lesser Bilby		

Sophia Z. Kovachevich

The Great Barrier Reef

The Great Barrier Reef, is the world's largest coral reef system comprised of 2,900 individual reefs and 900 islands. It lies off the north-east coast of Australia off the coast of Queensland. It extends over 2,300 kilometres. Along with many fascinating and harmless creature in its waters there are also some fascinating and potentially dangerous living creatures lurking in its water. Some of the most dangerous ones are: jellyfish, sea snakes, several species of fish including the reef stonefish which has highly toxic poison in the 13 spines on its back which cause extreme pain and even death; certain species of shellfish and octopus.

There are about 300 species of coral that form the coral reef. It also has many species of anemones, sponges, worms, gastropods, lobsters, crayfish, prawns, crabs, multiple varieties of fish and sea birds. The most destructive reef animal in this reef is the crown-of-thorns. It is a starfish that feeds on the living corals.

The Great Barrier Reef is one of the most beautiful and diverse reefs in the world, in my opinion with a fascinating array of flora and fish, shellfish and sea mammals. It has an incredible 80% of marine species, endemic to Australia. Many of the species living here are now endangered or threatened. It is the last remaining healthy tropical sea – according to global studies. It is incumbent on us to maintain that now. In 1981 it was declared a world Heritage Site. It has been named a Queensland iconic state symbol by the Queensland National Trust.

There are serious threats to the reef. The mining boom has greatly endangered the reef. It is also being systematically raped by human environmental pressure on the reef itself and its ecosystem. One of the dangers that the reef faces is from elevated levels of fertilizers and other pollutants from runoffs.

These cause phytoplankton that The COTS (Crown of Thorns) larvae eat. Climate Change has also affected it. In 2016 and 2017 there were 2 heatwaves that killed off 50 of the shallow corals. The rate of coral reproduction had also dropped. Besides this the corals are also at risk from the Crown of thorns starfish (COTS) which is a voracious coral eater. It can eat its own body weight in one evening. They have already stripped 150 coral reefs here and damaged more than 500 in the following years. They are the second greatest danger to coral. Now underwater robots are used to attack the COTS and keep them in check.

Endangered species in the Great Barrier Reef

These are some of the endangered and vulnerable species that inhabit the Reef:

The hawksbill sea turtle (*Eretmochelys imbricate*) is critically endangered. They are preyed on by large fish, sharks and humans. They live most of their time in shallow lagoons and coral reefs. However, they also spend time in the open oceans. They feed on fish, algae and crustaceans though their main food is coral reef sponges.

The flatback sea turtle (*Natator depressus*) inhabits Australia's shallow coastal waters and sandy beaches. They are a mixture of olive-green, green and grey colour. They can be found on continental shelves, bays, lagoons, estuaries and soft sea-beds. They feed on soft corals, sea cucumbers, jellyfish, shrimps, mollusks and other invertebrates.

The Olive Ridley Sea Turtle (*Lepidochelys olivacea*) inhabits the warm, tropical waters of the Pacific and Indian Oceans. It is predominantly a carnivore in its growing stage. It and feeds on jellyfish, sea-urchins, snails, crabs, shrimps, rock lobsters and such-like creatures as an adult. Its eggs are eaten by feral dogs, coyotes, sunbeam snakes, pigs, opossums, ghost crabs, caimans and others.

The green sea turtle (*Chelonia mydas*), also known as the green turtle, black sea turtle, or Pacific green turtle is found in the tropical and sub-tropical seas around the world. There are two distinct species of this turtle endemic to the Atlantic and Pacific Oceans. This species changes its dietary habits with age. The young turtles eat fish eggs, mollusks, jellyfish, worms, sponges, algae and such like things. As they mature, they become omnivorous but mainly herbivorous

The leatherback sea turtle (*Dermochelys coriacea*) is the largest sea turtle. The adults feed mainly on jellyfish, tunicates and cephalopods. They are preyed upon by predatory fish and cephalopods. They are endangered due to plastic bags floating in the waters which they often mistake for jellyfish.

The dugong (*Dugong dugon*) is a medium-sized marine animal related to the Steller's Sea Cow that is now extinct. The Great Barrier Reef is its primary food supplier.

They are endangered because people have hunted them for their meat and oil. It is still hunted in the Pacific Islands and North Australia.

Humpback grouper (*Cromileptes altivelis*) is called the Barramundi cod in Australia. It is a medium sized fish that lives in the clear waters of reefs and lagoons. It likes silty areas. It eats small fish and crustaceans. It is a rare fish due to overhunting by humans which is due to the high value placed on it in the live fish trade. The other threat to this is habitat degradation.

The Queensland grouper is Australia's largest bony fish found in coral reefs throughout the Indo-Pacific region. It feeds on small sharks, juvenile turtles and other similar marine creatures. They are hermaphrodites. All are born females though with age some become males.

The longcomb sawfish or green sawfish (*Pristis zijsron*) is found in tropical waters of the Indo-West Pacific Oceans - from the Red Sea and East New Guinea, north to southern China and south to New South Wales in Australia. This fish has a blade-like snout. It is critically endangered as their numbers have declined by 80% over three generations due to overfishing for its meat and fins and blade-like snout and getting entangled in nets as bycatch.

The Maori Wrasse (*Cheilinus undulatus*) or Humphead wrasse lives in coral reefs in the Indo-Pacific region. It breeds slowly but lives longer. It has become endangered due to ocean acidification and reduction of coral due to calcification. This is because of the increase in CO_2 in the atmosphere which causes acidification and so disturbs reef activities. Other threats to this are destructive fishing techniques like bombs and cyanide and removal of live-reef food for fish trade.

The sperm whale (*Physeter macrocephalus*) is the largest toothed whale and predator. Mature male whales are solitary creatures except for mating times. The females live in pods with the young. They give birth every four or 20 years. Sperm whales are a prime target for the whaling industry for their oil for use in lamps, as lubricants and candles. What a shame!

The blue whale (*Balaenoptera musculus*) is a baleen whale. It is the largest animal to have existed in the world. This whale is at high risk from Orcas and ocean vessels. They are also much affected by the change in ocean temperature that affects its food supply.

The fin whale (*Balaenoptera Physalus*) belongs to the sub-order of baleen whales and is the second largest mammal after the Blue Whale. It is one of the fastest cetaceans. They are endangered by colliding with large ocean-going vessels and from the whaling industry.

The great white shark (*Carcharodon carcharias*) is a species of the mackerel shark. It is the world's largest extant fish. It is a top predator of other marine mammals, birds, and fish. They are strong and fast swimmers. They are endangered due to a serious drop in their numbers caused by overhunting and unregulated trade.

The sand tiger shark (*Carcharias taurus*): these inhabit the waters in subtropical and temperate waters around the world. They live on continental shelves from sandy shorelines to reefs. They are endangered by fisheries and exploitation by humans.

The giant clam (*Tridacna gigas*) belongs to the large species of clams and is found in coral reefs of the Indian and Pacific Oceans. They are hermaphrodites and produce both eggs and sperm. But they cannot self-fertilize. It has become endangered due to intensive exploitation of the reef by bivalve fishing vessels.

The Irrawaddy dolphin (*Orcaella brevirostris*) is an oceanic dolphin which resembles a beluga whale. However, it is more closely related to the killer whale. They feed on fish, crustaceans and cephalopods. They are shy creatures. They have been raised to the endangered list as their numbers have shrunk due to human activities. They have been reduced by 50% in the last 60 years according to the ICUN Red List.

The Barrier Reef is a renowned tourist attraction and one not to be missed when visiting Queensland, Australia.

Coral | Photo by Sophia Z Kovachevic

Floods

A flood is an excessive amount of water at a place and time when it is not wanted. In 2011 the Australian government issued a standard definition for flood to avoid any ambiguity for insurance purposes: *The covering of normally dry land by water that has escaped or been released from the normal confines of: any lake, or any river, creek or other natural watercourse, whether or not altered or modified; or any reservoir, canal, or dam.*

Floods may have both positive and negative effects. On the positive side is that floods can occur after a drought when the ecosystem is in need of water. On the negative side, it can be very destructive. And costly.

Some floods develop slowly while others come up very fast without any visible sign of rainfall. Floods can affect a restricted area or can impact entire river basins. They can sometimes be very destructive. A flood occurs when water inundates land that's normally dry, which can happen in a multitude of ways - excessive rain, a ruptured dam or levee, rapid melting of snow or ice, and climate change. In the past 30 years there have been a lot of floods all over the world that have brought destruction and loss of life in their wake. Global warming is a major cause as evaporation is increased and more water is available for precipitation to take place.

Other factors that can contribute to flooding are:

- Volume, spatial distribution, intensity and duration of rainfall over a catchment
- Ground cover
- Capacity of the watercourse or network to carry away the runoff
- Topography

- Tidal influences
- Catchment and weather conditions before rainfall

One or more of these factors can cause flooding.

There are many types of floods:

Areal floods: These are when floods occur in low-lying or flat areas. The ground gets saturated due to heavy rainfall or snow melt. The water cannot infiltrate or run off.

Riverine floods: These are floods that occur most commonly in large river and stream channels in humid zones to generally dry channels in dry areas. They may be worse if there are obstructions like landslides, ice, debris or beaver dams. They generally occur in low-lying areas. In Australia they occur in the flat inland regions, where they may spread over thousands of square kilometres and last up to many weeks. Flood warnings are often issued in advance so that the inhabitants are somewhat prepared. In Australia's mountain and coastal region flooding generally occurs very rapidly and without warning or on very short notice – a few hours at most.

The Great Dividing Range extends along eastern Australia. It provides a natural boundary between the shorter, faster moving river on the east side and the slower, longer west flowing river. Sometimes blockages at the river mouths also cause flooding.

Slow rising floods generally occur more in large rivers with catchments. The increased flow from these could be because of sustained rainfall or rapid snow melt or monsoon rains or tropical cyclones.

Flash flooding also known as overland flooding usually occurs more often in small rivers, rivers with steep valleys, rivers that flow over impermeable terrain or those with dry channels. They can occur at any place that has a short, intense burst of rainfall as during a thunderstorm. This can result in the drainage system being unable to cope with the downpour. Flash flooding is generally localized. Flash floods can be deadly because they are unpredictable.

Riverine floods occur in relatively low-lying areas adjacent to rivers and streams in Australia.

Estuarine and coastal flooding: The former is caused by a combination of storm surges and large waves. While the latter is caused *by a combination of storm surges caused by winds and low barometric pressure and large waves meeting high upstream river flows (Wikipedia).*

Coastal areas can be hit and flooded by the combination of storm surges and high tides which can lead to waves over-topping the flood defences and so leading to flooding. Flooding can also be caused by tsunami, tropical cyclones or extratropical cyclones. Flooding of coastal areas is worst when the storm surges coincide with spring tides. The storm tides under such circumstances can reach to 20 feet or even more.

Urban Flooding: this happens when land or property in built environments get inundated with water. This is more specially the case in densely populated urban areas. When flooding occurs in such areas the drainage system gets overwhelmed. Urban flooding is sometimes triggered by flash flooding or snowmelt. It is often characterised by repetitive systemic impacts on communities that can occur whether or not the area is located within designated flood plains or near a body of water.

The effects of floodwaters can be exacerbated by paved roads and impervious surfaces as the water gathers and cannot drain away. This poses a danger to the population as well as to the infrastructure like the summer flooding of 2010-2011 in Queensland, (Rockhampton, Bundaberg) and Brisbane Australia.

Catastrophic Flooding: This type of flooding is generally associated with major problems as the collapse of a dam, landslide, earthquake or volcanic eruption including tsunamis.

Floods and Australia

Floods are quite a common phenomenon in Australia especially the south-eastern part of Australia. This is not to say that other parts of Australia cannot be flooded – one never knows where it might occur next – perhaps as a result of a typhoon or heavy thunderstorm or excessive rainfall and precipitation. One of the worst floods in our history was I think, that of 2010-2011. There was extensive flooding in the Lockyner Valley, Ipswich and Brisbane in January 2011. There were 35 deaths – that is 35 too many lives lost, there were a lot of injuries, the emotional and psychological toll was great, 20,000 people lost their homes and in economic cost it was about 6.64 billion Australian dollars. It was a terrible time.

Between 1967 and 2013 the average annual cost was about 943 million Australian dollars in direct costs and about 943 million dollars overall. That is not counting other costs.

The other bad flood that I remember was that of 2017. It was when Cyclone Debbie hit Queensland. It became a category 4 cyclone. It caused a lot of damage and flooding in the densely populated South East Queensland and Northern River areas. The total damage was 3.5 billion Australian dollars. 14 people died as a result of the severe flooding. It was the worst cyclone that hit Australia in a long time.

Then in February 2018 parts of Queensland and NSW saw heavy rainfall and flash floods. On 24th -25th February 2018 there were flash floods in the Australian Capital Territory (ACT). It was the highest recorded for a February day.

SES (State Emergency Services) Queensland says there were over 750 calls for assistance in less than a week. They also had to help in cleaning up the flood debris and in erecting temporary flood defences. Many cars were stranded in the flood water from the rain.

On 27th February, Casino in NSW saw 125.8 mm of rain in just one hour affecting homes and businesses. From 27 to 28 February Nelly Bay recorded 229 mm of rain; Pallarenda 170mm; Saunders Creek 173 mm and Stony Creek 170 mm. It was a very hard time. They are all in Queensland. Both New South Wales (NSW) and Queensland were badly affected by the flash floods. The cities of Townsville and Bowen (QLD) were also affected by very heavy rainfall.

In 2018 Sydney and other places in NSW saw a month- long rain. This was followed on 28th November by flash floods and wind damage. Firefighters and SES workers had to be called out to help those who were stranded.

According to BoM it was the wettest day since 1984. Most of the rain fell within two hours. The wind gusted over 90km/h.

Emergency teams were kept busy rescuing people trapped in the flood. They also had to deal with downed power lines and falling trees. More than 50 flights were cancelled. Public transport services were delayed.

Flood Chart

Date	Location	State/ Territory	Fatalities	Comments
June 2007	Hunter Valley/ Maitland floods	NSW	10	Between **1967 & 2013** average annual cost was$943 million overall
June 2007	Gippsland Floods	VIC	0	cost included in above figure
Feb 2008	Mackay Floods	Qld	0	
March 2010	Queensland floods	QLD		
Sept 2010	Victorian floods	VIC	0	
Dec 2010	Carnarvon/ Gascoyne	WA		
Dec 2010-Jan 2011	Queensland floods	Qld	35	a lot of damage; worst to date; costing $664.5million
Jan 2011	Victorian floods	VIC	2	cost included in above figure
Aug 2011	Gippsland floods	VIC	1	cost included in above figure
Feb-Mar 2011	Eastern Australia	NSW, VIC Qld	3	
Mar 2011	Gippsland & Koowerup	VIC	0	
Jan-Feb 2013	Eastern Aust. floods	Qld & NSW	6	
April 2015	Hunter Valley, Central Coast, Sydney	NSW	8	
May 2015	S-E Qld Flash floods	QLD	5	
Sept 2016	Central west Riverina	NSW	1	
Feb 2017	Western Aus.	WA	2	

Date	Location	State/ Territory	Fatalities	Comments
Late Mar 2017	Eastern AUS, caused by Cyclone Debbie	South Qld, North NSW	12	Category 4 force total damage $$3.5 million
Feb 2020	Widespread flooding of Sydney Basin & Blue Mountains, flooding in Central & west to north NSW, Caused by tropical Cyclone Damien & Karrath	NSW&WA	0	

Drought and Bushfires

According to the Bureau of meteorology drought conditions are when there is scanty rainfall over a period of three months. This water shortage can be over a prolonged period of scanty water supply due to precipitation. The drought can last from 15 days to months or even years.

Droughts always have a great impact on the ecosystem, agriculture and economy of the affected country or state. Annual dry seasons generally significantly increase the chance of droughts.

There are three main kinds of drought;

- **Meteorological** – over a prolonged period of time with less than average precipitation. It usually precedes other kinds of droughts
- **Agricultural** –independent of any change in precipitation when either of which affects crops and the ecology of the place. This can happen when increased irrigation or soil conditions and erosion is triggered by poor agricultural planning and severe water shortage
- **Hydrological** – occurs when water reserves in aquifers, lakes and reservoirs fall significantly below normal levels.

When a drought persists over a long period of time it takes a significant toll on the population wild life, animals and economy of a country.

The **effects** of droughts and water shortages can be divided into three groups – environmental, social and economic.

Environmental – this affects the lower surface and subterranean water levels, increases pollution of surface water, dries out wetlands, poses a direct danger to amphibians, larger and more frequent fires, loss of biodiversity, appearance of pests and dendroid diseases and affects tree health.

Social: It affects the health and safety of people in the affected area. It may lead to conflicts when there is not enough water to go around. It leads to forced change in lifestyle and there is the added threat of the beginning of fires in those areas.

Economic – this could include lower agricultural produce, loss of forests and game and fishing; higher costs for food production.

The BoM (Bureau of Metrology) records that since the 1860's Australia has had a severe drought every 18 years. However the worst droughts have occurred in Australia in the 21st century – in 2003, 2012, 2017 and worst of all in 2019-2020 when it was followed by terrible bushfires. Since 1994 there has been a marked decrease in the precipitation levels. Between 2017 and 2019 severe drought conditions developed over much of eastern and inland Australia including Queensland, New South Wales and Victoria and extending into South Australia. Some of the worst droughts to affect Australia were the Federation Drought (1902-1903), the drought of 1937-1947, the 1960 drought that severely affected Tasmania and ended in the Tasmanian fires of 1967 where 62 people died and 1,400 homes were lost; the Queensland drought of 1991, 1994 and 1995 which was broken by the El Niño. And the trend continued. In 2019 BoM declared that drought to be the worst on record. Many farmers lost their livelihood. The land was extremely dry and parched. Food shortages began including animal feed. Exacerbating this, temperatures were unusually high. Bushfires began. This came to be known as the black summer. Conditions were very bad. There was no rain and the land was parched dry. By March 2020 the fires had burnt 18.6 million hectares and destroyed over 5,900 buildings. Firefighters came from overseas (New Zealand,

Canada, USA, Singapore among others) to help fight the fires. The Australian firefighters put in their all. The smoke from the fire could be felt far from the outbreaks as the land was sheathed in a pall of smoke. By January smoke from the Australian fire could be seen in Chile and Argentina. NASA estimated that 306 million tonnes of CO_2 had been emitted.

The fires raged from September 2019 until March 2020 leaving behind death and destruction. About a billion animals were lost and many have now become extinct. Bird, insects, amphibians have also been lost.

Fire Chart

State/territory	fatalities	homes lost	area in hectares	comments
ACT (Australian Capital Territory)	1	0	86,464	1 fatality, area impacted. No major bushfires. Smoke blew in from NSW causing dangerous pollution 1 died as a result of smoke inhalation
NSW (New South Wales)	25	2, 439	5,500,000	V severely affected. Most fatalities occurred here. Most damage & loss of homes
NT (Northern Territory)	0	5	6,800,000	Mainly scrub fires which are within the area burnt by bushfire every year. No fatalities
QLD (Queensland)	0	48	2,500,000	Area includes scrub fires and homes. No fatalities

State/territory	fatalities	homes lost	area in hectares	comments
SA (South Australia)	3	151	490,000	3 dead after air tanker accident. Bodies retrieved later. Homes lost, areas impacted
TAS (Tasmania)	0	2	89.000	No fatalities. Area somewhat impacted 2 homes lost
VIC (Victoria)	5	396	1,500,000	Fatalities, homes & area impacted. Not as bad as NSW but second most damage
WA (Western Australia)	0	1	2,200,000	area includes scrub impacted
Total	**34**	**3,500+**	**18,736,070**	**Current figures are probably higher. Some fatalities firefighters. Mid Feb 2020**

https://en.wikipedia.org/wiki/2019%E2%80%9320_Australian_bushfire_season#Overview
https://en.wikipedia.org/wiki/2019%E2%80%9320_Australian_bushfire_season

Latest figures for homes lost in AU 3,500; fatalities 34 animals 1 billion, insects and invertibrates and bird about 1 billion March and December hotter than usual

40 animal species on the threatened list.
Extinct species rose to 91

Australian Icon: I wish there was food for my joey
Photo by Mike(Miroslav) Jokic

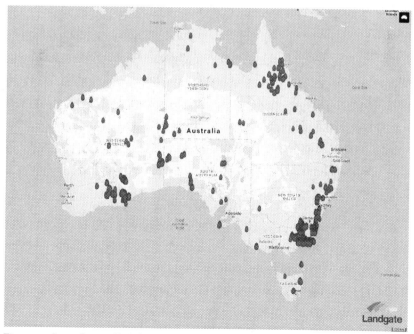

Fire map from: https://myfirewatch.landgate.wa.gov.au/

The **prognosis** is that fires will begin earlier, last longer and be more intense. Bushfires and grass fires are an intrinsic part of the Australian environment. Natural ecosystems here have evolved with the fires and the biodiversity and ecology have been shaped through fires past and present. Many of our native plants are fire prone and readily combustible while other species are regenerated by fires. The indigenous Australians have always used the fire to clear land for agriculture.

Grass fires cause less damage. Bush fires are more intense and last longer especially if they reach the crown of the canopy. Fires have always caused damage but with proper precautions the effect can be minimised by implementing mitigation strategies which would reduce the potential impact to the most vulnerable areas.

Bush fires occur when the conditions are there. These include fuel load, fuel moisture, ambient temperature, humidity, wind speed and slope angle.

- **Fuel load** is the amount of fallen bark, leaf, small branches, twigs etc. that are littering the ground. The more the ground litter, the more intense will be the fire. Dense ground litter will make the fire burn longer as will large branches or tree trunks. The less compacted the ground litter and the smaller and drier the pieces they will burn faster. Tree trunks need a long time to burn and continue to do so after the fire front has passed. The oil in eucalyptus trees promotes combustion
- **Fuel moisture** when the ground cover is dry it will burn quicker but damp fuel if it burns at all, burns slowly. When there is drought bushfires are more likely. After rains, it is less likely to occur and less severe if it does occur.
- **Ambient temperature** determines the speed and intensity of a bushfire. The higher the ambient temperature, the faster the fire will spread

- **Humidity** – dry air promotes the speed and intensity of a fire. Plants become more flammable at low humidity because they release the oil more easily.
- **Wind speed** - wind supplies the oxygen the fire needs. It brings the fire to ignition. Wind also facilitates the rapid spread of the fire and in igniting new ones. Spotting can occur up to 30 km downwind of a fire. The threshold speed of the wind around a fire is between 12 and 15 km. Even a slight change will help or hinder the fire. Heavy fuel loads cause the fire to burn more slowly. The width of the fire front also has an effect on the rate of spread of the fire.
- **The slope angle** – radiation and convection preheat the fuel source. The steeper uphill the slope the fire would accelerate whereas on a downward slope it would decelerate. With every 10° increase in the slope the fire would travel faster than on flat areas.
- **Ignition source** – Fires predominantly originate naturally through lightning or they can be a deliberate or accidental act. Deliberate or accidental fires are more common near populated areas and these have a higher impact on the infrastructure.

All natural disasters are terrible, but I think fires are the worst. Too many animals, birds, insects died as there was no escape from the fast spreading, unforgiving fire.

Sophia Z. Kovachevich

Australia – extinct and endangered species

Australia's oceans are some of the richest and most diverse on our blue planet.

Global studies have revealed that the northern oceans are some of the last remaining healthy tropical seas in the world. In the cool southern oceans, an incredible 80% of the marine species there occurs nowhere else on Earth.

This means that if they are lost, they are lost from the world forever.

Australians love our dolphins, seals and sea turtles, but many species are under threat from commercial fishing. Much of our marine wildlife has suffered from historical hunting and capture in fishing gear. Today, many species of seabirds, turtles, sharks and marine mammals are legally recognised as threatened – their future at risk. We must protect them from overfishing, pollution and climate change.

We need to protect the precious threatened and endangered animals in Australia's oceans.

Extinct Australian animals 1788 to 2020

Extinct species are those that are no longer found in our world. Some have been hunted to extinction while others became extinct due to disease or introduced species. The interesting thing here is that 80% of Australian mammals are endemic to the island continent which was a direct result of its isolation from other continents since it broke away from Gondwana 40 million years ago. The monotremes and marsupials were both also present in Gondwana. Now the monotremes are only found in Australia and New Guinea while the marsupials are found in

Australia as well as in North and South America, New Guinea, and Indonesia. Many mammal species and fauna in Australia are similar to those of New Guinea because they were once connected by a land bridge.

Extinct Birds

Common name/species	location	comment
Tasman starling/Aplonis Fusca	Norfolk Island, Lord Howe Island NSW	Last seen in 1923. Predation from introduced species and black rats
White throated pigeon/ Columba vitiensis godmanae	Lord Howe Island	Last recorded 1853. Extinct due to over hunting
Red crowned parakeet /Cyanoramphus Novaezelandiae subflavescens	Lord Howe Island	Last recorded 1869. Due to persecution for predation in gardens and crop
Rufous bristlebird/ Dasyornisbroadbenti litoralis	Western Victoria South Australia	1 species is extinct; Not seen since 1906 Other 2 are threatened with habitat loss
Roper river scrub-robin/ Drymodes superciliaris colcloughi	Northern Territory	Last recorded 1910
Norfolk ground dove/Gallicolumba norfolciensis	Norfolk Island	last seen 1850's
Lord Howe gerygone/ Gerygone insularis	Lord Howe Island	Last recorded in 1928. Due to introduction of black rats on ship *SS Makambo* in June 1918
New Zealand pigeon/Hemiphaga novaeseelandiae spadicea	Norfolk Island	Last seen in 1850's
Norfolk Island long-tailed triller/Lalage leucopyga	Norfolk Island	extinct
Norfolk Island kaka/ Nestor productus	Norfolk Island	last seen 1851

Common name/species	location	comment
Southern boobook/ Ninox novaeseelandiae albaria	Lord Howe Island	last seen 1950's
Common name/species	location	comment
Norfolk Island boobook/ Ninox novaeseelandiae undulata	Norfolk Island	last seen 1996
White gallinule/ Porphyrio albus	Lord Howe Island	extinct since 1894
Lewin's water rail/Rallus pectoralis clelandi	WA	Last recorded 1932
Paradise parrot/ Psephotus pulcherrimus	NSW, QLD	Around 1927. Starvation - lack of grass seed after drought; introduction of the prickly pear, overgrazing, fires
Macquarie island rail/ Gallirallus philippensis Macquariensis	Macquarie Island	1932 – last recorded
Lord Howe fantail/ Rhipidura cervina	Lord Howe Island	Last recorded in 1924. Due to introduction of black rats on ship *SS Makambo* in June 1918
Norfolk Island Thrush/ grey headed blackbird/ Turdus poliocephalus	Norfolk Island	Last recorded in 1924. Due to introduction of black rats on ship *SS Makambo* in June 1918
White chested, white-eye Norfolk Island silvereye/ Zosterops albogularis	Norfolk Island	IUCN considers them endangered. Not seen 30+ years
Robust white-eye/ Zosterops strennus	Lord Howe Island	Last recorded in 1923. Introduction of black rats on *SS Makambo* in June 1918

Mammals

Name/species	Location	Comments
Kangaroo Island emu/ Dromaius Novaehollandiae baudinianus	Kangaroo Island	1827 Extinct due to over-hunting and deliberate brush fires
King Island Emu/ dwarf emu/Dromaius Novaehollandiae minor	King Island	Last 2 died 1822 in captivity overhunting and human started brush fires
Tasmanian emu/ Dromaius Novaehollandiae diemenensis	Tasmania	1850. Extinct due to over-hunting and deliberate brush fires
Lesser Stick Nest Rat	Australia	Built large nests with twigs. Hunted as food by humans for its tasty meat. Last sighted in 1970. IUCN hopes some still live in interior Australia
Bulldog Rat	Christmas Island(External Australian territory	Weighed about a pound when wet. Succumbed to diseases brought by the Black Rat on European ships
Big –Eared Hopping Mouse	Australia	European settlers cleared their habitat for agriculture & was mercilessly preyed upon by their dogs and cats
Horned turtle (Meiolania	Australia, New Caledonia & Vanuatu	In Vanuatu hunted to extinction by the Aborigines
Giant monitor lizard(Ankylosaurus Meiolania)	Australia	An apex predator 25 ft long 2 tons, fed on the megafauna e.g. giant short-faced kangaroo. Extinct due to climate change & loss of food source

Name/species	Location	Comments
Wonambi (Wonambi naracoorthsis & Wonambibarriei)	Australia	Over 100 lbs, 18 foot long could kill a giant wombat – a prehistoric snake. Disappeared when the Aborigines came to Australia

Amphibians

Common name/species	location	comment
Gastric-brooding frog/ Rheobactrichus silus	Qld	Last wild specimen recorded in 1981
Eungella gastric-brooding frog/ Rheobactrichus vitellinus	Qld	Last wild specimen recorded in 1985
Sharp-snouted day frog or torrent frog/ Taudactylus acutirostris	Qld	Last wild specimen recorded in 1997
Southern-day frog or Mt Glorious day frog/ Taudactylus diurnus	Qld	Last wild specimen recorded in 1979
Quinkana(long legged, very sharp-toothed crocodile)	Australia	Fed on the megafauna. Extinct due to being hunted as food by the aborigines & loss of usual prey

Reptiles

Common name/species	location	comment
Christmas Island forest skink/emoia nativitatis	Christmas Island	Last captive specimen died May 31, 2014
Victorian grassland earless dragon/ Tympanocryptis pinguicolla	VIC	Last wild specimen died 1969. Possibly first recorded extinct reptile on the mainland

Reptiles

Name/species	location	comment
Jamaican Giant Waspcelestius occiduus (amnguid lizard)	Caribbean (Jamaica, Cuba, Puerto Rico, Costa Rico)	Last seen in 1840's. Night hunters; shy mysterious creatures
Cape Verde Giant Skink/ Chioninia cocteri)	Cape Verde Islands	Type of lizard. Extinct since early 20th Century due to inability to adapt to resident humans. Killed for its oil. Extinct also because of aridification of its natural habitat
Kawekaweau (Delcourt's giant gecko)	native to New Zealand	Extinct in 1873 when a Maori chief killed the last one. Largest ever gecko over 2 feet long
Rodrigues Giant Tortoises 2 kinds Cylindraspis peltastes & Cylansraspis vosmaeri	350 miles off Mauritius in the Indian Ocean	Extinct 19th century – hunted to extinction by man for amusement at its social behaviour
Horned turtle (Meiolania)	Australia, New Caledonia & Vanuatu	In Vanuatu hunted to extinction by the Aborigines
Giant monitor lizard(Ankylosaurus Meiolania)	Australia	An apex predator 25 ft long 2 tons, fed on the megafauna e.g. giant short-faced kangaroo. Extinct due to climate change& loss of food source
Wonambi (Wonambi naracoorthsis & Wonambibarriei)	Australia	Over 100 lbs, 18 foot long could kill a giant wombat – a prehistoric snake. Disappeared when the Aborigines came to Australia
Quinkana(long legged, very sharp-toothed crocodile)	Australia	Fed on the megafauna. Extinct due to being hunted as food by the aborigines & loss of usual prey

Sophia Z. Kovachevich

Name/species	location	comment
Big –Eared Hopping Mouse	Australia	European settlers cleared their habitat for agriculture & was mercilessly preyed upon by their dogs and cats
Bulldog Rat	Christmas Island(External Australian territory)	Weighed about a pound when wet. Succumbed to diseases brought by the Black Rat on European ships
Dark Flying Fox	Reunion & Mauritius Islands Brazil	A fruiting bat crowding in caves. Eaten by the Islanders & settlers on the Islands. Hunted for their meat, fat & the young during summer. In autumn & winters hunted by Europeans with guns.
Indefatigable Galapagos Mouse (Nesoryzomys indeffesus)	Galapagos archipelago	Killed by human settlers, loss of habitat, lethal introduced diseases (from the hitch-hiking Black rats)
Giant Vampire Bat (Desmodus draculae)	South America & Brazil	Slightly larger than the common bat; was a blood sucker preyed on mega fauna. Extinct probably due to climate change
Lesser Stick Nest Rat	Australia	Built large nests with twigs. Hunted as food by humans for its tasty meat. Last sighted in 1970. IUCN hopes some still live in interior Australia
Puerto Rican Hutia	Puerto Rico,& Cuba	Believed to have been eaten By Columbus for its tasty meat when he landed in the West Indies; hunted by the indigenous people for years; Extinct due to diseases brought by Black Rats

Name/species	location	comment
Sardinian Pika Corsican Pika	Sardinia Corsica	They were larger than rabbits. Had succulent meat& hunted by the indigenous Nuragici (Sardinian). Extinct in the 19th century

Name/species	location	Comments
Vespucci's Rodent	Islands of Fernando de Noronha off the coast of Brazil	Named after Amerigo Vespucci; extinct in the late 19th century due to pests brought by Europeans – rats, cats & mice.
White-Footed Rabbit Rat	Australia	Quite large, the size of a kitten. Made its nest of leaves in tree hollows. Became extinct in the mid-19th century due to loss of habitat and the invasive Black rats and cats

Mammals

common name/species	location	comment
Boodie burrowing bettong/Bettongia lesueur graii	WA (inland), Sa, Vic, western NSW	predation by foxes & feral cats; poisoned by early farmers, loss of habitat; extinct
Brush tailed bettong/ Bettongia pencillata	NSW, NT, SA, VIC, NA, WA (southeast mainland)	2 species was seriously endangered reintroduced into NSW
Desert rat kangaroo / Caloprymnus campestris	Qld, SA, NT	Last recorded 1935
Pig-footed bandicoot/ chaeropus ecaudatus	NSW, NT, SA, VIC, WA	Last recorded 1950's
White-footed rabbit rat/ Conilurus albipes	NSW, Qld, SA, VIC	Last recorded 1857
Central Hare wallaby/ Lagorchestes asomatus	NT	Last recorded 1935

common name/species	location	comment
Rufous hare-wallaby/ Lagorchestes hirsutus	NT, SA, WA (southwest mainland)	vulnerable
Eastern hare wallaby/ Lagorchestes leporides	NSW, Qld, SA VIC	Last recorded 1890
Banded hare wallaby/ lagostrophus fasciatus albipilis	WA (mainland)	reintroduced on Faure Island
Tammar wallaby/ Macropus eugenii	SA	Population rediscovered in New Zealand
Toolache wallaby/ Macropus greyi Name/species	SA, VIC	Last recorded 1932
Lesser wallaby/Macrotis leucura	NT, Qld, SA	Last recorded 1931
Bramble Cay melomys/ Melomys rubicola	Bramble Cay Qld	Last recorded 2016
Long-tailed hopping mouse/Notomys longicaudatus	NT, SA, WA	Last recorded 1901
Big-eared hopping mouse/Notomys macrotis	WA	Last recorded 1843
Darling Downs hopping-mouse/Notomys Mordax	NSW, Qld	Last recorded 1846
Crescent nail-tail wallaby/ Onychogalea lunata	SA, WA	Last recorded 1956
Western barred bandicoot/ peramelesbougainville,)	NSW, VIC (mainland	smallest species, endangered
Desert bandicoot/ Perameles eremiana	NT, SA, WA	Before 1960
Christmas Island piistrelle/Pipistrellus murray	Christmas Island	Last recorded 2009
Broad-faced potoroo/ Potorous playtops	WA	Last recorded 1865
Blue-grey mouse/ Pseudomys glaucus	NSW, Qld	Last recorded 1956
Gould's mouse/ Pseudomys gouldii	NSW, Qld, SA, VIC, WA	Last recorded 1857

common name/species	location	comment
Dusky flying fox/ Pteropus brunneus	Qld	Last recorded in late 1800's
Maclear's rat/Rattus Maclear	Christmas Island	Last recorded 1908
Bulldog rat/Rattus navtivitatis	Christmas Island	Last recorded 1903
Thylacine Tasmanian tiger/Tasmanian wolf/ Thylacineus cynocephalus	Tasmania	It was the largest known carnivore marsupial of modern times. Extinct due to being overhunted and loss of habitat; Last one died of neglect. It was locked out of its sleeping quarter in the freezing cold. Its name was Benjamin & died on September 7am 1936
Christmas Island shrew/ Crocidura trichura	Christmas Island	Last recorded 1985
1985 Lesser stick-neck rat/Leporillus apicalis	NSW, NT, SA, VIC, WA	last recorded 1933
Lord Howe long-eared bat/ Nyctophilus howensis	Lord Howe Island	extinct since August 2009
Christmas Island pipistrelle/Pipistrellus murrayi	Christmas Island	last recorded August 2009

Also Extinct

Tasmanian Tiger, Red–Fronted Parakeet, Gastric–brooding Frog, Lesser Bilby. All became extinct due to our exploitation and callousness to nature's gifts.

Invertebrates

A number of Australian invertebrates have been listed as extinct by the World Conservation Union.

common name/species	location	comment
LakePeddarWorm/ Hypolimnuspedderenis	Tasmania	Last recorded in 1972. Extinct status in 2000
Campbell's Island snail/ Advena campbelli	Norfolk Island	
Norfolk snail/Nancibella quintelia	Norfolk Island	
Lord Howe snail/ Tornelasmias capriconi	Lord Howe Island	
Macquarie slug/Angrobia dulvertonensis		last recorded 1996
Lord Howe Slug/ Placostylus bivaricosus etheridgei	Lord Howe island	

Australian Vulnerable animals

Koala	Blobfish	Giant clam
Quokka	Possum	Wallaby
Antechinus	Numbat	Eastern Bettong
Tree kangaroo	Australian Sea Lion	Dingo
Australian Sea Lions	Dugongs	Dolphins.
Hammerhead Sharks.	Cassowary	Tasmanian Devil
Wombat	Gouldian Finch	Spotted Quoll
Night Parrot	Bandicoot	Greater Bilby
Giant cuttlefish	Giant Clam	

Extinction means that there are no more of a particular type of plant or animal living on the earth — they are extinct. A clear example of extinction is the dinosaurs. They disappeared from the face of the earth 65 million years ago. Extinction is an ongoing process of evolution. It is estimated that over 90% of all animals that ever lived, since life began on the earth, are now extinct. Extinction is usually a slow process that takes many hundreds if not thousands of years.

In recent time however, due to human activities, the number of species becoming extinct has accelerated at an alarming rate. Some species have become extinct in just a few years.

In Australia the Tasmanian tiger became extinct in just 100 years after European settlement. Similarly in America, the passenger pigeon, which once numbered in the hundred of millions, became extinct in less than a hundred year because of indiscriminate hunting by European settlers

Threatened Species

- Great Barrier Reef, Australian Sea Lions. Australian sea lions are a type of seal that are native only to our shores. ...
- Dugongs. Dugongs are shy, elusive marine mammals that depend on healthy seagrass meadows ...
- Dolphins. 15 species of dolphins and one species of porpoise live in Australian waters. Plastic is a huge hazard for them
- Hammerhead Sharks. Hammerhead sharks are an iconic species inhabiting Australia's waters but

Endangered Species

cassowary	Tasmanian Devil	wombat
Gouldian Finch	Spotted Quoll	Night Parrot
Bandicoot	Greater Blby	
whales	Turtles	Sharks

Australia is home to the most incredible ocean wildlife on earth, but many of our species are threatened or endangered. Our threatened marine life like our turtles, whales and sharks including the tiger shark 71% decline in last 3 decades along

Australia's east coast according to the AMCS (Australian Marine Conservation Society),and the HIS (Human Society International).

One reason given for this was that commercial fishing was decimating the tiger shark population and causing their numbers to plummet over the past 33 years. Another reason was Queensland's lethal Shark control programme.

Critical list

Snapping Turtle	Leadbeater's Possum	corroboree frog
Plains Wanderer	Handfish	Northern Wombat
Swift Parrot	Gilbert's Potoroo	Night Parrot
Woylie		

An Australian Icon – Kanga and joey in the woods
Photo by Janice M Davis

Some unusual and Interesting Australian creatures

- **Koalas** are cuddly tree-dwelling marsupial mammals with large noses. They sleep up to 20 hours a day. They were on the verge of extinction in the 1900's due to being hunted for their fur. They recovered but the bush fires of 2020 saw a large number of them wiped out. Now they are on the vulnerable/endangered list

- **Gilbert's Potoroo** (Ngilkat) is the world's rarest marsupial. It has long front limbs with curved claws with which its digs for underground fungi (truffles). There are only 30-40 animals left in the wild

- **The Southern Cassowary,** with dagger-like claws and a very powerful kick, is the most dangerous bird in the world. They are also the world's second-largest bird. There are only about 1,500 of these dinosaur-like rainforest birds left in the wild in northern QLD

- **Blobfish** have jelly-like bodies and live in the ocean at depths of over 1,000m. At this depth, they look like fat-headed fish shaped like a tadpole. Some claim that this fish is vulnerable. However, there is no definitive proof of this. They live in deep waters off the Australian mainland coast and, Tasmania and New Zealand

- **Tasmanian Devil** is a scary and boisterous marsupial with blood-curdling screams like a devil. It is the world's largest marsupial carnivore. It was listed as endangered in 2008. It has recovered somewhat.

- **The Giant Cuttlefish** is the largest cuttlefish and an expert at camouflage and colour change. It is impacted by overfishing and habitat degradation and listed as protected species. It is feared that it may become extinct due to low numbers

- **The Northern Hairy-Nosed Wombat** is a solidly built burrowing herbivorous marsupial with a large head and short, sturdy legs and claws. It may appear clumsy and slow, but it can gallop at over 40 km/h. There are only 250 northern hairy-nosed wombats in the wild. It is listed as critically endangered

❖ **Giant Clams** can take over a hundred years to grow up to 1.5 meters and weigh 230kg. They have large protruding brilliant iridescent lips. The clam eats sugars and proteins produced by billions of algae that live in its tissues. It is endangered because of harvesting by humans and accidents from bivalve fishing vessels

❖ **The Woylie** is a very rare nocturnal marsupial with a long tail with a black brush at the end, which it wraps around a bundle of nesting material and transports it home. Their primary diet is underground fungi. The woylie was once abundant across southern Australia. Now it is endangered (1982). Their decline is a result of grazing animals and land clearing, predation by red foxes and feral cats, and feral rabbits

❖ **Dingoes** are native wild dogs brought to Australia by humans 5,000 years ago. Dingoes are not endangered as such but are listed as vulnerable because of the decline of the "pure" breed dingo as a result of interbreeding with domestic dogs.

❖ **Gouldian Finches** are beautifully coloured grass finches found in Northern Australia. They all but extinct in the wild, with only about 2,500 left. Luckily they survive in captivity as popular pets.

❖ **The Corroboree Frog**, is a highly poisonous amphibian with striking yellow and black longitudinal markings. It is found in the Kosciuszko National Park in New South Wales. There may be as few as 50 adult southern corroboree frogs left in the wild. They are critically endangered

❖ **Possum** are tree-dwelling, nocturnal marsupials very nimble and capable of climbing up vertical surfaces and even electric power lines. They are found in VIC and are endangered

❖ **Dugongs** are plant-eating marine mammals. Because of their sleek, smooth appearance and large teats ancient sailors thought they were mermaids. They are listed as vulnerable

❖ **The Northern Quoll** is the size of a small cat. It is the smallest of all quolls and also the most aggressive. Predation by feral cats and being poisoned by eating cane toads has seen their numbers decline drastically. They are endangered

❖ **The Swift Parrot** is a small green and yellow parrot with long pointed wings. This rather noisy bird is the fastest parrot in the world. It flies from Tasmania to the Australian mainland to feed and returns to Tasmania in the spring to breed. There are only 2,000 in the wild, and they are projected to become extinct by 2031 due to predation and habitat loss. They are critically endangered

❖ **Loggerhead Turtle** is the largest turtle of them all. It is called a leatherback because it doesn't have a hard shell but has leathery skin instead. It is carnivorous, feeding mainly in the open ocean on jellyfish and other soft-bodied invertebrates. It is found world-wide. It is endangered since 1978

❖ An estimated 4,000 **Quokkas** live on mainland Australia and are threatened by habitat loss due to logging and land clearing of the wetland – its habitat, and predation from foxes, dogs, and cats. Another 7,000 live on Rottnest island animal sanctuary.

❖ **Wallabies** are small hopping marsupials having two large hind legs, small forelimbs, and a large thick tail. They are very similar to kangaroos but smaller. They are endangered since the colonisation of Australia and loss of their habitat in more recent times

- **Numbats** are small marsupial anteaters that eat termites which they scoop up with their long, sticky tongue. They are also called Banded or Marsupial Anteaters. They forage for termites during the daylight. One species became extinct in the 1960s. They are indigenous to Australia

- The **Antechinus** is a ferocious little marsupial mouse with a pointy nose that feeds on small insects. There are 15 species of antechinus. They are endemic to Australia. They are endangered from habitat destruction and threats from introduced animals like cats

- **The White-Throated Snapping Turtle** is also known as the bum-breathing turtle because it breathes through its bottom. By doing so, it can remain submerged for days. It is critically endangered. Humans are destroying their habitat by the building of dams and weirs in its territory in QLD

- **Night Parrots** are small ground-dwelling nocturnal parrots of Australia. They inhabit the remote, semi-arid areas of Australia especially WA. They are critically endangered. Only 250 survive in the wild

- **Greater Bilbies** are small, nocturnal, omnivorous marsupials with rabbit-like ears and pointy pink snouts. These small marsupials are endangered because introduced rabbits are destroying their habitat and predation by feral foxes and cats. They are endemic to Australia and especially found in QLD

- **Leadbeater's Possums** are critically endangered fast-moving marsupials that live in the forest canopy. However their habitat is restricted to small pockets of alpine ash, mountain ash and snow gums in Central VIC. It was once thought to be extinct until a small population of animals was rediscovered.

- **Bandicoots** are small native omnivorous marsupials with pointy snouts, large hind feet and they hop. There are many species of bandicoots in Australia, however the Northern Bandicoot is now extinct

❖ **Handfish** prefer to walk on their pectoral and pelvic fins rather than swim. They are critically endangered due to habitat loss and destruction, pollution and climate change

❖ **Tree kangaroos**, obviously live in trees. They climb by wrapping the forelimbs around a tree and hopping up with their powerful hind legs. They are critically endangered due to severe reduction of their habitat. There are about 50 remaining tree kangaroos

❖ **Australian Sea Lions** hunt fish, squid and other sea creatures. Relentlessly hunted until 1920, the population has never recovered. There are only about 10,000 left. They are still hunted for their coat and are often killed or hurt by fishing boats. Their numbers are <u>not</u> increasing

❖ **Plains-Wanderers** a type of quail–like bird are critically endangered and under imminent threat of extinction. It is because of loss of habitat and food source. These small ground birds prefer to run rather than fly and fall easy prey to foxes.

❖ **The Eastern Bettong,** often described as a tiny kangaroo became extinct on the mainland of Australia in the 1920s as the result of the introduction of the red fox and rabbit. A very small population still exists in Tasmania but is listed as near threatened

❖ **Green Turtles** feed mostly on sea grasses but they are one of the few animals that also eat the venomous box jellyfish. They are listed as an endangered species but are still killed for their meat and eggs. Their numbers are also reduced due to propeller accidents, getting caught in fish nets and destruction of their habitat by human encroachment

Melbourne's important waterways

The Aboriginal people lived close to waterways throughout Victoria. Rivers and creeks often formed boundaries between clans and provided meeting points and places for ceremonies. There were many wetlands which were great sources for food and water.

When the European settlers came, they chose to establish Melbourne on the confluence of the Yarra and Maribyrnong rivers. But from the 1840's Melbourne's creeks and rivers became dumping ground for waste from homes and businesses.

The 1934 very heavy rains made it clear, when the rivers broke their banks and flooding up to 12 metres above the usual resulted, that improved drainage was needed. By the late 1960's pollution of the rivers became a problem and you could read captions focusing on the *dying Yarra*. Environmental issues became a feature by the early 1970's.

Now in the 2020's the waters are far more polluted than could have been envisaged. It is time to clean up the waterways. It is time for change!

Port Melbourne

For many years now (since the 1980's) Port Melbourne has allowed water contaminated with massive levels of cancer-causing arsenic to leach from one of its properties into the Maribyrnong River.

Arsenic can and does cause cancers and organ and skin damage.

Till 2005 many people fished within a kilometre of the arsenic poisoning at Yarraville, in Melbourne's Inner West. The fishermen, mostly local Vietnamese, often ate their catch or sold it to the local shops. No one had been warned about the risk to their health.

Neither the Port authorities nor the EPA – which knew since the 1970's about the contamination with extremely high arsenic levels – warned the fishermen. Or tested the fish. Then in 2005 the environmental watchdogs managed to extract a clean-up plan from the Port authorities.

When the Port authorities bought the land they knew about this most contaminated piece of land but still they signed a release form that exempted the previous owners – the Pivot fertiliser company from any liability to clean up the site. This piece of land has been the site of a chemical plant, and an acid and fertiliser plant since the 1840's. The pollution here is a toxic mix of heavy metals and other poisonous substances. This is in shallow groundwater which is in direct contact with the Maribyrnong River. The arsenic levels are particularly high and it is environmentally very unsafe. It is also very dangerous for human contact.

Roger Parker, an independent auditor conducted a survey and found that the groundwater was leaking copper into the Maribyrnong River at 154,000 times the safe EPA limit. Zinc was being leached at 5000 times the safe limit; and lead (Pb) up to 250 times more; the level of ammonia too was very high -33,500 the amount set for human contact.

The arsenic is leached from iron oxide which was used since a long time to fill the lower banks of the Victorian rivers. This is believed to be six feet deep in places and certainly in at least half the total area of the former Pivot site.

The Age newspaper carried out an investigation in 2001 and found:

- EPA knew and was concerned about the arsenic levels in the Maribyrnong since the early 1990's and certainly by 1995 when they got a report stating that arsenic leaching was about 3,000 times more than was acceptable. Nothing was done with the report.
- In 2003 a laboratory tested the groundwater but the findings were never interpreted though the test had showed that the arsenic in the water was the highest level in eight years.
- The Department of Human Services conducted a research into the consumption of fish but again, nothing was done

Cobalt, iron, manganese, mercury, nickel, selenium, molybdenum and cadmium were all also being leached into the Maribyrnong River.

In November 2003 the first, formal EPA notice to clean up the river was received.

In November 2019 EPA began construction of a new web site to report contamination of the rivers with among others, solvents, arsenic, lead and other heavy metal and pesticides. This was an attempt to prevent contamination of the environment.

The Maribyrnong River

The Maribyrnong River begins near the town of Lancefield, passes by the Tullamarine airport, makes its way past Keilor, Essendon, Footscray and Yarraville till it joins the Yarra River near the Westgate Bridge. This river has been called a saltwater river. It is contaminated and has been so for quite some time. Since the past few years, The Port of Melbourne authorities has allowed contaminated water having massive amounts of arsenic to leach into the Maribyrnong River at Yarraville in Melbourne's inner west. People fish there and eat their catch. The river has not been tested for arsenic since the 1970's though people (Port Melbourne authorities and EPA) knew it was contaminated with arsenic. It is also polluted with a toxic mix of heavy metals and other noxious substances. The arsenic levels show that it is 20,000 times higher than is regarded as environmentally safe. The test measured the pollution flowing into the river and not levels in the river itself. It also found that copper is leaking into it at 154,000 times the safe level, zinc at 5,000 times; lead up to 250 times. The levels of ammonia leaking in, is 33,500 times the safe level for human contact.

The arsenic is leaching from iron oxides that have been used to fill the river banks. The ground water is also leaching cobalt, iron, manganese, mercury, molybdenum, nickel, selenium, aldrin, dieldrin, cyanide and cadmium into the Maribyrnong. Long term exposure to arsenic can cause cancers and organs and skin problems. Testing of the waters has also found high levels of PFAS (poly-fluorinated alkyl substances) in the river. There are also elevated levels of PCBs. People have now been advised not to consume fish upstream from Solomon's Ford in Avondale Heights or from Arundel Creek. The fish is contaminated here and those who fish here too, eat their catch. Over time it will lead to health problems. Earlier people had been advised not to fish, swim, go boating or water the stock or irrigate the land with the Maribyrnong River waters

The Yarra River

The natural corridor that the Yarra provides is indispensable to the lives of Melbournians. It provides a natural setting for recreation. It is also a rich habitat for different species of plant and animal life. Unfortunately however, this area is shrinking due to urban growth and other developmental projects that are connected with urbanisation.

In the 1880's the falls across the Yarra River were blasted to facilitate shipping further upstream but this increased the salt levels in the water which in turn impacted the environment. It also increased pollution. The pollution became so bad that it was recommended building a sewage treatment farm in Werribee that treated the water flowing into the Yarra.

In the 1990's Melbourne developed very fast and a lot of the wetlands were drained or filled for human habitation. The flow of rivers and creeks were altered.

In 1934 there was heavy rain and the Yarra River rose to 12 metres making it clear that the drainage system was not adequate. And by the 1960's it became apparent that the rivers, creeks and bay were extremely polluted. The focus was on the *dying Yarra.* In 1968 urban runoff commenced.

In 1970 the Environment Protection Act was introduced. Sewage could not go to the Yarra directly but needed to be treated. Many outer suburbs and rural area sewage was connected to the sewerage system.

Later tests showed that there were a number of hot spots including the Yarra River and that 3,500 tonnes of nitrogen, phosphorous and silica entered the bay from the sewerage system.

In the late 1990's a new scheme was introduced to protect and improve waterway health and manage litter in the bay. Urban growth has led to more pollution and loss of wetlands. But despite the efforts to clean up the Yarra high levels of pollution, including raw sewage, used syringes, cigarette butts and spray cans are still flowing into the Yarra.

Besides this runoffs from the road and other hard surfaces, carrying heavy metals like zinc, lead, copper, car brakes and tyres, plastics, litter and chemicals from homes, offices and buildings and water from urban stormwater systems all pour in and pollute the Yarra. During high rainfall times, raw sewage overflows from sewage treatment plants and enters the Yarra as diluted raw sewage. These are major problems.

Another problem that arose was with litter traps. In order to control the flow of litter into the Melbourne waterways, litter traps were introduced into the Port Philip bay at two points: St Kilda main drain and Sandringham drain. This has had partial success. The traps, trapped litter as well as marine life including dolphins that drown when caught in the litter traps.

The Yarra River has 16 hectares of grassland a third of which is envisaged to become 2,500 houses and apartments for 5,000 residents. Another third of the grassland will be turned into hard surfaces. That will mean added pollution and loss of habitat for the birds.

Landfills

Landfills are the oldest form of waste disposal. In prehistoric times these were middens. Into the midden went domestic waste – animal bones, human excrement, mollusc, shells, left over food, shards, lithics (stone) in short the unwanted remains of daily life. Middens were open in olden days and they stank. However middens now provide a very useful resource for archaeologists to study habits, culture etc. of olden times. Middens are damp and supply anaerobic (where no free oxygen is present) conditions that are good for preserving organic remains that have been disposed in them. Along with these also go sediments. Water and wind interact and animals may also dig in them. All these factors interact and create a matrix that provides a lot of information to scientists including climatic and seasonal information.

A landfill now is a tip, dump, rubbish dump into which goes all recyclables and other household rubbish. Landfills as we now know came to be used from the 1940's. It is a designated area of hollow land into which goes household waste, construction waste and other such things. It is supposed to be a covered space.

There are different categories for what can go into which landfill. Category A is high hazard waste and there is supposed to be strict rules for the dumping of such waste. Category B is industrial waste like contaminated soil, packaged asbestos and seafood processing wastes. Category C is low hazard waste which is generally accepted by most landfills.

Landfills are an important part of Victoria, Australia's waste management programme. Only one landfill in Victoria is allowed to accept Category B (industrial waste). I do not know about Category A waste. Category C is allowed in most landfills.

Different gases are produced in landfills as a result of anaerobic digestion by microbes. In well managed landfills these gases are collected and used for other purposes like electricity generation. If care is not taken, these gases can end up causing harmful symptoms in people.

Leachate which is produced in landfills is liquid that while passing through the waste matter extracts the soluble or suspended solid organic or inorganic matter. It is putrefied industrial waste. It has harmful substances that can enter the environment and pollute it. It enters the surrounding soil and groundwater or surface water due to movement in the landfill. It can and does lead to severe pollution problems when care is not taken.

The Leachate that is produced in landfills differs in composition depending on the age of the landfill and its contents. There are three important negative consequences of having landfills near human habitation. They are

- Toxins –
    - o Arsenic – present in pesticides. It is linked to cancer, cardiovascular diseases, respiratory diseases, skin disease, birth defects and reproductive problems
    - o Cadmium affects the central nervous system developing embryos, causes cancer, kidney damage and breathing problems
    - o Chromium. – Chromium has been linked to genetic mutations, cancer, skin allergies, eye problems, and respiratory diseases
    - o Mercury. – Mercury negatively impacts the cardiovascular system, central nervous system, risk of cancer and eye problems
    - o Lead – affects the central nervous system, causes mental retardation, physical development & growth

in children, reproductive problems, brain damage and kidney damage

o Nickel – Nickel is a substance that is known to be highly allergic. Causes eye irritation, breathing problems kidney & liver damage and is linked to increased risk of cancers

o Chloroform – linked to cancer, liver and kidney damage, gastrointestinal damage and central nervous system damage

o Ethylbenzene causes liver and kidney damage, central nervous system and respiratory system damage

o Benzene – Benezene is is an extremely toxic chemical. It is very carcinogenic and causes genetic mutations and central nervous system damage. It also has been linked to damage to the peripheral nervous system, blood cell disorders, gastrointestinal disorders, skin and eye irritation

Not all these are present in every landfill. But many are present in pesticides that are there in with seven other household chemicals which also go into landfills. Discarded electronics contain dangerous chemical. Plastics are not recyclable but breakdown into dangerous chemicals

Landfills not only contaminate the soil surrounding them, but also seep into the water table and contaminate it. They also leach into the air and contaminate that too. This affects humans for generations.

- Leachate which is the liquid formed when waste material breaks down and filters into the groundwater

- Greenhouse gases that the landfills produce. Cadmium. Cadmium affects the central nervous system. Often referred to as GHG. It absorbs & radiates energy within thermal infrared ranges. It causes greenhouse effect on the earth. The main greenhouse gases of the earth are water vapour, (H_2O), Carbon dioxide (CO_2), Methane (CH_4), Nitrous oxide (N_2O) and ozone (O_3). Without these the earth would be very cold

To summarise health hazards that landfills pose to humans are:

- respiratory illnesses
- cancer
- birth defects
- diseases spread by the increase in vermin in the area along with the toxins mentioned above.

These toxins leach into the groundwater and the soil and become a health hazard and an environmental hazard for years to come. One example of this would be the dumping of electronic waste in a landfill.

Landfills are dumping sites in many countries in the world. In Canada they are regulated by the provincial agencies and the environmental protection legislation. Older sites are monitored for leaching. Some have been converted into parkland.

In the EU individual states regulate and monitor their own but have to comply with EU regulations at the same time.

Denmark, Sweden, Finland, Germany, Poland, Belgium, the Netherlands, Austria and Slovenia have very strict regulations concerning landfills. They have in place regulations and laws banning or severely restricting the disposal of household waste in landfills.

Each country has its own rules and regulations. In Australia, each state and territory regulates its landfill programme.

In Victoria (Australia) the State government along with the EPA are responsible for safe management of landfills. They are expected to follow best practice measures to ensure that the locations of landfills are acceptable to the public.

In Victoria only one landfill is licensed to accept Category B, industrial waste. Category C low hazard industrial waste can be accepted by most landfills.

Victoria even though it is the second largest city has relatively less landfills, most situated in the Western suburbs of Melbourne.

In recent years there was a lot of anger over a landfill very close to residential dwellings in the St Albans and Kealba suburbs. Most of the residents were very upset about the pollutions level and the noise level emanating from the landfill site. It appears that the old EPA council knew about it seven years ago but did nothing. The present EPA is trying to redress the problem.

Explosive confidential advice to Brimbank city council late last year said, that a 2013 report the council gave to the EPA, identified a "high risk to residents" as well as "off-site workers and the public" from the former Sunshine Landfills, which contained radioactive materials, solvents, paints, oil, acids, poisons, manure and other household and industrial waste (By Chris Vedelago and Michael Bachelard Feb 27, 2020). But it appears that the high risk posed by the close presence of the landfill site was regarded as *acceptable* and that *no urgent intervention* was necessary to protect the residents.

The residents were unaware of the risk posed by the landfill so close to them. Since then a number of residents have sold their properties without informing the new buyers of the landfill. It also has come out that in 1978 contamination had leaked from the landfill into Port Philip Bay through the ground water. The Brimbank Council had then informed the residents that there was a tip beneath their properties. Recently residents from the area complained of a smell in the air and noise pollution. This is not the first time that the residents of Brimbank have complained to the relevant authorities. They even took the matter to court but the case was decided against the dwellers. The citizens; health was not deemed important enough.

Landfills are important for the deposit of industrial and household waste but care must be taken as to their location. This is another way in which our environment is getting raped.

Landfills are well-known for their pollution because of what goes into it. It is a major cause of soil pollution. Toxic and hazardous substances are constantly leaking from it into the soil causing and nullifying the supporting life in the soil. The contaminants are many and dangerously toxic, among them industrial waste, household waste, sewage, chemicals, waste from factories, radioactive waste from nuclear plants, oily sludge waste from oil refineries etc. There are more and more landfills and often things are dumped by households which shouldn't go into landfills.

Then as population increases so does the need for homes. Urbanisation is still on the rise. Deforestation takes place to get the raw materials for the housing projects. Construction always results in pollution. Concrete and debris are pollutants which end up in the landfills increasing the landfills to capacity. Other construction wastes like oils and paints are also hazardous. When they are not properly disposed of, they too pollute the soil. Deforestation is another disadvantage – it causes soil erosion. This in turn leads to land pollution and the soil is eroded by wind and rain. This results in nutrients and organic matter being lost leaving the soil infertile.

Floods are also linked to deforestation. Where there are no trees the water has nowhere to go so it rushes downstream causing severe floods which then ultimately reach the ocean polluting that too with the debris and toxins it has picked up on the way.

As the population increases so does the need for food. Farmers have to increases their yield. But the soil is not fertile enough to maintain larger crop yield. Therefore fertilisers are needed to correct the soil deficiency and then pesticides are used to kill unwanted pests and fungi from the crops. These pesticides and toxins are washed into streams and rivers and ultimately reach the oceans polluting all in its path.

As the population increases so does the need for raw materials. Metals, coal, precious and semi-precious stones are raw materials much in demand. These have to be extracted through mining. Mining has a huge negative impact on the soil. Surface mining destroys plants and trees. Other kinds of mining need land structures to carry out the work. So the area is destabilised and soil erosion is facilitated. The rocks need to be disposed. They go into the landfills further polluting and contaminating it.

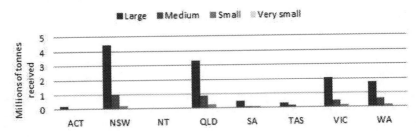

https://theconversation.com/

PART VIII

NEW ZEALAND

New Zealand or as it is also known as - Aotearoa is a sovereign island mass in the south west Pacific ocean. It has two islands North Island where the capital Wellington is located and the largest city, Auckland is also situated. Then there is the South Island. It has a number of smaller islands too. It is a multicultural island with the largest population being Europeans. The indigenous people who came to New Zealand between 1280 AD and 1350 AD came from Polynesia. They are the Maoris.

In 1642 the Dutch explorer Abel Tasman sighted New Zealand. Then in 1840 UK representatives signed a treaty – the Treaty of Waitangi with the Maori chiefs that claimed New Zealand as UK territory. Unlike Australia, New Zealand was never a penal colony. In 1907 it became an independent Dominion and part of the Commonwealth

New Zealand was the largest country in Polynesia before it was annexed by Great Britain in 1840. Then it was a crown colony, a self-governing colony (1856), and finally a dominion (1907).

Due to its geographic isolation, its ecology is very distinctive. About 82% of its indigenous vascular plants are endemic to the country. New Zealand also has a very wide variety of fungi which too are endemic to the country. The two main types of trees found there are the broadleaf trees with emergent podocarps (belonging to the genus of conifers) and the southern beech trees that grow in the cooler areas. The vegetation is mainly tussock and grassland.

Before human arrival about 80% of the land was covered in forests and with wet, infertile treeless volcanic areas. But once people started arriving, deforestation on an unprecedented rate occurred.

Since the time that New Zealand became populated by humans, about half the vertebrates of the country have become extinct including 51 species of birds, 3 species of frogs, 3 species of lizards 1 species of bats and 1 species of freshwater fish. A large number have become endangered. Conservationists in New Zealand are trying to help endangered species to recover in various ways. The giant Haast eagle died out when the Maoris came. This was because the new inhabitants hunted the Moa which was the eagle's main prey until they became extinct. Another reason for the disappearance of the endemic birds was the introduction of mammals like the ferrets, rats and cats.

When the Polynesians arrived about half the forests were lost to fires to clear the land. A lot of the remaining forests were cleared after the arrival of the Europeans. Logging took place too, to clear the land for pastoral farming. Only 23% of forest land survived. Another dependent relationship was between the now extinct huia (bird) and the mite that lived on its skin. That particular mite is now extinct too. The New Zealand bat species are also dependent on the bat fly as is the woodrose.

New Zealand had a lot of flightless birds like the moa, kiwi (endangered), kakapo, weka, and takahē. This was probably because there were no mammals to hunt them and the ground was full of food. New Zealand had lots of birds and some very unusual reptiles like the tuatara which is often regarded as a living fossil. It had many amphibians. There were no mammals.

The only fossil is that of a mouse-like mammal has been dated at least 16 million years old. It has a lot of marine animals. They also have more penguin species than any other country in the world.

The total number of creatures threatened with extinction in New Zealand has increased from 416 to 2,788 according to the *New Zealand Threat Classification System* lists (2005) published by the Department of Conservation. In 2007 a report by the *State of New Zealand Environment* maintained that the 10 most threatened species are still the same.

Recent research has shown that there is possibly a strong connection between the pollution index and the Corona virus COVID 19. Most countries that have a high pollution index have had a lot more cases than countries with a low pollution index.

The pollution level index in New Zealand is much lower than in Europe, USA or South America. It seems that is why the number of Coronavirus cases was very low too and very quickly contained.

The years I spent there taught me to appreciate the land and its inhabitants. New Zealanders make really good friends. I'm the richer for having known them.

New Zealand's most endangered species

The following is a list of the most endangered species in New Zealand. There has been no change in their status.

The Maui dolphin is the smallest dolphin. It is related to Hector's dolphin. It is now found only in shallow coastal waters off the North Island. There are between 48 and 69 mature dolphins left alive.

Mokohinau stag beetle is the largest beetle and is only found in Mokohinau Island east of Auckland. It is a rat-free island. The male beetle has large stag like antlers. There are none to be found on islands that have rats.

Canterbury knobbled weevil was thought to be extinct but was rediscovered in 2004 in speargrass in Burke's Pass, South Canterbury. The total population is less than 100 weevils.

Isoetes is a primitive kind of aquatic fern or quillwort. It was found on a number of Northland lakes but as the quality of water became polluted, they disappeared. An extensive search led to finding 12 of these. They are now in an aquarium.

New Zealand fairy tern is the most endangered endemic bird of New Zealand. There are only about 12 surviving pairs in beaches between Whangarie and Auckland. A major threat to these birds is human activity in their vicinity. In 1983 there were only 3 or 4 breeding pairs but the conservation programme has successfully managed to bring it up to 12 breeding pairs.

Limestone cress is a plant that is found on only one limestone outcrop. There are about 50 plants. Why they are endangered is not known but it is believed it is because of animals and insects like the white butterfly, snails, slugs, rodents and rabbits; and because of excessive shade and by their susceptibility to diseases and fungi as a result of the introduction of cabbage. There is a conservation programme underway to protect them.

Chesterfield skink was discovered in the 1990's in Chesterfield between Hokitika and Greymouth in Westland. Their numbers have reduced dramatically in recent years and they do not seem to be found in any other place.

Coastal peppercress was only found around the Nelson coastline. Conservation efforts failed and it is now classified as extinct.

Eyelash seaweed looks like human eyelashes and shows remarkable similarity to the oldest fossils of multicellular organisms. They are found on only two boulders in separate sites on the Kaikoura coast. The numbers fluctuate for no known reason.

Dune swale daphne is a small shrub that inhabits moist sand flats on the coasts of Manawatu, Whanganui and Christchurch. Recently all disappeared except for one site where a few plants have survived. Conservationists are trying to cultivate these plants. Its habitat has been swamped by grass and weeds and grazed on by animals. The area too, is infested with rabbits and snails. Perhaps that is why they are disappearing.

Wood pigeons are also on the decline. They are the only large bird left in New Zealand that can disperse seeds of native trees like the tawa, miro, karaka, taraire and the puriri trees.

New Zealand's extinct species

Auckland Island Shore Plover Extinct 1840	Bush wren extinct 1972	Chatham Island fern bird 1895
Chatham Island bellbird/ Anthornis Melanocephala Extinct 1906	Chatham rail/Cabalus modestus 1900	South Island kokako/ Calleas cinera 1967
Little Barrier Island snipe Extinct 1870. Only 1 was caught	Stewart Island snipe 1960's	New Zealand quail 1875
Dieffenbach's rail 1872	Huia December 1907	New Zealand little bittern 1890's
Auckland Island Merganser Extinct Jan 1902	Laughing owl July 1914	Stephen's Island rail (Lyall's Wren)1875? Certainly by 1894
South Island piopio 1963	North Island piopio 1955	Chatham Island penguin 1872?
Greater Short tailed Bat (last sighted 1967 on Solander Island) Only NZ mammal	New Zealand grayling fish (last sighted 1930's or 1940)	Mecodema punctellum (insect) extinct 1931
Hawkins rail Extinct late 19th century	Saint Bathans mammal one of the 2 mammals found on the island Extinct before human arrival	Mysterious starling 1774
land snail -6 species extinct -recently	Upland moa 16th century	North island snipe 1870
Crested Moa extinct 1850	New Zealand Sealion marine mammal fossils found in Moa Hunter middens 1875	North Island Takahē extinct 1894?
Kawekaweau (Delcourt's giant gecko) Extinct in 1873 A Maori chief killed the last one. Largest ever gecko over 2 feet long native to NZ		Hooker's Sealion subantarctic species repopulated Otago

	Bird extinct since Maori settlement	
NZ Owlet/nightjar extinct 13th century	Waitaha penguin 14th century	Coastal moa 16th century
North Island Adzebill Extinct 16th century	South Island Adzebill 16th century	Eyles' Harrier 1777
Coastal moa Extinct 16th century	Eastern moa 16th century	Scarlett's duck 16th century
Haast Eagle Extinct 16th century	Giant Chatham Island rail 1900	Hodgen's Waterhen 16th century
Snipe Rail Extinct 13th century	Chatham Island Coot fossil remains found in 1892	Giant Chatham Island Snipe
New Zealand Raven Extinct 16th century	South Island Raven 16th century	New Zealand Musk Duck 16th century
Chatham Island Duck Extinct 17th century	New Zealand Pink-eared Duck Bones discovered in 1903	Finsch"s Duck 1870
North Island Goose Extinct 16th century	South Island Goose 16th century	New Zealand Swan 16th century
Bush Moa 15th century	Upland Moa 16th century	Heavy-footed Moa 16th century
Crested moa Extinct 1850's	Mappin's Moa extinct	Stout-legged Moa extinct
Chatham raven Extinct	Long billed wren 14th century	North Island Giant Moa 16th century
Giant Moa Extinct 16th century	Waitaha penguin 14th century	Stereospondyl Extinct
NZ geese extinct 16th century	Scarlett's duck 16th century	Scarlett's shearwater 13th century
Stout legged wren extinct		
	Extinct Reptiles	
Kawekaweau** extinct 1870	Narrow-bodied Skink 1955	Northland Skink late Holocene period
	Extinct Amphibians	
Aurora Frog	Markham's frog	Waitomo frog
	Extinct Molluscs	

Placostylus ambagiosus gardneri extinct recently	Placostylus ambagiosus hinemoa recently extinct	Placostylus ambagiosus lesleyae recently extinct
Placostylus ambagiosus priscus Extinct recently	Placostylus ambagiosus spiritus recently	Placostylus ambagiosus worthy recently
Tokea Orthostichon NZ earthworm extinct 1861	NZ Grayling (**Fish**) extinct 1931	Mecodema punctellum Insect extinct 1931 was found on Stephen Island

**The kawekaweua is believed to have been endemic to New Zealand. It was the world's largest gecko that had a beautiful haunting call similar to pipe organs.

PART IX

SUMMING UP

*Human action has triggered a vast cascade of environmental problems that now threaten the continued ability of both natural and human systems to flourish. Solving the critical environmental problems of global warming, water scarcity, pollution, and biodiversity loss are perhaps the greatest challenges of the 21st Century. **Britannica.com.***

Our environment needs care. It has been badly treated over the past few centuries. We have misused the planet's benefits to such a degree that if we continue at this rate this will become a barren planet. And when we render the air, soil and water toxic, it impacts on OUR health too as we are inhabitants of this earth. We breathe the air it provides we eat the bounty that Nature offers us and in return we rape the land, the sea, the forests - everything. This will not do. It cannot be allowed to go on. It is time to take care of our inheritance – the gorgeous world we inhabit and its marvellous inhabitants.

To sum up the main environmental issues are the following

❖ Air pollution – toxic fumes are injected into the atmosphere in many ways like vehicle fumes, aircraft pollution, industrial fumes, nitrates, carbon dioxide, metal and plastic poisons. We can reduce the amount of toxins we produce and try to transfer totally to renewable energy but it will take years to clean up our present mess.

- ❖ Water Pollution - acid rain, urban sprawl, agricultural activities, sewage, industrial waste, landfills all pollute the water. It has become a major issue in the 21st Century as more and more bodies of water become contaminated as well as the fish in it which we eat. The animals also drink the polluted water. We consume their meat polluting our health further. We can redress this issue by not dumping refuse and industrial and other waste in the water.

- ❖ Soil pollution – this includes the land. That too is polluted through the degradation of the land. Some of these activities would be mining, weapons of war especially mines and bombs, deforestation, agricultural waste that seeps into bodies of water, industrial toxins and plastic usage. We should avoid using plastic as much as possible and look for alternate methods that are less corrosive to our earth.

- ❖ Agricultural pollution – Present day agriculture uses a lot of pesticides and other related toxins and fertilizers to deal with localised pests. Some of the chemicals seep into the ground and contaminate the water and plants. The farmers often use this water for irrigation. Toxins thus enter the human food chain

- ❖ Global warming & climate change. – is the trapping of Carbon dioxide, with other air pollutants to form greenhouse gas. This gas absorbs radiation from the sun and traps it, warming up the earth. This in turn leads to melting ice caps, freak weather, appearance of new diseases, unstable weather conditions and so on. This can be redressed by cutting down pollutants that cause the Carbon dioxide to form and instead, using renewable energy as we should all be doing these days.

- ❖ Increased Carbon footprints – is the amount of carbon dioxide released into the atmosphere as a result of the activities of a particular individual, organization, or community. Carbon footprint depletes the resources of the earth and causes more greenhouse gas to form. It is imperative that we try and reduce the carbon footprint.

❖ Genetic engineering – is manipulating the genes of something like soybean, corn, canola, rice and cotton seed oil. These affect us by introducing foreign bodies into our system which can make some people who are hypersensitive, very sick.

❖ Marine life –The toxins that our industries and landfills and factories produce and those that are leached into the water primarily affect the shellfish and corals but also affect all other fish and the marine life. We eat that fish and it then affects us aggravating some diseases like osteoporosis

❖ Loss of biodiversity – Our negative impact on the environment has led to the loss of biodiversity. Too many animals, fish, birds and insects have become extinct. Many more are endangered or vulnerable. It is time to take stock and change our ways to be more in step with nature.

❖ Deforestation – From the time of the Industrial revolutions, forests have been chopped down at a very fast rate to accommodate new structures. This means that the oxygen that the trees reduce is lost and the greenhouse effect is stronger. We should now begin afforestation.

❖ Ozone layer depletion – The ozone layer protects the earth from very strong ultraviolet rays. It is getting depleted and there are large holes in it. This has led to a sharp increase in skin cancer some of which kill not just people but also other living creatures.

❖ Waste – Both industrial waste and household waste is not disposed-off safely. Richer countries produce more waste than poorer countries. Unsafe waste is often dumped in landfills and oceans where whales, sharks and other water mammals get snared in the plastic and drown. We should try and produce less junk. In Australia and New Zealand, plastic shopping bags are out and environmentally friendly ones are in. This is a good sign but other rubbish should also be reduced.

❖ Overpopulation – This has become a major environmental problem. In some countries this has led to rampant disease and starvation. At this rate of population explosion, it will become unsustainable. There should be some form of population control.

❖ Acid rain –The fossil fuels that we burn for energy, vehicles and heavy machinery and in manufacturing, oil refineries and other similar industries include any form of precipitation with acidic components like Nitric and Sulphuric acid. These acids combine with water and oxygen and fall as Acid Rain. This falls on the earth as snow, hail, for or even dust which is acidic. We can limit the amount of fossil fuel we use and cutback on the others for the long-term benefit of mankind.

❖ Depletion of Natural Resources (non-renewable resources) – Natural resources take a very long time to form but we are depleting it at an alarming rate. This also leads to global warming. To make matters worse, mining for resources not only bring toxins to the surface but it also poisons the water, soil and air. Many countries have reduced mining. The USA, however, last year reopened coal mines as it withdrew from the Paris Accord. The Paris Agreement is under the UN framework and was signed in Nov-Dec 2015. It was signed by 196 countries and was a move in the right direction. Unfortunately the USA which produces the maximum carbon dioxide and other toxic substances withdrew from the agreement.

❖ Urban sprawl – is when there is unrestricted growth of commercial and residential housing as well as commercial development and of roads without taking into consideration urban planning. It is the relocation of people from high density to low density provincial zones.

This results in these zones spreading outwards which leads to environmental problems and health problems.

❖ Medical waste is what comes from hospitals, medical centres etc. Medical waste is things like syringes, needles, contaminated gloves, tubes, blades and medicinal containers which can pose a serious danger to the public.

❖ Light and Noise Pollution – is a very common phenomenon in the modern world. Heavy machinery, heavy traffic, extremely loud music, airplanes and aircrafts all cause noise pollution and can have negatives effect on the health of those affected by it.

❖ A healthy environment produces healthy inhabitants. In the 21st century more and more people have various allergies, are gluten intolerant, lactose intolerant, fructose intolerant. I believe simply because of what we eat. There are also a lot more serious illnesses and types of flu that affect us regularly.

❖ Wars from the 20th century onwards keep going on and on. The land gets polluted with the armaments; dead bodies often cannot be buried and add to the contamination. Bombs, mines, bombers all add to the pollution and the countries that begin war are in countries far away countries from the country that begin the war. So the effects of such wars are not faced by the attacking countries on their own soil. We always seem to take it to other countries – not on our own turf. The air, soil and water contamination spreads to other countries. So in the end we are all at risk.

Another world war will destroy our natural world as all the above will be impacted. We do not need to rape the earth further. **It is enough!**

I am ashamed of being a human learning what we have done and are still doing to our mother earth and its creatures that have as much right as we do to live on the earth.

Post Script

Just before the book is going for publication good news has arrived at last.

Today December 15, 2020 the vaccine has arrived but not enough for all to be vaccinated. However we should still practice wearing masks, distancing and hand hygiene because no one knows what the virus might do next and all must be vaccinated all over the world for us all to be safe. Some people in A few European countries hand in the States (today) have begun getting vaccinated.

PART X

BIBLIOGRAPHY

https://www.ancienthistorylists.com/wp

https://www.bing.com/search?q=the+Inca+Civilisation&form=PRAUEN&httpsmsn=1&msnews=1&refig=1bf2f5ac00564fb98b67398da4e903fe&sp=-1&pq=the+inca+civilisation&sc=7-21&qs=n&sk=&cvid=1bf2f5ac00564fb98b67398da4e903fe

www.reference.com/history/were-major-accomplishments-aztec-mayan-civilizationshttps://www.bing.com/search?form=NINENH&mkt=en-au&PC=NBWS&qs=n&sk=&q=what+the+Persian+empire+gave+to+the+world

https://www.ancienthistorylists.com/ancient-civilizations/10-oldest-ancient-civilizations-ever-existed/

21&qs=n&sk=&cvid=1bf2f5ac00564fb98b67398da4e903fe

http://www.environmentalpollution.in/essay/man-and-environment-essay-on-man-and-environment/21

https://www.theguardian.com/environment/2019/may/06/human-society-under-urgent-threat-loss-earth-natural-life-un-report

https://en.wikipedia.org/wiki/Holocene_extinction#Activities_contributing_to_extinctions

https://www.socialistalternative.org/global-warning/humans-nature

https://www.history.com/topics/industrial-revolutions/

https://www.britannica.com/topic/industrialization

https://en.wikipedia.org/wiki/Second_Industrial_Revolution

https://www.economist.com/leaders/2012/04/21/the-third-industrial-revolution

https://en.wikipedia.org/wiki/Chemical_industry#Industrial_Revolution

https://www.weforum.org/agenda/2016/01/the-fourth-industrial-revolution-what-it-means-and-how-to-respond/

www.businessinsider.com/historical-people-that-died-of-curable-things-2015-5

https://www.bing.com/search?q=people+who+have+been+cryogenically+frozen&qs=BT&pq=people+who+have+been+cyrogenics&sc=1-31&cvid=A76B3CB6081C40A8AFF3DBD59AECBD34&FORM=QBRE&sp=1

https://www.coolweirdo.com/12-amazing-cases-of-people-who-were-cryogenically-frozen.html

https://www.bing.com/search?q=The+economic+implications+are+profound

https://animals.howstuffworks.com/endangered-species/top-10-most-endangered-fish.htm

http://www.marinemammalcenter.org/science/Working-with-Endangered-Species/vaquita.html

http://www.iucnredlist.org/details/

https://greentumble.com/top-10-endangered-marine-mammals-in-the-world/

https://www.independent.co.uk/news/world/americas/donald-trump-administration-ends-measure-endangered-sea-animals-caught-fishing-nets-environmental-a7787541.html

https://www.thoughtco.com/recently-extinct-fish-1093350

https://www.bing.com/search?q=Endangered+water+mammals&form=PRAUEN&httpsmsn=1&msnews=1&refig=d7b301145a2c4850930c6bc38df06f8a&sp=1&pq=endangered+water+mammals&sc=1-24&qs=n&sk=&cvid=d7b301145a2c4850930c6bc38df06f8a

https://bestreviewof.com/top-10-most-endangered-fish-species-that-you-need-to-know/

https://greentumble.com/top-10-endangered-marine-mammals-in-the-world/

https://www.lifeadvancer.com/most-endangered-animals/

https://www.ranker.com/list/animal-suicides/beth-elias

https://www.psychologytoday.com/us/blog/all-dogs-go-heaven/201801/new-look-animal-suicide

https://www.oddee.com/item_98725.aspx

https://education.seattlepi.com/nuclear-bombs-affect-environment-6173.html

https://www.ultimate-survival-training.com/anti-personnel-mines/

https://www.bing.com/search?q=shaped+charge+bomb&FORM=R5FD3

https://www.scienceabc.com/nature/how-much-do-vehicles-really-contribute-to-air-pollution.html

https://www.aef.org.uk/issues/air-pollution/

https://www.smh.com.au/national/the-same-coronavirus-strain-turned-up-in-an-australian-and-a-tiger-how-20200622-p554wq.html

https://www.un-habitat.org/endangered-animals-arctic-region/

https://www.sciencedaily.com/releases/2018/09/180910111237.htm

https://www.britannica.com/science/conservation-ecology/Fire-suppression-as-habitat-https://www.livescience.com/arctic-ice-refuge-vanishing.html oss#ref959658

https://australianstogether.org.au/discover/australian-history/colonisation/

https://www.bing.com/search?form=NINENH&mkt=enau&PC=NBWS&qs=n&sk=&q=extinct+Australian+fish

https://theconversation.com/au/topics/australian-endangered-species-4363

https://deepoceanfacts.com/endangered-species-in-the-great-barrier-reef#:

https://panique.com.au/trishansoz/animals/australia-endangered-animals.html

https://www.ga.gov.au/scientific-topics/community-safety/bushfire

https://www.theage.com.au/national/arsenic-leaked-into-river-20050822-ge0qfz.html

https://www.epa.vic.gov.au/for-community/current-projects-issues/...

https://www.sciencedaily.com/releases/2018/09/18091011 1237.htm

https://www.britannica.com/topic/Paris-Agreement-2015

https://www.sbs.com.au/news/last-year-was-the-worst-on-record-for-australia-s-environment

https://www.ucsusa.org/resources/global-warming-happening-and-humans-are-primary-cause

https://www.thealternativedaily.com/9-dangerous-toxic-chemicals-present-in-landfills/

https://www.conserve-energy-future.com/causes-effects-melting-glaciers-humans-environment.php

https://www.greenmatters.com/p/australian-bushfires-everything-you-need-to-know

Sophia Z. Kovachevich

https://openweather.co.uk/blog/post/influence-temperature-plant-productivity-agriculture-accumulated-temperature

https://www.wwf.org.au/what-we-do/climate/impacts-of-global-warming#gs.lhjpdz

https://en.wikipedia.org/wiki/Drought_in_Australia

https://www.bing.com/search?q=endangered+seal+in+the+antarctic&form=PRAUEN&httpsmsn=1&msnews=1&refig=30bbe5026e8f43a698893f47d1521142&sp=1&qs=HS&pq=endangered&sk=PRES1&sc=8-10&cvid=30bbe5026e8f43a698893f47d1521142

https://www.bing.com/search?q=endangered+hammerhead+sharksin+the+antarctic&qs=n&form=QBRE&sp=-1&pq=endangered+hammerhead+sharksin+the+antarctic&sc=0-44&sk=&cvid=CADE5E2A95514020A966F7E0E229DC66

https://www.ga.gov.au/scientific-topics/community-safety/flood

https://www.theguardian.com/australia-news/2019/feb/10/floods-fire-and-drought-australia-a-country-in-the-grip-of-extreme-weather-bingo

https://reneweconomy.com.au/rba-says-climate-change-already-having-profound-impact-on-australian-economy-38695/

https://www.thebalance.com/economic-impact-of-climate-change-3305682

www.britannica.com/science/pollution-environment

https://medical-dictionary.thefreedictionary.com/land+mines

en.wikipedia.org/wiki/Birds_of_Macquarie_Island

nhc.net.nz/

https://www.rnz.co.nz/news/national/288243/new-plan-to-protect-nz's-most-endangered-species

https://www.lifeadvancer.com/most-endangered-animals/

https://www.theguardian.com/environment/2019/may/06/human-society-under-urgent-threat-loss-earth-natural-life-un-report

https://www.socialistalternative.org/global-warning/humans-nature

https://www.economist.com/leaders/2012/04/21/the-third-industrial-revolution

https://www.weforum.org/agenda/2016/01/the-fourth-industrial-revolution-what-it-means-and-how-to-respond/

https://www.bing.com/search?q=Endangered+water+mammals&form=PRAUEN&httpsmsn=1&msnews=1&refig=d7b301145a2c4850930c6bc38df06f8a&sp=1&pq=endangered+water+mammals&sc=1-24&qs=n&sk=&cvid=d7b301145a2c4850930c6bc38df06f8a

https://www.bing.com/search?form=NINENH&mkt=enau&PC=NBWS&qs=n&sk=&q=extinct+Australian+fish

https://www.thoughtco.com/recently-extinct-fish-1093350

https://animals.howstuffworks.com/endangered-species/top-10-most-endangered-fish.htm

Sophia Z. Kovachevich

http://www.marinemammalcenter.org/science/Working-with-Endangered-Species/vaquita.html

http://www.iucnredlist.org/details/

https://greentumble.com/top-10-endangered-marine-mammals-in-the-world/

https://www.ucsusa.org/resources/global-warming-happening-and-humans-are-primary-cause

www.businessinsider.com/historical-people-that-died-of-curable-things-2015-5

https://www.bing.com/search?q=people+who+have+been+cryogenically+frozen&qs=BT&pq=people+who+have+been+cyrogenics&sc=1-31&cvid=A76B3CB6081C40A8AFF3DBD59AECBD34&FORM=QBRE&sp=1

https://en.wikipedia.org/wiki/Chemical_industry#Industrial_Revolution

https://www.coolweirdo.com/12-amazing-cases-of-people-who-were-cryogenically-frozen.html

https://www.bing.com/search?q=Endangered+water+mammals&form=PRAUEN&httpsmsn=1&msnews=1&refig=d7b301145a2c4850930c6bc38df06f8a&sp=-1&pq=endangered+water+mammals&sc=1-24&qs=n&sk=&cvid=d7b301145a2c4850930c6bc38df06f8a

https://bestreviewof.com/top-10-most-endangered-fish-species-that-you-need-to-know/

https://www.ga.gov.au/scientific-topics/community-safety/bushfire

https://greentumble.com/top-10-endangered-marine-mammals-in-the-world/

https://www.un-habitat.org/endangered-animals-arctic-region/

https://www.independent.co.uk/news/world/americas/donald-trump-administration-ends-measure-endangered-sea-animals-caught-fishing-nets-environmental-a7787541.html

https://education.seattlepi.com/nuclear-bombs-affect-environment-6173.html

https://github.com/liammagee/sealand

www.witpress.com,

https://theconversation.com/explainer-how-much-landfill-does-australia-have-78404

web@nhc.net.nz

REFERENCES

Australian Marine Conservation Society – Ingrid Neilson on 0421 972 731

Bell, B.D. 1994. A review of the status of New Zealand Leiopelma species

New Zealand *Journal of Zoology*, Vol. 21: 341–349.

Behrendt, L. 2012, Indigenous Australia for Dummies, Wiley Publishing Australia PTY LTD, Milton, Australia, pg. 94

Claire Hopley, "A History of the British Cotton Industry." British Heritage Travel, July 29, 2006

Dahlman, Carl T.; Gilmartin, Mary; Mountz, Alison; Shirlow, Peter (eds.). Key Concepts in Political Geography. Key Concepts in Human Geography. London:pp115-116

Ekechi, Felix. "The Consolidation of Colonial Rule, 1885–1914." In *Colonial Africa, 1885–1939*, vol. 3 of *Africa*, ed. Toyin Falola. Durham: Carolina Academic Press, 2002.

Gavin Weightman, The Industrial Revoultionaries: The Making of the Modern World 1776-1914. New York:Grove Press, 2007

Gilmartin, Mary (2009). "9: Colonialism/imperialism". In Gallaher, Carolyn;

Governor Phillip to Lord Sydney, 13th February 1790, Historical Records of New South Wales, I, ii, pg. 308

Harris, J. 2003, *"Hiding the Bodies: the myth of the humane colonisation of Australia", in Journal of Aboriginal* History, Vol. 27, pg. 79-104

Harris, J. 2013, pg. 27, O*ne Blood* (electronic resource): Two hundred years of Aboriginal encounter with Christianity, Concilia LTD, Brentford Square, pg. 255

Harris, J. 2003, "Hiding the Bodies: the myth of the humane colonisation of Australia", in Journal of Aboriginal History, Vol. 27, pg. 79-104

Heiner Lasi, Hans-Georg Kemper, Peter Fettke, Thomas Feld, Michael Hoffmann: Industry 4.0. In: Business & Information Systems Engineering 4 (6), pp. 239-242

Humane Society International –Australian Marine Conservation Society

Humane Society International – Rhiannon Cunningham on 0406 017 588 or (02) 9973 1728

Iweriebor, Ehiedu E. G. "The Psychology of Colonialism." In *The End of Colonial Rule: Nationalism and Decolonization*, vol. 4 of *Africa*, ed. Toyin **Falola. Durham**: Carolina Academic Press, 2002.

IUCN Red List of Threatened Species. IUCN. 2008: e.T14260A4427606. doi: 10.2305/IUCN.UK.2008.RLTS

"IIOT AND AUTOMATION".

Jump up to: [a][b][c] Hermann, Pentek, Otto, 2016: <u>Design Principles for Industrie 4.0 Scenarios</u>, accessed on 4 May 2016

John Handmer, Monique Ladds and Liam Magee (December 2016), Disaster losses from natural hazards in Australia, 1967–2013. (Report with AGD)

Jürgen Jasperneite:*Was hinter Begriffen wie Industrie 4.0 steckt* in *Computer & Automation,* 19 December 2012 accessed on 23 December 2012

Kagermann, H., W. Wahlster and J. Helbig, eds., 2013: Recommendations for implementing the strategic initiative Industrie 4.0: Final report of the Industrie 4.0 Working Group

Ladds, MA, Magee, L, Handmer, J (2015) AUS:DIS - Database of losses from disasters in Australia 1967-2013

Ladds M, Keating A, Handmer J and Magee L (2017) How much do disasters cost? A comparison of disaster cost estimates in Australia. *International J of DRR.* 10.1016/j.ijdrr.2017.01.004

Marr, Bernard. "Why Everyone Must Get Ready For The 4th Industrial Revolution". Forbes. Retrieved 14 February 2018

Matthew White, Georgian Britain: "The Industrial Revolution." <u>British Library</u>, October 14, 2009

Monica Watchman: *List of endangered animals in the Arctic Tundra*

Musson, Albert Edward and Robinson, Eric (1969). *"Science and technology in the Industrial Revolution".* University of Manchester, University Press.

New Zealand Journal of Zoology, Vol. 21: 341–349

Queensland Department of Agriculture and Fisheries Shark Control Program catch data.

Oyebade, Adebayo. "Colonial Political Systems." In *Colonial Africa, 1885–1939, vol. 3 of Africa*, ed. Toyin Falola. Durham: Carolina Academic Press, 2002.

Peter Raven, former president of the American Association for the Advancement of Science (AAAS), in the foreword to their publication AAAS Atlas of Population and Environment

Queensland Department of Agriculture and Fisheries Shark Control Program catch data.

References. IUCN Red List of Threatened Species. IUCN. 2008: e.T14260A4427606. doi: 10.2305/IUCN.UK.2008.RLTS.

Reynolds, H. 2006, The Other Side of the Frontier: Aboriginal resistance to the European invasion of Australia, University of New South Wales Press LTD, pg. 126

Shestakova I. G. New temporality of digital civilization: the future has already come // // Scientific and Technical Journal of St. Petersburg State Polytechnical University. Humanities and social sciences. 2019. # 2. P.20-29

Sniderman, Brenna; Mahto, Monika; Cotteleer, Mark J. "Industry 4.0 and manufacturing ecosystems Exploring the world of connected enterprises" (PDF). Deloitte. Retrieved 25 June 2019.

Stannard, David E. *American Holocaust: The Conquest of the New World*. Oxford University Press, 1993. p. 151

Stilwell, Sean. "The Imposition of Colonial Rule." In *Colonial Africa, 1885–1939, vol. 3 of Africa*, ed. Toyin Falola. Durham: Carolina **Academic Press, 2002**

Temple S. A. (1986). The problem of avian extinctions. Ornithology.

Tuckfield Journal, Manuscript 655, pg. 138-140, 152, State Library of Victoria William Rosen, <u>The Most Powerful Idea in the World: A Story of Steam, Industry and Invention</u>. New York: Random House,2010

Wilson, E. Argus 17th March 1856, in Harris, J. 2013, One Blood (electronic resource): Two hundred years of Aboriginal encounter with Christianity, Concilia LTD, Brentford Square, pg. 209

ABOUT THE AUTHOR

Sophia Z Kovachevich is and has been at different times, a lecturer, a teacher, a lay preacher, a peace activist, a political commentator, a counselor, a playwright and a poet.

She has a Masters Degree in English Literature and Language; and a Masters Degree in English Linguistics and a TELTA. She also has a few Bachelor degrees, Diplomas, and Advanced Certificates. She is very familiar with the disciplines of Literature, Linguistics, Theology and Ecology. She also has an incomplete PhD degree.

She has lived in 17 countries in 5 continents. She is widely travelled and has been to at least 50 countries around the world.

Sophia used to speak 8 languages in varying degrees of fluency.

She loves animals and believes in justice and fair-play for all irrespective of race, religion, colour or creed and also in always fights for the underdog.

Printed in the United States
By Bookmasters